Philip Holt

Head of Mathematics, Wimbledon College, London

Nelson

Thomas Nelson and Sons Ltd
Nelson House Mayfield Road
Walton-on-Thames Surrey
KT12 5PL UK

51 York Place
Edinburgh
EH1 3JD UK

Thomas Nelson (Hong Kong) Ltd
Toppan Building 10/F
22A Westlands Road
Quarry Bay Hong Kong

Distributed in Australia by

Thomas Nelson Australia
480 La Trobe Street
Melbourne Victoria 3000
and in Sydney, Brisbane, Adelaide and Perth

© Philip Holt, 1989
First published by Thomas Nelson and Sons Ltd 1989
ISBN 0-17-431046-3
NPN 987654321

Printed in Great Britain by
Thomson Litho Ltd, East Kilbride, Scotland

All Rights Reserved. This publication is protected in the United
Kingdom by the Copyright Act 1956 and in other countries by comparable
legislation. No part of it may be reproduced or recorded by any means
without the permission of the publisher. This prohibition extends
(with certain very limited exceptions) to photocopying and similar
processes, and written permission to make a copy or copies must
therefore be obtained from the publisher in advance. It is advisable
to consult the publisher if there is any doubt regarding the legality
of any proposed copying.

Credits for photographs in this volume are due to the following:
All-Sport (p.4); All-Sport, Adrian Murrell (p.57); All-Sport, Simon Bruty (p.15); All-Sport, Trevor Jones (p.6); Canberra Cruises Ltd (p.123); Chris Ridgers Photography (pp.13, 16, 38, 41, 52); Ed Barber (pp.28, 40, 42, 56, 140); Jo Hidderley (p.61); Regent Productions (p.62); Sally & Richard Greenhill (pp.49, 79); Survival Anglia Ltd, Maurice Tibbles (p.36); Zefa (UK) Ltd (pp.29, 67).

Cover photograph: The Photo Source.

Preface

This is the second of two books which are designed to provide practice at questions of the type likely to appear in GCSE Mathematics examinations. It is mainly suitable for students who are either Level 3 (Higher Level) or on the borderline between Levels 2 and 3 and seeking to test their ability at questions of Level 3 standard before a final decision is made. Students who are clearly Level 2 may be better advised to use Book A, as it contains less material which is unsuitable for them.

The main exercises are set out in pairs (1A, 1B; 2A, 2B; etc.) which cover the same material and are of roughly equal length and difficulty. Thus the first member of the pair might be used for classwork or exposition by the teacher while the second is used for homework. There are also a few 'quick revision' exercises to provide practice in the more important basic techniques. When an exercise contains *only* Level 3 material this is indicated by the words 'Level 3' in the margin and by a shaded panel down the edge of the page. Otherwise the exercises are suitable for both Level 2 and Level 3 students.

For Level 3 there is considerably more material to be covered than for Levels 1 and 2, and a larger number of minor differences between the syllabuses of the four English examining groups. I have sometimes indicated where an exercise, or part of an exercise, is not appropriate for all students, but it will be essential nevertheless for teachers and students to use their own judgement in this matter and omit exercises or questions which are not required by their particular syllabuses.

At the end of the book three 'GCSE papers' are provided. These consist entirely of questions taken from the specimen papers issued by the four English examining groups.

Philip Holt
1989

Contents

Numerical Topics

Types of numbers, number patterns and sequences
Exercise 1A — 1
Exercise 1B — 3

Percentage and everyday arithmetic
Quick revision exercise 2 — 5
Exercise 3A — 6
Exercise 3B — 8

Decimal places, significant figures
Exercise 4A — 10
Exercise 4B — 11

Approximation and estimation
Exercise 5A — 12
Exercise 5B — 14

Ratio and proportion
Exercise 6A — 15
Exercise 6B — 17

Rate
Exercise 7A — 20
Exercise 7B — 21

Practical graphs
Exercise 8A — 23
Exercise 8B — 27

Indices, standard form
Exercise 9A — 31
Exercise 9B — 32

Zero, negative and fractional indices (Level 3)
Exercise 10A — 33
Exercise 10B — 34

Set Theory (Level 3)

Language and notation
Exercise 11A — 35
Exercise 11B — 37

Numerical problems
Exercise 12A — 39
Exercise 12B — 42

Statistics

Exercise 13A — 45
Exercise 13B — 49

Probability

Elementary techniques
Exercise 14A — 53
Exercise 14B — 56

Harder problems
Exercise 15A — 58
Exercise 15B — 60

Algebra

Some basic techniques
Exercise 16A — 63
Exercise 16B — 64

Linear equations and inequalities
Exercise 17A — 65
Exercise 17B — 66

Construction and solution of linear equations from given data
Exercise 18A — 67
Exercise 18B — 69

Further factorisation (Level 3)
Exercise 19A — 70
Exercise 19B — 71

Quadratic equations (Level 3)
Exercise 20A — 72
Exercise 20B — 73

Transformation of formulae — new subject in one term only
Exercise 21A — 74
Exercise 21B — 75

Transformation of formulae — harder problems
Exercise 22A — 77
Exercise 22B — 78

Simultaneous equations (Level 3)
Exercise 23A — 78
Exercise 23B — 79

Variation (Level 3)
Exercise 24A — 80
Exercise 24B — 82

Algebraic fractions (Level 3)
Exercise 25A — 84
Exercise 25B — 85

Graphs of equations
Exercise 26A — 86
Exercise 26B — 88

Further graphical techniques (Level 3)
Exercise 27A — 90
Exercise 27B — 92

Geometry

Simple angle properties, symmetry, polygons
Exercise 28A — 94
Exercise 28B — 96

Congruence
Exercise 29A — 99
Exercise 29B — 101

Similarity, enlargement
Exercise 30A — 102
Exercise 30B — 104

Reflection, rotation, translation
Exercise 31A — 106
Exercise 31B — 108

Angle in a semicircle, angles made by tangents and radii
Exercise 32A — 110
Exercise 32B — 112
Further arc properties (Level 3)
Exercise 33A — 113
Exercise 33B — 115

Trigonometry, Pythagoras' Theorem

Quick revision exercise 34 — 117
Problems involving right-angled triangles in two dimensions
Exercise 35A — 120
Exercise 35B — 121
Simple three-dimensional problems; harder two-dimensional problems on right-angled triangles (Level 3)
Exercise 36A — 123
Exercise 36B — 124
Trigonometric graphs (Level 3)
Exercise 37A — 126
Exercise 37B — 127
Sine rule, cosine rule, the formula $A = \frac{1}{2}ab \sin C$ (Level 3)
Exercise 38A — 128
Exercise 38B — 130

Mensuration

Quick revision exercise 39 — 132
Elementary techniques
Exercise 40A — 134
Exercise 40B — 136
Arcs, sectors, segments; further standard bodies (Level 3)
Quick revision exercise 41 — 137
Exercise 42A — 139
Exercise 42B — 140

Matrices (Level 3)

Basic rules and operations
Exercise 43A — 142
Exercise 43B — 144
Matrix transformations
Exercise 44A — 145
Exercise 44B — 148

Vectors (Level 3)

Parallelogram and triangle laws, column vectors
Exercise 45A — 151
Exercise 45B — 152
Vector geometry
Exercise 46A — 154
Exercise 46B — 155

GCSE Specimen Papers

Paper 3 — 157
Paper 4 — 160

Answers to Exercises — 164

Answers to GCSE Specimen Papers — 183

Numerical Topics

Types of numbers, number patterns and sequences

Exercise 1A

1. Describe the numbers in each of the following sequences and in each case state the next two numbers:
   a 1, 3, 5, 7
   b 4, 8, 12, 16
   c 1, 4, 9, 16
   d 3, 9, 27, 81

2. The first four **triangular numbers** are
   $$1, 3, 6, 10$$
   Explain with the aid of diagrams why these numbers are called triangular numbers and state the next three numbers in the sequence.

3. Write down the next three numbers in each of the following sequences:
   a 2, 8, 14, 20
   b 46, 39, 32, 25
   c $-14, -11, -8, -5$
   d $7, 10\frac{1}{2}, 14, 17\frac{1}{2}$

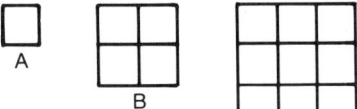

4. The sequence of patterns on the left, A, B, C, could be made with matches.
   a Draw the next pattern, D, in the sequence.
   b Count the number of squares of the size of A in each pattern, and write down the number of squares of this size that occur in patterns E and F.
   c Copy and complete the following table:

Pattern	A	B	C	D
Number of matches	4	12		
Number of extra matches		8		

   d By considering the sequences in the table, work out the number of matches that would be needed for patterns E and F.

5. The first five of the numbers of a certain type are
   $$2, 3, 5, 7, 11$$
   Name these numbers and give the next four of them.

6 Write down the next two numbers in each of the following sequences:
 a 2, 10, 50, 250
 b 400, −200, 100, −50
 c $\frac{1}{16}, \frac{1}{8}, \frac{1}{4}, \frac{1}{2}$
 d 16, 24, 36, 54

7 Work out how many of the following kinds of numbers there are in the interval $30 < x < 50$:
 a natural numbers,
 b square numbers,
 c multiples of 4,
 d prime numbers.

8 In each of the following cases say whether the given number is rational or irrational:
 a $2.\dot{3}$ **b** π **c** $\sqrt{7}$ **d** $\sqrt{6\frac{1}{4}}$ **e** $5\frac{2}{7}$

9 In the following sequence, each number after the first two numbers is obtained by adding the two numbers just before it:

$$0, 1, 1, 2, 3$$

The sequences below are formed in a similar way. In each case find the missing terms:
 a 1, 5, 6, *, *, *
 b 2, *, 5, *, *, *
 c 1, *, *, 7, 11
 d *, *, *, 26, 42

10 As shown on the left two lines can cross in, at most, one point, and three lines can cross in three points at most.
 a If a fourth line is added to the second diagram, what is the maximum number of **extra** crossing points that it can make?
 b From your answer to **a**, work out the maximum number of crossing points that four lines can make.
 c Using similar reasoning, work out the maximum number of crossing points that five lines can make.
 d Copy and complete the following table:

Number of lines	2	3	4	5	6	7
Maximum number of crossing points	1	3				

 e What are the numbers in the second row of the table called?

11 By finding a pattern in the **differences** between successive numbers, work out the next two numbers in each of the following sequences:
 a 2, 3, 5, 8, 12
 b 1, 2, 5, 10, 17
 c 4, 10, 15, 19, 22
 d 0, 1, 5, 12, 22
 e 50, 49, 46, 41
 f 42, 32, 24, 18

12 In the following sequence of equations, work out the values of a, b, x and y:

$$2(3 - 1) = 4$$
$$3(5 - 1) = 12$$
$$4(7 - 1) = 24$$
$$\vdots$$
$$7(a - 1) = b$$
$$\vdots$$
$$x(y - 1) = 180$$

Exercise 1B

Note: *In this exercise 0 will be regarded as a natural number.*

1 Describe the numbers in each of the following sequences and in each case state the next two numbers:
   a 2, 4, 6, 8
   b 5, 10, 15, 20
   c 2, 4, 8, 16
   d 1, 8, 27, 64

2 Write down the first five terms in the sequence formed by squaring the odd numbers. (The first two terms are 1 and 9.) Work out also the differences between successive terms of this sequence and say what these numbers are called.

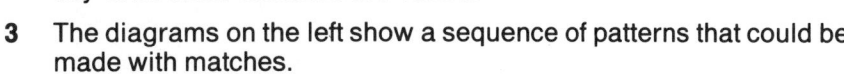

3 The diagrams on the left show a sequence of patterns that could be made with matches.
   a Draw the next pattern in the sequence.
   b Count the number of squares in each of the patterns, and write down the number of squares in the fourth, fifth and sixth patterns of the sequence.
   c Count the number of matches in each of the patterns, and write down the number of matches in the fourth, fifth and sixth patterns of the sequence.

4 Work out
   a the number of natural numbers in the interval $-7 < x \leqslant 10$,
   b the number of prime numbers in the interval $80 < x < 100$,
   c the number of non-natural integers in the interval $-12 \leqslant x < 12$.

5 Write down the next two numbers in each of the following sequences:
   a 5, 12, 19, 26
   b 68, 57, 46, 35
   c 11, 8, 5, 2
   d $-10\frac{1}{2}, -8, -5\frac{1}{2}, -3$

6 Write down the next two numbers in each of the following sequences:
   a 7, 14, 28, 56
   b $1, \frac{2}{3}, \frac{4}{9}, \frac{8}{27}$
   c $-168, 84, -42, 21$
   d $\frac{1}{12}, \frac{1}{2}, 3, 18$
   e 256, 192, 144, 108

7 In each of the following cases say whether the given number is rational or irrational:
  a $-4\frac{2}{3}$ **b** $3\frac{1}{7}$ **c** $\sqrt{2}$ **d** $\sqrt[3]{100}$ **e** $1.\dot{6}$ **f** 5.049

8 In the following triangle (which is called **Pascal's triangle**), the numbers at the ends of the rows are all ones, and each other number is obtained from the two numbers just above it:

$$\begin{array}{ccccccc} & & & 1 & & & \\ & & 1 & & 1 & & \\ & 1 & & 2 & & 1 & \\ 1 & & 3 & & 3 & & 1 \end{array}$$

  a Copy the triangle and add the next three rows.
  b Find the sum of the numbers in each row. Name the numbers you obtain.
  c Without listing the numbers, find the sum of the numbers in the ninth row of the triangle.

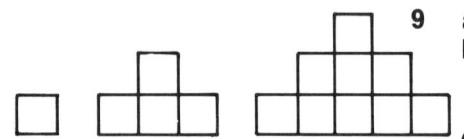

9 a Draw the next pattern in the sequence of patterns on the left.
  b Find the number of squares (of the size of the first square shown) in each of the first four patterns. What are these numbers called?
  c Without drawing the pattern, find the number of squares in the sixth pattern of the sequence.
  d Count the number of vertices (points where lines cross) in each of the first four patterns.
  e Without further drawing, find the number of vertices in the fifth, sixth and seventh patterns of the sequence.

10 In each of the following sequences each number (except the first two) is obtained from the two numbers just before it. Find the next two numbers in each sequence:
  a 1, 3, 4, 7, 11
  b 1, 2, 2, 4, 8
  c 16, 10, 6, 4, 2

11 By finding a pattern in the differences between successive numbers, work out the next two terms in each of the following sequences:
  a 4, 5, 7, 10, 14
  b 0, 2, 8, 18, 32
  c 20, 18, 14, 8
  d 5, 6, 8, 12, 20

12 In the following sequence of equations, work out the values of *m*, *p* and *t*:
$$(1 \times 2) - 2 = 0$$
$$(2 \times 3) - 4 = 2$$
$$(3 \times 4) - 6 = 6$$
$$\vdots$$
$$(m \times 12) - p = t$$

13 Some football teams play in a league in which the rule is 'all play all twice'. If there were just three teams (A, B and C) in the league, the following table would show all the games that had to be played.

a By drawing similar tables (where necessary), work out the total number of games that would have to be played in leagues with two teams, with three teams, with four teams and with five teams.

b By considering the pattern in the sequence of numbers you have obtained, work out the number of games that would have to be played in leagues with six teams and with seven teams.

c State the relationship between the numbers in your pattern and triangular numbers.

Percentage and everyday arithmetic

Quick revision exercise 2

1 Express the following percentages as fractions in their lowest terms:

   a 10%   **e** $33\frac{1}{3}$%   **i** 40%   **m** $12\frac{1}{2}$%   **q** $22\frac{1}{2}$%
   b 43%   **f** 5%   **j** 65%   **n** 58%
   c 25%   **g** 95%   **k** $2\frac{1}{2}$%   **o** $8\frac{1}{3}$%
   d 6%   **h** 28%   **l** 84%   **p** $37\frac{1}{2}$%

2 Express the following fractions and decimals as percentages, giving inexact answers to one decimal place:

   a $\frac{7}{10}$ **d** 0·74   **g** 0·08   **j** 0·253   **m** $\frac{7}{8}$
   b 0·3   **e** $\frac{13}{50}$ **h** $\frac{2}{3}$ **k** $\frac{4}{13}$ **n** 0·0029
   c $\frac{4}{5}$ **f** $\frac{4}{7}$ **i** $\frac{11}{25}$ **l** $\frac{29}{200}$ **o** $\frac{53}{57}$

3 Work out:

   a 25% of 44   **e** $37\frac{1}{2}$% of 24p   **i** $1\frac{1}{4}$% of 1600
   b 7% of £5   **f** $9\frac{1}{2}$% of 2 million   **j** $66\frac{2}{3}$% of 9·6
   c 60% of £2·45   **g** 15% of £8·40
   d 84% of 4250   **h** 73% of £319

4 Work out:

   a 24% more than 325   **f** 35% less than 760
   b 5% less than £6·80   **g** 15% more than £23·60
   c 75% less than 56   **h** 42% less than £6·50
   d 17% more than £806   **i** $8\frac{1}{2}$% less than £9400
   e $3\frac{1}{2}$% more than £2000

5 In each of the following cases find the percentage profit or loss, giving inexact answers to one decimal place:

   a cost price = £40, selling price = £52
   b cost price = £3·50, selling price = £3·99
   c cost price = 75p, selling price = 60p
   d cost price = £2400, selling price = £2200
   e cost price = 37p, selling price = 31p
   f cost price = £126·30, selling price = £185·50

6 Find the cost price of an article in each of the following cases:
  a selling price = £60, profit = 25%
  b selling price = £2·80, profit = 12%
  c selling price = £448, loss = 20%
  d selling price = £3660, loss = 70%
  e selling price = 92p, profit = 15%
  f selling price = £3·78, loss = 28%

Exercise 3A

1 It is calculated that, on average, 12% of a tennis player's services are faults and $2\frac{1}{2}\%$ are aces.
  a In 75 of the player's services, how many faults are likely to occur?
  b In 320 services, how many aces are likely to occur?

2 A car costs £6000 when new. In its first year of use it loses 25% of its original value, and in its second year it loses 20% of its value at the beginning of the year. Work out
  a the car's value when one year old,
  b the car's value when two years old,
  c the percentage of its original value that the car loses in its first two years of use.

3 One evening Fatima has $1\frac{1}{4}$ hours of spare time, and spends half an hour of it reading the newspaper. She then spends 60% of the remaining time watching a video.
  a What percentage of her spare time does she devote to reading?
  b How many minutes does she spend watching the video?

4 A double-glazing company gives an estimate of £800 for fitting some replacement windows. It has to add VAT at 15%, but it offers a discount of 5% for paying cash. Work out how much is saved by paying cash
  a if the discount is calculated before VAT is added,
  b if the discount is calculated after VAT is added.

5 Nicola's salary is £920 per month. Her national insurance and superannuation cost her £164 altogether, and she is charged income tax on the rest at 29%. Work out
  a the amount of her monthly salary on which Nicola pays income tax,
  b the amount of tax she pays per month,
  c her net monthly salary.

6 A cricket ground which can seat 24 000 spectators has a crowd of 16 750 on the first day of a test match. On the second day of the match, the attendance increases by 8%. Work out
  a the percentage of seats which are filled on the first day, to one decimal place,
  b the number of spectators on the second day.

7 Two married couples stay for one night at a seaside town. They book bed and breakfast at an hotel, which costs £24 per person plus VAT at 15%, and they also have dinner at a restaurant, for which they pay £32·40 for the whole party plus a service charge of 10p in the pound. Work out
   a the hotel bill,
   b the bill for the dinner,
   c the total cost of the stay at the town.

8 **a** The number 216 is mistakenly written 261. Find the percentage error, to the nearest whole number.
   b Some students measure the side-length of a square, obtaining readings which vary between 27·4 cm and 27·8 cm. Each student then uses his or her reading to calculate the area of the square. Given that the true area is 763 cm^2, work out, to one decimal place, the maximum percentage error that occurs in the students' estimates of the area.

9 A shopkeeper buys eggs in batches of 120 for £8 per batch. On average, 5% of the eggs get broken. The rest are sold in boxes of six.
   a How many boxes of six eggs will normally be obtained from a batch of 120?
   b If the shopkeeper needs to make a profit of at least 12% on his outlay, what is the minimum price he can afford to charge for a box of six eggs?

10 A building society offers two savings accounts in the advertisement on the left.

Mr Potok requires immediate access to his money. He invests £400 in the Deposit Account on 1 January and withdraws £120 of it 6 months later. On the following 31 December, work out
   a how much interest he receives on the £120 he withdrew,
   b how much interest he receives on the rest of his investment,
   c how much he has in his account after the interest is added.

Mrs Alford wants the highest possible interest. She invests £640 on 31 March in the Gold Star Account. On the following 31 December, work out
   d how much interest is added to her account,
   e how much extra interest she obtains by using the Gold Star Account rather than the Deposit Account.

11 An electrical shop offers a discount of 5% for cash.
   a A personal stereo is priced in the window at £27·40. What does it cost for cash?
   b A dishwasher is obtained by paying £418 cash. What was its price before the discount?
   c A hair dryer is bought for cash at a discount of 40p. How much is paid for it?

12 **a** A motorbike is sold at a profit of 35% for £3834. What did the motorbike cost?
   b A man's salary is cut by 6% to £13 348. What was his salary before the cut?

13 By taking a train rather than a bus I reduce the average time of my journey to work by 15% but raise the cost of the journey by 12%. The train takes, on average, 34 minutes and the train fare is 84p. Work out
  a the average time taken by the bus,
  b the fare for the bus journey.

Exercise 3B

1 In a $2\frac{1}{2}$ hour examination, Jamila spends half an hour on the first question. She then devotes 5% of her remaining time to reading the other questions.
  a What percentage of her total time does Jamila spend on the first question?
  b How long does she spend reading the other questions?

2 On average, Chelsea football team wins 32% of its matches and draws 36% of them.
  a In 75 matches, how many times is Chelsea likely to win?
  b In how many matches will Chelsea normally achieve 45 draws?

3 A clothes shop displays the notice on the left in its window. A man buys three T-shirts priced at £9·50 each and a pair of shorts priced at £6.25, while a woman buys a denim jacket priced at £29.90 and two pairs of jeans at £17·30 each. Work out how much is actually paid
  a by the man,
  b by the woman.

4 In a mock general election at a school, 450 pupils vote Conservative, 320 vote Labour and 280 vote for other parties. A month later the election is repeated, when 18% of the original Conservative supporters vote for other parties and 5% of the original Labour supporters vote for other parties. Of those who originally voted for other parties, $2\frac{1}{2}$% now vote Labour.

In the second election, how many pupils vote
  a Conservative?
  b Labour?
  c for other parties?

5 Kirsty Andrews buys a house in 1978 for £20 000. In 1982 she sells it to Vijay Shah for £28 000, and in 1985 Vijay himself sells it, making a profit of 25% on his own purchase price. Work out
  a the profit Kirsty makes as a percentage of her purchase price,
  b the price Vijay obtains for the house,
  c the total increase in the house's value between 1978 and 1985,
  d the total increase as a percentage of the house's value in 1978.

6 Paula works as a trainee camera operator and earns a salary of £14 000 per year. Her employers, Frisbee Feature Films, deduct 12% of this for national insurance and superannuation, and Paula pays tax on the rest at 29%. Work out her net annual income.

7 Rob earns £7·50 per week at his part-time job in a supermarket, and spends 60% of the money on clothes. After a year at the job

he is given a 14% wage rise, but does not alter the amount he spends on clothes. Work out
a how much Rob spends per week on clothes,
b his new weekly wage,
c to one decimal place, the percentage of his wage that he spends on clothes after the rise.

8 Marvin owns 160 books, of which 24 are on badminton, 16 are on tennis and the rest are on non-sporting subjects. Work out the percentage of the books which are on
a sport,
b badminton.

He later buys some more books, increasing the total number by 20%. Given that he buys 14 non-sporting books and increases the number of books on tennis by $37\frac{1}{2}\%$, work out
c the percentage increase in the number of books on badminton,
d the percentage increase in the number of books on sport.

9 A salesperson working for an insurance company receives a fixed payment of £450 per month and a commission of 20% on the policies she sells. One month she makes a total of £700.
a Work out the value of the insurance policies she sells.

In the following month her sales drop by 8%. Work out
b the commission she receives that month,
c the percentage decrease in her total salary, to one decimal place.

10 A quarterly telephone bill is presented as follows:

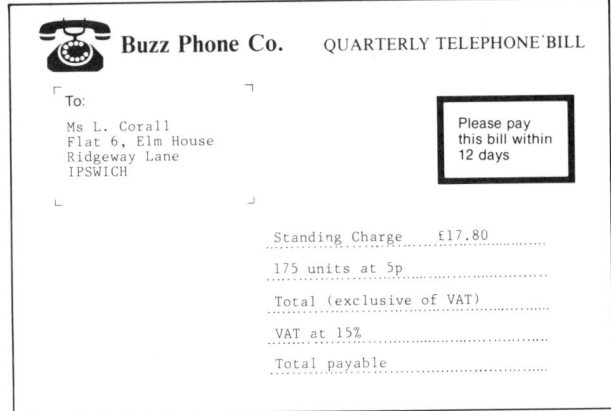

Work out
a the four amounts which should go in the right-hand column,
b the cost of the units used as a percentage of the total cost, to the nearest whole number.

In the following quarter Ms Corall increases the number of units she uses by 16% and the standing charge is increased by 4%. The cost of each unit is unchanged. Work out
c the new total payable, to the nearest penny,
d the percentage increase in the total payable, to the nearest whole number.

11 A car depreciates by 30% in its first year of use and by 25% in its second. After this it depreciates by 20% each year. Given that the car is worth £8400 when one year old, work out
 a its value when four years old,
 b its value when new.

12 a After appreciating by 20% a house is worth £57 840. What was its original value?
 b After spending 6% of my money I am left with £8·93. How much did I have originally?

13 An estate agent's charge for selling a house is 2% of the price obtained for the house plus VAT at 15%. The agent's final bill to a client is £1104. Work out
 a the agent's charge before the addition of VAT,
 b the price of the house that was sold.

Decimal places, significant figures

Exercise 4A

1 Express to two decimal places:
 a 5·342   b 0·816   c 12·084   d 1·298

2 Express to one decimal place:
 a 9·21   b 17·349   c 0·753   d $8\frac{2}{3}$

3 Express to two significant figures:
 a 847   b 0·0324   c 1062   d 0·5964   e 145 704

4 Express to three significant figures:
 a 6·231   b 12 496   c 0·005 013 6   d 20·082   e 6297

5 Express to one significant figure:
 a 473   b 0·000 639   c twenty-six million

6 The population of a town is 214 700. Express this
 a to three significant figures,
 b to two significant figures.

 State also
 c which of these answers gives the population to the nearest thousand people.

7 A garden which is approximately rectangular is 21 m 18 cm long and 15 m 70 cm wide. Estimate the area of the garden, in m²,
 a to three significant figures,
 b to two decimal places.

 State also
 c which of the two answers would be the more reasonable estimate to use.

8 To two significant figures, the number of children in a school is 530. Write down

a the smallest possible number of children in the school,
   b the largest possible number of children in the school.

9 A woman has to pay bills of £146, £61·09 and £117·80. She wants to know the total bill, to two significant figures.
   a Express each of the three bills to two significant figures.
   b Add up your answers to **a** and give the total to two significant figures.
   c Add up the exact bills and give the total to two significant figures.
   d Say which of your last two answers the woman should use as her estimate of the total bill.

10 The area of a square is 15 m². Work out (with a calculator) the length of each side, giving the answer
   a to three decimal places,
   b to one decimal place.

11 A car travels 300 miles in 3 days. Given that it travels 75·3 miles on the first day and 102·75 miles on the second, work out how far it travels on the third day, giving the answer
   a to one decimal place,
   b to three significant figures,
   c to one significant figure.

12 To one decimal place, the weight of a bar of chocolate is 82·9 g. Say which one of the following could be the exact weight of the chocolate:
   81·89 g, 82·97 g, 83·02 g, 82·86 g.

13 Seventy sheets of paper have a total thickness of 3·56 mm. Estimate the thickness of one sheet of paper in millimetres, giving the answer
   a to three decimal places,
   b to three significant figures.

Exercise 4B

1 Express to one decimal place:
   a 0·63   b 12·28   c 5·606   d 28·457

2 Express to two decimal places:
   a 4·854   b 0·899   c 17·3649   d $2\frac{1}{3}$

3 Express to two significant figures:
   a 28·6   b 163·84   c 12 375   d 0·00527   e 646 073

4 Express to four significant figures:
   a 12·459   b 0·402 138   c 160·14   d 0·040 719   e 54 237 814

5 The diameter of the earth is about 12 740 km. Express this
   a to three significant figures,
   b to two significant figures.

   State also
   c which of these answers gives the diameter to the nearest thousand kilometres.

6 To three significant figures, the total number of runs scored by a cricket team in a season is 11 400. Write down
   a the smallest possible number of runs scored by the team,
   b the largest possible number of runs scored by the team.

7 The mass of a pin is 0·026 37 g. Express this
   a to three significant figures,
   b to three decimal places.

State also
   c which of these answers gives the mass to the nearest milligram.

8 A boy finds that in 25 ordinary paces he walks a distance of 16 m 36 cm. Work out the average length in metres of one pace, giving the answer
   a to three decimal places,
   b to one decimal place.

State also
   c which of these answers would be the more reasonable to use as an estimate of the average pace.

9 The population of a country is 20 610 730. How many significant figures are being given when this is expressed
   a to the nearest thousand?
   b to the nearest hundred thousand?
   c to the nearest million?

10 Use your calculator to obtain a value of π, and express this value
   a to four significant figures,
   b to four decimal places,
   c to six significant figures.

11 The capacity of a ketchup bottle is 329 ml to three significant figures. Say which one of the following could be the exact capacity of the bottle:
        329·7 ml, 330 ml, 328·57 ml, 327·9 ml

12 The length of a rectangle is 7·3 cm and its area is 31·4 cm^2. Work out the width of the rectangle, giving the answer
   a to two decimal places,
   b to five significant figures.

Approximation and estimation

Note: *Do not use a calculator in Exercises 5A and 5B.*

Exercise 5A

In questions **1–8**, estimate the values of the given quantities by first rounding off each number to one significant figure.

1. 21.4×3.82
2. $59 \div 5.06$
3. 0.693^2
4. $\dfrac{77 \times 0.016}{0.39}$
5. $\dfrac{4.1^2 + 6.83^2}{7.9^2 + 8.2^2}$
6. $\dfrac{0.38^2}{0.17^2}$
7. $\sqrt{2\pi\left(\dfrac{1.03 + 2.87}{0.503}\right)}$
8. $\sqrt{\dfrac{0.032 \times 4.1^2}{0.0061}}$

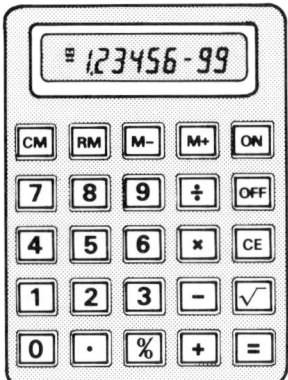

9. The calculator shown on the left, which is drawn to scale, is 7.53 cm wide. Estimate its length, to the nearest centimetre.

10. A jewellery shop owner is supplied with gold chains in boxes of 40. The chains have an average mass of 797 mg and the boxes have an average mass of 12.1 g. Estimate
    a the total mass, to the nearest gram, of one box of gold chains,
    b the number of boxes of gold chains that would have a mass of just over 1 kg.

11. Kelvin needs half a pound of sultanas for a recipe. In his local grocers the sultanas are sold in packets of 150 g, 200 g, 250 g and 300 g. He knows that there are about 28 grams to the ounce. Which packet should he buy to have just enough for the recipe with as little as possible left over?

12. To find out roughly how thick an ordinary piece of paper is, a girl measures the thickness of 100 pages of one of her books. She obtains a reading of 0.52 cm. Estimate the thickness in millimetres, to one significant figure, of
    a one page,
    b 76 pages.

13. Cambridge is about 350 miles from Glasgow and Brighton is about 240 km from Bristol. Taking 5 miles to equal 8 km, estimate
    a the distance from Cambridge to Glasgow, in kilometres,
    b the distance from Brighton to Bristol, in miles.

14.  A man knows that the height of his room is either $2\tfrac{1}{2}$ m, $3\tfrac{1}{2}$ m or $4\tfrac{1}{2}$ m, but he cannot remember which. He can tell, however, that the room is about $1\tfrac{1}{2}$ times his own height, and he is just under 6 feet tall. He remembers, furthermore, that 1 metre is about 3.3 feet. Which of the three lengths is the probable height of his room?

Exercise 5B

In questions **1–8**, estimate the values of the given quantities by using suitable approximations for each number.

1. 0.24×80.3

2. $\dfrac{4.03}{19.82}$

3. 0.018^2

4. $\dfrac{187 + 406}{78 \times 5.13}$

5. $\dfrac{8.8^2 - 1.9^2}{3.9^2 - 3.1^2}$

6. $\dfrac{0.00486 \times 0.062}{0.028 \times 0.104}$

7. $\sqrt{\dfrac{6.2\pi}{448}}$

8. $\sqrt{\dfrac{0.51 \times 0.182}{98.8 \times 0.247}}$

9. Say which of the quantities listed below is nearest to
   a the length of an ordinary car,
   b the weight of a piece of chalk,
   c the capacity of an ordinary bathroom washbasin.

   1500 ml, 0·02 kg, 380 cm, 1·9 m, 3 litres,
   1·4 g, 12 m, 50 litres, 20 mg, 1000 cl

10. On a small bridge there are cars of mass 1490 kg, 2·6 t and 3250 kg, and also eight people who have an average mass of 67 kg. The bridge can safely support a load of 25 t. Work out, to the nearest tonne, the extra mass that the bridge can safely hold.

11.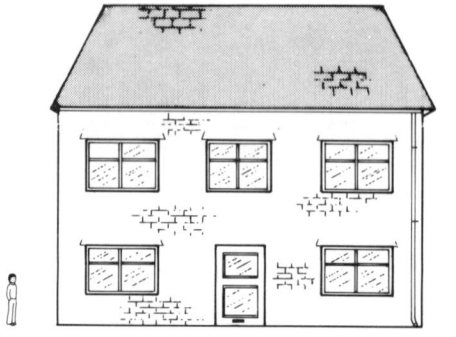

    Given that the boy shown above is 4 feet 4 inches tall, estimate the height of
    a the door,
    b the tree,
    c the house.

12. An Indian takeaway sells portions of rice in foil containers. On average, the containers weigh 15 g and each one holds about 175 g of rice.
    a Estimate, to the nearest 100 g, the total weight of seven portions of rice in containers.
    b How many portions would be needed to provide just over 2 kg of rice?

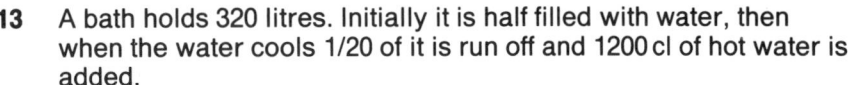

13 A bath holds 320 litres. Initially it is half filled with water, then when the water cools 1/20 of it is run off and 1200 cl of hot water is added.
  a How much water is now in the bath, in litres?
  b Given that 1 gallon is about $4\frac{1}{2}$ litres, estimate the number of gallons of water now in the bath, giving the answer to the nearest gallon.

14 Mr Campbell, who has entered for the London Marathon, decides to start his training by jogging at least 5 km per day. He is told that his local sports ground has a perimeter of 700 yards, and he knows that 1 foot is about 0·3 metres. Work out
  a the approximate perimeter of the sports ground, in metres,
  b the minimum number of complete circuits Mr Campbell needs to make to fulfil his training requirements.

Ratio and proportion

Exercise 6A

1 Express the following ratios as simply as possible:
  a 27:36
  b 16:24:40
  c $1\frac{1}{2}:3\frac{1}{2}$
  d 30:18:54
  e $\frac{1}{4}:\frac{1}{8}$
  f $1\frac{1}{3}:2:2\frac{2}{3}$
  g 1·75:2·25
  h 0·18:0·04:0·12
  i $3\frac{1}{2}:8\frac{1}{6}$
  j 60 cm to $1\frac{1}{2}$ m
  k 0·2 t to 160 kg
  l 35 cl to 0·5 litres
  m 8·4 mm to 0·63 cm

2 Neville divides the time he spends on history, English and science homeworks in the ratio 3:4:5. One evening Neville spends 1 h 5 min on science. How long does he spend
  a on history,
  b on English?

  Over the whole of 1 month Neville spends $7\frac{1}{2}$ h on history. How long does he spend
  c on English,
  d altogether on the three subjects?

3 On a map of London, 2 km is represented by 5 cm.
  a On the map, two underground stations are 12 cm apart. What is their true distance apart?
  b On the map, a road is represented as 3·2 cm long. What is its true length?
  c A hospital and a school are in fact 7 km apart. How far apart will they be shown on the map?

4 A model is made of a house on a scale of 4:55.
  a In the model, the kitchen is 36 cm long. How long is the real kitchen, in metres?
  b The real house is 16·5 m high. How high is the model, in centimetres?

5 Divide
   a 12 in the ratio 1:3
   b 25 in the ratio 3:2
   c 21 in the ratio 4:3
   d 32 in the ratio 1:2:5
   e 42 in the ratio 2:1:3
   f 80 in the ratio 5:3:2
   g £5·20 in the ratio 6:7
   h £18·45 in the ratio $1\frac{1}{4}:4\frac{3}{8}$

6 In her will, a woman leaves £30 000 to be divided among her three children in the ratio $2:2\frac{1}{2}:3$. How much does each child receive?

7 An alloy consists of copper, zinc and tin in the ratio 5:2:1 by weight.
   a How much copper will be contained in 120 kg of the alloy?
   b Find the weight of a piece of the alloy in which there is 9 kg more copper than zinc.

8 A cricket team plays 45 games in a season, achieving wins, losses and draws in the ratio 3:2:4.
   a Work out the numbers of wins, losses and draws.

   The following season the team plays the same number of games, but wins three fewer. The ratio of losses to draws stays the same.
   b Work out the numbers of wins, losses and draws for the second season.

9 Copy and complete the following tables, given that in each case y is directly proportional to x:

a
x	2	3	5	20	30
y	8	12			

c
x			10		
y	3	9	15	27	60

b
x	1	2	3	4	5
y			16·5		

d
x	2	8	12	16	24
y				36	

10 The current in amps flowing through a wire is directly proportional to the potential difference in volts between the ends of the wire. Given that the current is 3·6 amps when the potential difference is 96 volts, find
   a the current when the potential difference is 60 volts,
   b the potential difference which produces a current of 4·5 amps.

11 An experiment is performed in which weights are hung on the end of a spring and the extensions of the spring are measured. The results are as follows:

Weight	250 g	500 g	1 kg	1·5 kg	2 kg
Extension	0·6 cm	1·2 cm	2·4 cm	2·6 cm	4·8 cm

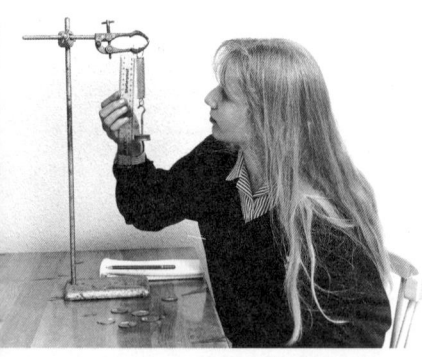

   a Which extension in the table appears to be a mistaken reading and what would be the correct extension?
   b What extension would be caused by a weight of $1\frac{3}{8}$ kg?
   c What weight would produce an extension of 1·5 cm?

12 Copy and complete the following tables, given that in each case the two quantities are in inverse proportion:

a	1	2	3	4
	30	15		

b	3	4	8	12
	16			

c		12		
	0·5	1·5	2	4·5

d	2	8	10	20
	11			

13 Three workmen take 1 h 12 min to do a certain job. Assuming that all men work equally quickly, work out how long the job would take if done by
  a 6 men,
  b 1 man,
  c 2 men.

14 The time taken by a train for a journey is inversely proportional to the train's average speed. Given that the train takes 4 h 24 min for the journey when its average speed is 95 km h^{-1}, work out
  a how long the journey would take at an average speed of 76 km h^{-1},
  b the average speed, to the nearest whole number, at which the journey would take $3\frac{1}{4}$ h.

15 A teacher speculates that the percentage of students who obtain grade A at GCSE mathematics may be inversely proportional to the average number of students in the mathematics classes. One year 32% of the students obtain grade A and there is an average of 22 students per class. On the assumption that the teacher's speculation is correct, work out, to the nearest whole number
  a the percentage of students who will obtain A grades when there is an average of 15 students per class,
  b the average number of students per class when 26% of the students obtain A grades.

Exercise 6B

1 Express the following ratios as simply as possible:
  a 35:28
  b 24:36:60
  c $7\frac{1}{2}:10\frac{1}{2}$
  d 125:75:350
  e $2\frac{1}{3}:1:1\frac{2}{3}$
  f 0·44:1·21
  g $1\frac{1}{4}:1\frac{7}{8}:2\frac{1}{2}$
  h 0·8 km to 480 km
  i 25 mg to 0·04 g
  j 4·5 cm to 80 mm
  k 2 h 8 min to 1·6 h

2 A gardener makes up a mixture consisting of 7 parts of peat to 4 parts of sand.
  a How much peat should he use with 10 buckets of sand?
  b If he uses 35 litres of sand, how much of the mixture will he obtain?

3 In a map of Britain, 2 inches represent 125 miles.
  a On the map, Holyhead and Norwich are 5 inches apart. What is their true distance apart, to the nearest 10 miles?
  b Hull is 400 miles from Inverness. How far apart will these towns be shown on the map?
  c On the map, Oxford and Edinburgh are 5·8 inches apart. What is their true distance apart, to the nearest 10 miles?

4 A carpenter makes a scale drawing of a piece of furniture which he is designing, letting 20 cm represent $1\frac{1}{2}$ m.
  a Express the ratio of lengths in the drawing to real lengths as simply as possible.
  b In the drawing, the piece of furniture is 8·5 cm wide. What will be its real width?
  c The carpenter plans to make the piece of furniture 1·86 m high. Work out the height in the drawing, in cm and mm.

5 Divide
  a 14 in the ratio 5:2
  b 45 in the ratio 4:1
  c 72 in the ratio 1:3:4
  d 35 in the ratio 2:1$\frac{1}{2}$
  e $1\frac{1}{2}$ m in the ratio 3:2:5
  f £5·72 in the ratio 2:9
  g 4·5 in the ratio 2:1:6
  h £8·60 in the ratio $2\frac{1}{6}$:$3\frac{1}{4}$

6 A journey of 85 km is covered partly by train and partly by bus, the respective distances being in the ratio 14:3. Work out the distance covered by train.

7 A road 55 miles long has three roundabouts which divide its length in the ratio 2:1:3:4. Work out the distance between the second and third roundabouts.

8 Lisa has some reggae records and some soul records, the numbers being in the ratio 5:9. If Lisa has 32 more soul records than reggae records, what is the total number of records in her collection?

9 In a local election, the votes received by the Labour, Liberal, Conservative and Independent candidates are in the ratio 6:2:4:1.
  a Given that the Labour candidate's majority over the Conservative candidate is 3500, how many people voted altogether?
  b If 650 parliamentary seats were divided up in the ratio of the votes cast in the above election, how many seats would each party receive?

10 Copy and complete the following tables, given that in each case y is directly proportional to x:

a

x	1	2	5	10
y	15			

b

x	5	10	20	50
y			8	

c

x				35
y	15	35	75	175

d

x	4	14	19	33
y	5			

11 The number of car radios produced by a firm in a week is directly proportional to the number of assemblers employed by the firm. Given that the firm produces 240 car radios when it employs 56 assemblers, work out
  a the number of car radios that will be produced when 126 assemblers are employed,
  b the number of assemblers needed to produce 150 car radios.

12 Copy and complete the following tables, given that in each case the two quantities are in inverse proportion:

a

4	6	8	16
12	8		

c

	18		
1·5	2·5	4·5	7·5

b

1	2	3	4
120			

d

8	6	4·2	2·8
21			

13 To store a batch of screws, a factory needs 90 boxes when the average number of screws per box is 760. Work out
  a the number of boxes that would be needed if the average number of screws per box were 720,
  b the average number of screws per box if 80 boxes were used.

14 Say in each of the following cases whether the two quantities are in direct proportion, in inverse proportion, or neither:

a

2	6	8	20
16	48	80	160

d

2·4	3	4	12
0·5	0·4	0·3	0·1

b

3	5	10	20
100	60	30	15

e

5	10	15	20
10	15	20	25

c

150	120	90	72
25	20	15	12

f

0·2	1·2	1·8	2·2
50	300	450	550

15 In a physics experiment, wires of various resistances are connected to a pair of terminals and the current is measured. The following results are recorded:

Resistance (ohms)	5	8	12	15	20
Current (amps)	2	1·26	0·83	0·57	0·49

  a Which measurement of current appears to be a mistaken reading and what would be a reasonable reading to two decimal places?
  b To two decimal places, what current would you expect with a resistance of 22 ohms?
  c To the nearest whole number, what resistance would give a current of 0·17 amps?

Rate

Exercise 7A

1. Meryl earns a wage of £75 per week. Work out how much she earns in
   a 17 weeks,
   b a year.

   Work out also the time for which Meryl needs to work in order to earn
   c £1050,
   d £2175.

2. Simon's normal walking speed is $1.5\,\text{m s}^{-1}$. Work out how far in kilometres he will normally walk in
   a 15 minutes,
   b 1 h 20 min.

   Work out also the time Simon will normally take to walk
   c 570 m,
   d 3 km.

3. A car uses 2·3 gallons of petrol in travelling 85 miles on a motorway.
   a Work out, to the nearest whole number, how many miles per gallon the car is doing.
   b Given that the car has 5·7 gallons left in its tank, work out, to the nearest mile, how many more miles the car can travel before running out of petrol. (Assume that the petrol consumption does not change.)

4. a Work out the average speed in m s^{-1} of a car which travels 6·48 km in three minutes.
   b At this speed, how long to the nearest minute will the car take to travel 100 km?

5. The population of a country is increasing at an average rate of 38 people per day.
   a Work out, to the nearest 100, how much the population will increase by in two years.
   b Work out, to the nearest day, how long the population will take to increase by 5000.

6. At her top speed, a journalist can type 325 words in five minutes.
   a Work out her maximum rate of typing, in words per minute.
   b Work out the maximum number of words she can type in a quarter of an hour.

   Normally the journalist works at 4/5 of her top speed. Working at this speed, she types out a news article containing 1247 words.
   c How long does this take, to the nearest minute?

7. Andrew is going on holiday to Spain and needs to change some English pounds into pesetas. The exchange rate is 206 pesetas to the pound.
   a How many pesetas will Andrew obtain for £125·50?

When he returns to England, Andrew has 827 pesetas to convert back to pounds. The exchange rate is now 209 pesetas to the pound.
b How much English money does he obtain, to the nearest penny?

8. The first 45 miles of a 77 mile journey take $1\frac{1}{2}$ hours and the rest of the journey is covered at 16 mph. Work out
   a the average speed at which the first 45 miles is covered,
   b the time taken for the whole journey,
   c the average speed for the whole journey.

9. Jim Highgate, a best-selling author, sets out to write three pages of his new book on five days of each week. The pages contain, on average, 340 words each. Work out
   a how many pages Jim plans to write in four weeks,
   b how many words he plans to write per week.

   The book will eventually contain about 90 000 words. Work out
   c how many weeks altogether it is likely to take Jim to write the book, giving the answer to the nearest whole number.

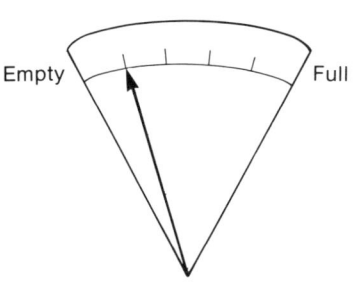

10. The figure on the left shows the petrol gauge of a car whose tank can hold 14 gallons of petrol. The car does an average of 27 miles to the gallon and the driver does not like to risk having less than half a gallon in the tank. Estimate to the nearest mile how far the car can travel before the driver needs to fill up.

11. A factory produces 180 toasters at a rate of 15 toasters per hour, then works at twice this rate for the next 3 hours. Work out
    a the total number of toasters produced,
    b the total time taken,
    c the average rate at which all the toasters are produced.

12. A woman walks a distance of $7\frac{1}{2}$ km at 5 km h^{-1}, then cycles for the same length of time. Her average speed for the whole journey is $8\frac{1}{2} \text{ km h}^{-1}$. Work out
    a the time she takes for the whole journey,
    b the total distance she covers,
    c the average speed at which she cycles.

Exercise 7B

1. In a mathematics test consisting of 48 short questions, Phillip answers the questions at a rate of $1\frac{1}{3}$ questions per minute.
   a How many questions will Phillip answer in the first half an hour?
   b How long will Phillip take to complete the first quarter of the test?
   c If he is allowed 40 minutes altogether, how long will Phillip have left at the end of the test for checking?

2. A car covers 225 km in $2\frac{1}{2}$ hours. Work out
   a the car's average speed in km h^{-1},
   b its average speed in m s^{-1},
   c how far the car will travel, at this average speed, in 6·4 s,
   d how far the car will travel, at this average speed, in 3 h 25 min.

3   Mrs O'Neill finds that in 423 km of town driving, her car uses 45 litres of petrol. Work out
    a the average number of kilometres per litre that Mrs O'Neill is getting from her car.

    On 5 days of each week Mrs O'Neill drives to and from her office, which is 12·5 km from her home. Work out
    b how many litres of petrol she will normally use per week for these journeys, to the nearest litre.

4   A long-distance runner trains by running at a steady speed of $5.2\,\mathrm{m\,s^{-1}}$. Work out
    a the distance in metres she runs in an hour,
    b her speed in $\mathrm{km\,h^{-1}}$.

    One day the runner maintains her normal training speed for 45 minutes, then jogs at half this speed for 20 minutes. Work out
    c how far she runs altogether, in kilometres.

5   A visitor to Australia receives 624 dollars for £260. Work out
    a the exchange rate, in dollars per pound,
    b the amount of Australian money that would be obtained for £430,
    c the amount of English money, to the nearest penny, that would be obtained for 500 dollars.

6   A bus travels at an average speed of $8\,\mathrm{m\,s^{-1}}$ for 30 s, then at an average speed of $12\,\mathrm{m\,s^{-1}}$ for 10 s. Work out
    a the total distance the bus travels,
    b its average speed for the two-stage journey.

    The bus then travels another 140 m at such a speed that its overall average speed for the three-stage journey becomes $10\,\mathrm{m\,s^{-1}}$. Work out
    c its speed for the third stage of the journey.

7   A theatre's prices for tickets are set out in the following table:

	IRVING THEATRE Seat Prices		
	Low rate	Middle rate	Peak rate
Stalls	£9	£10·50	£13·50
Lower gallery	£7	£8·50	£11
Upper gallery	£5·50	£6·50	£8·50

The peak rate is charged for the months of May to August inclusive, the low rate for the months of November to February inclusive, and the middle rate for the other months. There are no reduced rates for children.
    a A man wants to take his wife and two children to see *Julius Caesar* on 18 September. How much will this cost if he books tickets in the stalls?
    b A party of 20 children pays a total of £110 to see a performance of *Peter Pan*. Do they go in the winter or the summer, and where do they sit?
    c A woman books two tickets for *The Phantom of the Opera* for 25 April, but has to cancel and re-book for a fortnight later. The new tickets, which are for the same seats, cost an extra £5. What is the position of the seats?

8   A pipe delivers 240 litres of water at a rate of 400 litres per minute, then delivers water at $1\frac{1}{2}$ times this rate for 14 s. Work out the average rate of delivery in litres per second.

9   A 3-hour journey is covered in two stages at an overall average speed of 40 km h^{-1}. The distances covered in the two stages are in the ratio 3:1 and the times are in the ratio 3:2. Work out the ratio of the average speeds at which the two stages are covered.

10 A solicitors' office makes an average of 40 telephone calls per hour. The office works a 7-hour day and a 5-day week. Work out
    a the average number of telephone calls made by the office per week,
    b the time normally taken, in weeks and days to the nearest day, for the office to make 5000 calls.

    The calls cost, on average, 6·4p each. Work out
    c the office's average weekly telephone bill,
    d the approximate time it takes, in hours to the nearest whole number, for the office to spend £50 on telephone calls.

Practical graphs

Exercise 8A

1   The following conversion graph relates kilograms and pounds:

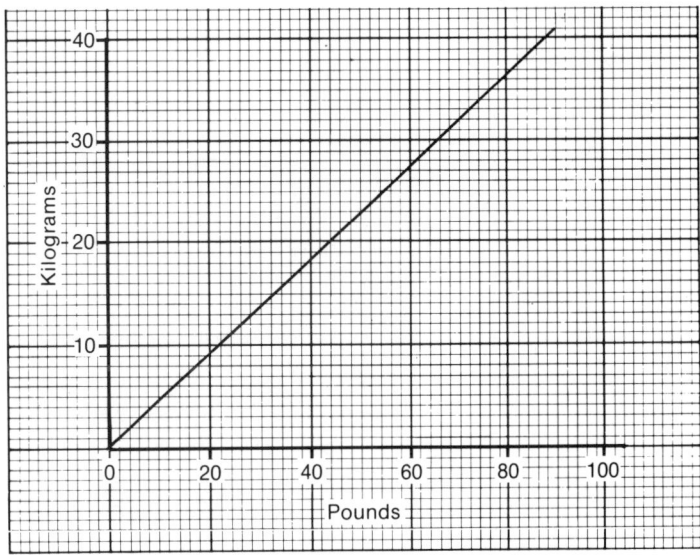

Use the graph to find, to the nearest whole number
a the weight in kilograms of a girl who weighs 82 lb,
b the weight in pounds of a chair which weighs 8 kg,
c the total weight in kilograms of four articles weighing 16 lb each,
d the total weight in pounds of three articles weighing 7·3 kg each.

2 A manufacturing firm finds that the time taken to make a certain product varies with the number of people working on the product as shown in the following table:

Number of people	5	10	15	20	25	30
Time taken	76	70	62	50	44	34

Draw a scatter diagram to represent these data on graph paper, letting 2 cm represent 5 people and letting 2 cm represent 20 days. Draw a line of best fit and use it to estimate
a the time that would be taken if 8 people were working,
b the number of people that would take 40 days to make the product.

3

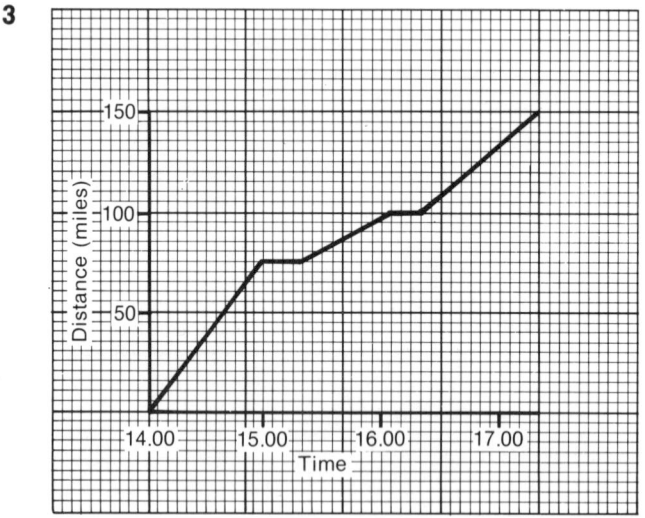

The above graph represents the journey of a train which travels 150 miles altogether and stops at two stations. Work out
a how long the train spends at each station,
b how far apart the stations are,
c the speed of the train on the first stage of its journey,
d the time at which it starts the final stage of its journey,
e its speed on the final stage of its journey,
f how long it spends in motion altogether.

4 From the following table construct a conversion graph relating English pounds and French francs:

Pounds	1·4	2·6	3·7
Francs	15	28	40

Use the graph to convert
a £3·50 to francs, to the nearest whole number,
b 23 francs to pounds and pence, to the nearest 10p.

5 The following table shows a car's petrol consumption at various steady speeds:

Speed (miles per hour)	20	30	38	55	70	80
Miles per gallon	33	40	43	42	32	22

Represent the above data as a series of points on graph paper and draw as smooth a curve as possible through the points. Use the graph to estimate
a the maximum number of miles per gallon that can be obtained, and the speed at which this occurs,
b the two speeds at which the car does 35 miles to the gallon.

6 A cyclist, a car driver and a runner each make the same 20 km journey, starting at the same time. The three journeys are represented by the travel graphs shown below.

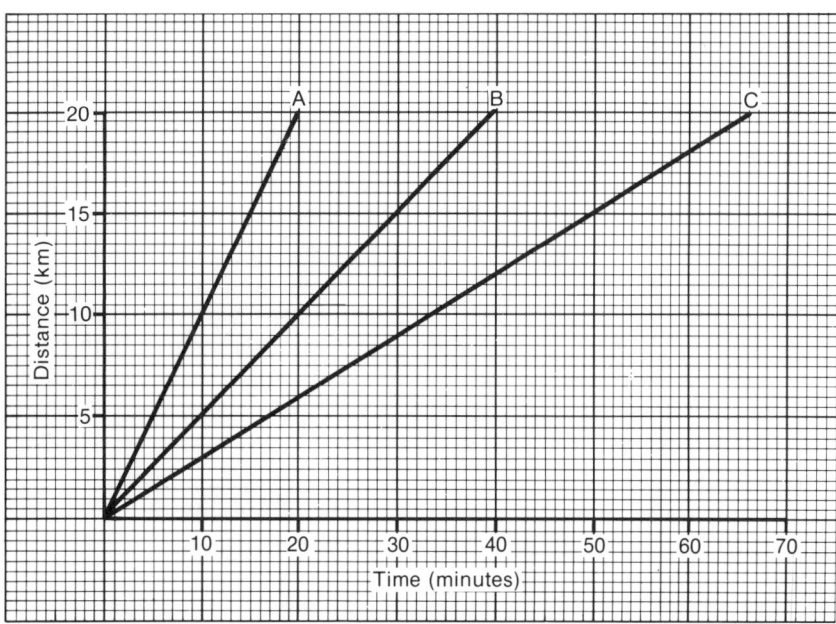

a Say which line represents which traveller and work out the speed of each.
b Work out the difference between the time taken by the runner and the time taken by the cyclist for the complete journey.
c When the car is at the halfway point, how far ahead of the runner is it?

Five minutes after completing the 20 km journey, the car is driven back to its starting point at constant speed, arriving exactly 1 hour after it originally set out. Work out
d the time at which the car passes the cyclist and their distance from the starting point at this time.

7. The charges made by a car-hire company for renting a small car for a day are shown below:

TRAVELRITE
— RENT - A - CAR —

▶ Low cost rental on ALL small cars

Distance covered in miles	0	50	100	150	200
Cost in pounds	30	40	50	60	70

▶ Extensive insurance cover

▶ Free delivery

Phone us now on
ASHWELL 68301

Draw a graph of distance against cost and use the graph to work out
 a the cost of hiring a car and driving it 115 miles,
 b the distance which can be covered for £48.

The cost of hiring a car can be considered to be made up of a standing charge and a charge of a certain amount per mile driven. Work out
 c the standing charge,   d the charge per mile.

Another company makes a standing charge of £10 and charges 40p per mile for the same type of car. On the same graph paper draw the graph of distance against cost for this case and work out
 e the distance for which the two companies charge the same amount.

8. The table below shows the numbers of pages and the weights of some of the books in a certain series of paperbacks.

Number of pages	80	170	290	410	530	690
Weight (grams)	60	120	185	260	335	430

Represent the data on a scatter diagram, letting 2 cm represent 100 pages and letting 4 cm represent 100 g. Draw a line of best fit and use it to estimate
 a the weight of a book containing 500 pages,
 b the number of pages in a book weighing 370 g,
 c the increase in weight which results from adding 50 pages to a book.

9. Mehmet and Denise visit each other's towns, which are 40 km apart, on the same afternoon. Their journeys are represented by the two travel graphs below.

 a Which of the two people takes the longer time for the journey, and by how much?
 b Estimate the time at which they cross.
 c For how long altogether is Denise stationary?

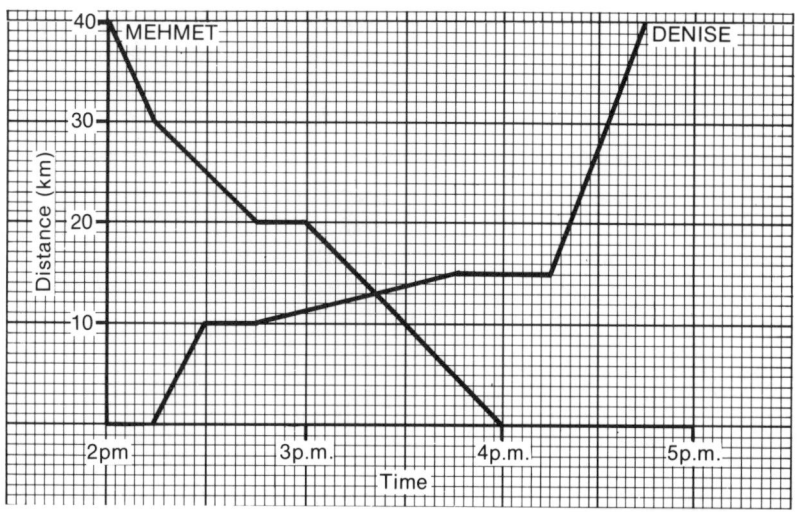

d How far does Mehmet travel while Denise stops for the first time?
e What is the highest speed at which either of the two people travels?
f What is the lowest speed at which either of the two travels?

Exercise 8B

1 The following graph shows how the temperature of a room changes through one night in winter. The room is warmed during the day by central heating, but the heating is turned off at night.

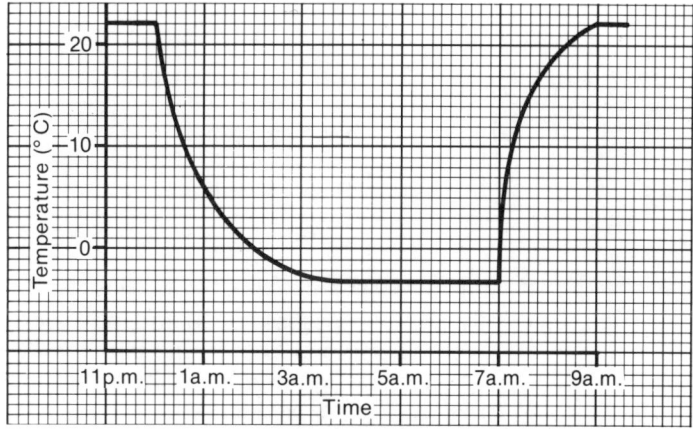

a For how long is the central heating turned off?
b What is the daytime temperature of the room?
c What temperature does the room fall to when the heating is turned off?
d To the nearest 10 minutes, what are the two times at which the temperature is 10°C?
e Approximately how long does the room take to rise from its lowest temperature to 16°C?
f How much does the temperature fall between 1 a.m. and 3 a.m.?

2 Andy walks from his home to his cousin's house to collect some tapes, chats to her for a few minutes, then walks home, calling in at the newsagents on the way back. This journey is represented by the following travel graph:

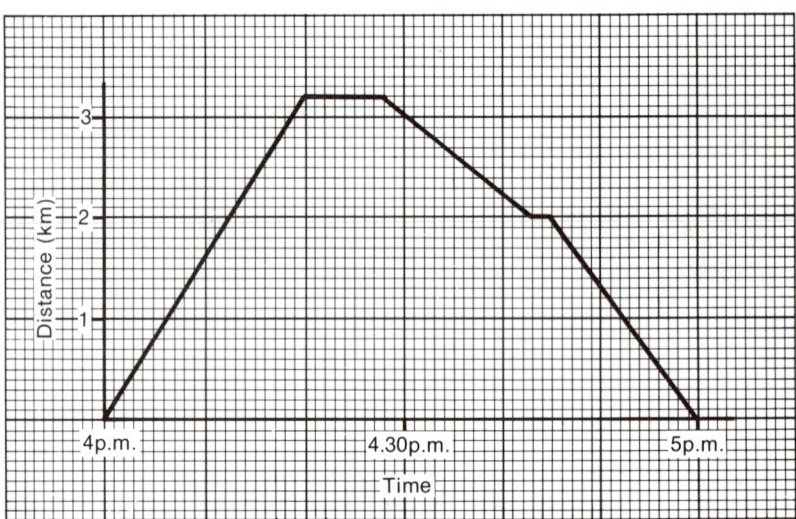

a How far from Andy's home does his cousin live?
b How long does Andy stay with his cousin?
c At what time does he arrive at the newsagents?
d How long does he take to get from the newsagents to his home?
e How fast does he walk from the newsagents to his home, in km/h?
f How fast does he walk to his cousin's house, in km/h?

3 One summer a travel company finds that the number of holidays it sells varies with the prices of the holidays as shown in the following table:

Price of holiday	£50	£120	£200	£280	£350	£430
Number of holidays booked	240	210	190	160	140	120

Display this information in a scatter diagram, letting 2 cm represent £100 and letting 4 cm represent 100 holidays. Draw a line of best fit and use it to estimate
a the number of holidays costing £230 that the company could expect to sell,
b the price of a holiday which would be likely to sell to 200 people,
c the number of people who would be likely to buy a £600 holiday.

4 From the following table draw a conversion graph relating German marks and Danish kroner:

Marks	21	30	42
Kroner	80	114	160

Giving the answers to the nearest whole number, use the graph to convert
a 14 marks to kroner,
b 126 kroner to marks.

5 On August Bank Holiday, the number of people at a funfair varies as shown in the following table:

Number of minutes after opening	0	20	50	80	110	150	190	230	290	360	450	600
Number of people at funfair	0	200	400	600	760	960	1080	1160	1160	1080	940	640

Plot this information as a series of points on graph paper. Let the horizontal axis represent time, with a scale of 2 cm to 100 minutes, and let the vertical axis represent the number of people, with a scale of 2 cm to 200 people. Draw as smooth a curve as possible through the points and use the graph to estimate
a the maximum number of people at the funfair, and the time at which this occurs,
b the two times at which there are 820 people at the funfair,
c the increase in the number of people at the funfair in the second hour after it opens,
d the time it takes for the number of people to fall from 1000 to 700.

6 A train leaves Carminster Station at 14·00 and travels at a constant speed to Bankwell Station, which is 90 km away. It arrives at Bankwell at 15·00, stays for 10 minutes then returns at constant speed to Carminster. On its return journey the train passes through Stratfield Station, which is 60 km from Carminster, at 15·40.

Draw a travel graph to represent this journey, letting 6 cm represent 1 hour and letting 2 cm represent 20 km. Work out from the graph
a the time at which the train arrives back at Carminster,
b its speed on the return journey,
c the time interval between the train's two visits to Stratfield Station.

At a distance of 18 km from Bankwell Station there is a level crossing. Work out
d the two times at which the train reaches the crossing.

7 Mr Jarvis owns a hamburger stall. The following table shows how his daily expenses depend upon the number of hamburgers he makes:

Number of hamburgers	8	12	20	32
Expenses	£4	£5·20	£7·60	£11·20

Draw a graph of expenses against the number of hamburgers made and use it to find
a how much Mr Jarvis spends when he makes 16 hamburgers,
b how many hamburgers he can make for £8·80.

Mr Jarvis's expenses are made up of an initial outlay together with a certain cost for each hamburger. Work out
c the initial outlay,
d the additional cost of each hamburger.

Mr Jarvis charges his customers 56p for each hamburger. Using the same graph paper, draw a second graph to represent the money he receives against the number of hamburgers he sells. Work out
e the minimum number of hamburgers Mr Jarvis must sell to make a profit,
f how much profit he makes if he sells 20 hamburgers.

8   The following travel graphs represent the journeys of two cars which are on the same road and are initially moving towards each other.

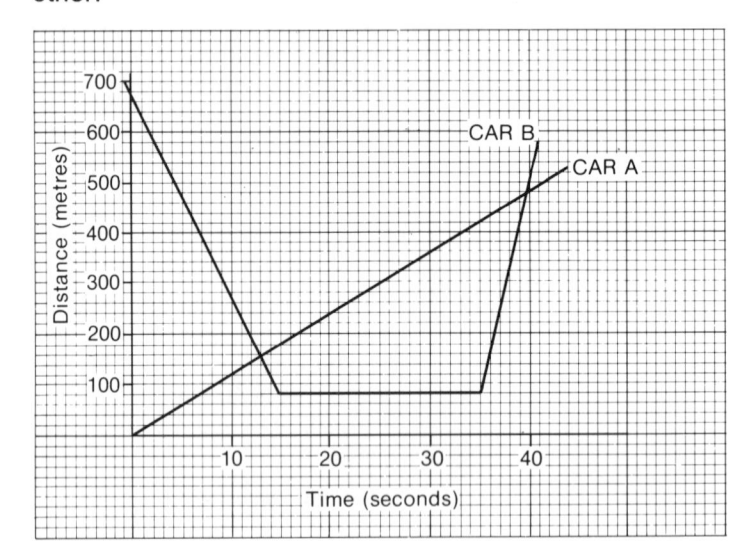

Use the graphs to work out
a the time for which car B is stationary,
b the time interval between the two moments at which the cars are together,
c the speed of car A,
d the initial speed of car B,
e the distance apart of the cars at the moment when car B starts to move in the same direction as car A,
f the distance travelled by car A while car B is stationary.

9   Each of the graphs on the left is of unemployment (on the vertical axis) against time (on the horizontal axis). In each case, say which of the graphs (i) to (vi) is being referred to:
a Unemployment is falling at a steady rate.
b Unemployment is rising more rapidly.
c Unemployment has been unchanged for some time.
d Unemployment has reached a peak and is now falling.
e Unemployment is falling, but by less and less each month.
f Unemployment is rising, but the rate of increase is going down.

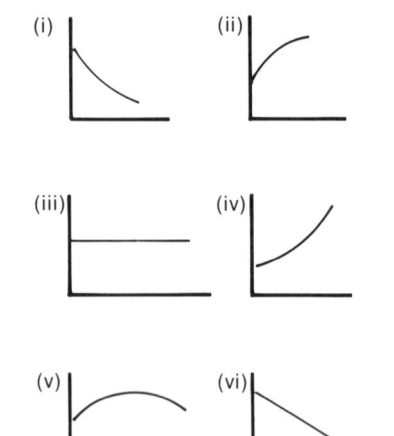

Indices, standard form

Note: *Do not use a calculator in Exercises 9A to 10B.*

Exercise 9A

1. Work out:
   a. 3^2
   b. 3^{-2}
   c. 2^3
   d. 2^{-3}
   e. 5^4
   f. 5^{-4}
   g. 7^{-2}
   h. 2^{-5}
   i. 6^{-3}

2. Work out:
   a. $\left(\frac{1}{4}\right)^{-2}$
   b. $\left(\frac{1}{3}\right)^{-4}$
   c. $\left(\frac{2}{3}\right)^{-1}$
   d. $\left(1\frac{1}{4}\right)^{-1}$
   e. $\left(\frac{2}{3}\right)^{-2}$

3. Work out, expressing the answers as fractions or whole numbers:
   a. 0.25^{-1}
   b. 0.2^{-2}
   c. 0.05^{-2}
   d. 0.9^{-1}
   e. 0.04^{-2}

4. Work out:
   a. 4.23×10
   b. 0.708×10^2
   c. 6.2×10^4
   d. $\dfrac{460}{10^2}$
   e. $\dfrac{29.7}{10^3}$
   f. 50×10^{-1}
   g. 7×10^{-2}
   h. 0.49×10^{-2}
   i. 64.23×10^{-3}
   j. 3700×10^{-8}

5. State in words the rules for
   a. multiplying a number by 10^n,
   b. multiplying a number by 10^{-n}.

6. Express in standard form:
   a. 857
   b. 0.24
   c. 0.000 541
   d. 236 000
   e. 72 million
   f. 0.000 009

7. Express in standard form:
   a. 0.3×10^{-2}
   b. 2600×400
   c. 0.07^2
   d. $\dfrac{0.0069}{0.3}$
   e. $\dfrac{4 \times 10^5}{2 \times 10^2}$
   f. $\dfrac{6 \times 10^3}{12 \times 10^7}$
   g. $\dfrac{2}{0.008}$

8. Express as a power of 2:
   a. $2^5 \times 2^3$
   b. $2 \times 2^4 \times 2^7$
   c. $2^x \times 2^y$
   d. $\dfrac{2^{11}}{2^4}$
   e. $\dfrac{2^2}{2^7}$
   f. $\dfrac{2^x}{2^y}$
   g. $\dfrac{2^9 \times 2^4}{2^5}$
   h. $\dfrac{2^5}{2^7 \times 2^4}$

9 Express as a power of 5:
  a $5^4 \times 5^{-1}$
  b $5^6 \times 5^{-8}$
  c $5^{-3} \times 5^{-2}$
  d $5^{4x} \times 5^{-8x} \times 5^{-2x}$

10 Express as a power of 3:
  a $(3^2)^3$
  b $(3^4)^5$
  c $(3^x)^y$
  d 9^4
  e 27^5
  f $9^5 \times 81^2$
  g $\dfrac{27^4}{9^3}$
  h $\dfrac{243}{81^4}$

Exercise 9B

1 Work out
  a 7^2
  b 7^{-2}
  c 2^{-6}
  d 10^{-3}
  e 3^{-4}

2 Work out:
  a $\left(\tfrac{1}{3}\right)^{-2}$
  b $\left(\tfrac{1}{2}\right)^{-4}$
  c $\left(\tfrac{2}{5}\right)^{-1}$
  d $\left(1\tfrac{2}{9}\right)^{-1}$
  e $\left(\tfrac{3}{4}\right)^{-2}$

3 Work out, expressing the answers as fractions or whole numbers:
  a $0 \cdot 1^{-1}$
  b $0 \cdot 25^{-2}$
  c $0 \cdot 6^{-1}$
  d $0 \cdot 02^{-2}$
  e $0 \cdot 05^{-3}$

4 Work out:
  a $0 \cdot 27 \times 10^2$
  b $0 \cdot 0069 \times 10^3$
  c $5 \cdot 8 \times 10^4$
  d 3×10^{-1}
  e 820×10^{-2}
  f $0 \cdot 72 \times 10^{-3}$

5 Express in standard form:
  a 9650
  b 0·053
  c a quarter of a million
  d 0·000 02
  e 4 684 000

6 Express in standard form:
  a $0 \cdot 02 \times 0 \cdot 003$
  b $0 \cdot 008 \times 10^5$
  c $4 \times 10^2 \times 7 \times 10^4$
  d $\dfrac{0 \cdot 00015}{0 \cdot 05}$
  e $\dfrac{12 \times 10^2}{3 \times 10^8}$
  f $\dfrac{9 \times 10^7}{15 \times 10^3}$

7 Express as a power of 3:
  a $3^6 \times 3^7$
  b $\dfrac{3^{12}}{3^{10}}$
  c $3^{2x} \times 3^{5x}$
  d $\dfrac{3^{7a}}{3^{2a}}$
  e $\dfrac{3 \times 3^6 \times 3^4}{3^7}$
  f $\dfrac{3^5}{3^4 \times 3^{10}}$

8 Express as a power of 7:
  a $7^6 \times 7^{-2}$
  b $7^2 \times 7^{-5} \times 7$
  c $7^{-3} \times 7^{-8}$
  d $7^{-3x} \times 7^{6x} \times 7^{-x}$

9 Express as a power of 2:
  a $(2^4)^2$
  b $(2^x)^5$
  c 8^3
  d 4^7
  e $4^5 \times 32$
  f $8^4 \times 16^3$
  g $\dfrac{16^6}{32^2}$
  h $\dfrac{64}{8^7}$

Zero, negative and fractional indices

Exercise 10A

Work out the values of the following quantities:

1 4^0
2 $9^{1/2}$
3 $\left(\tfrac{1}{4}\right)^{1/2}$
4 $8^{1/3}$
5 $125^{1/3}$
6 $27^{2/3}$
7 $16^{3/4}$
8 $36^{-1/2}$
9 $81^{-3/4}$
10 $343^{-2/3}$
11 $\left(\tfrac{1}{9}\right)^{-3/2}$
12 $\left(2\tfrac{1}{4}\right)^{-1/2}$
13 1^0
14 $\left(\tfrac{1}{64}\right)^{-1/3}$
15 $(0.25)^{-2\tfrac{1}{2}}$
16 $\left(11\tfrac{1}{9}\right)^{-0.5}$
17 $32^{-0.4}$
18 $\left(5\tfrac{4}{9}\right)^{0.5}$
19 $625^{-0.75}$
20 $\left(3\tfrac{3}{8}\right)^{-1\tfrac{1}{3}}$
21 $\dfrac{4^0 - 4^{1/2}}{4^{-1} - 4^{-1\tfrac{1}{2}}}$
22 $(3^{-1} + 3^{-2})^{-1/2}$

23 Given that $f(x) = 9^x$, work out the values of
  a $f(0)$
  b $f(-1)$
  c $f(-0.5)$
  d $f(2.5)$

24 Given that $f(x) = x^{-1/3}$, work out the values of
  a $f(8)$
  b $f(1/27)$
  c $f(0.216)$

25 Solve the equations
  a $25^x = \tfrac{1}{5}$
  b $x^{-1\tfrac{1}{2}} = 343$
  c $64^x = 32$

Use the index laws to simplify the following quantities, then work out their values:

26 $3^{1\frac{1}{2}} \times 3^{2\frac{1}{2}}$

27 $4^{1\frac{1}{4}}/4^{3/4}$

28 $(5^{1/2})^4$

29 $(16^{0\cdot6})^{1\cdot25}$

30 For a certain period the population of a country roughly obeys the equation $N = 16(1\cdot25)^t$, where N is the population in millions and t is the time in years after 1 January 1980. Work out
 a the approximate population on 1 January 1980,
 b the approximate population on 1 January 1982,
 c the approximate date on which the population is $8\sqrt{5}$ million.

Exercise 10B

Work out the values of the following quantities:

1 $49^{1/2}$
2 $121^{1/2}$
3 7^0
4 $27^{1/3}$
5 $256^{1/4}$
6 $8^{2/3}$
7 $625^{3/4}$
8 $100^{-1/2}$
9 $\left(\frac{1}{144}\right)^{-1/2}$
10 10^0
11 $64^{-2/3}$
12 $(6\frac{1}{4})^{1\frac{1}{2}}$
13 $128^{5/7}$
14 $\left(\frac{125}{512}\right)^{-2/3}$
15 $(0\cdot125)^{-2\frac{2}{3}}$
16 $4\cdot84^{-0\cdot5}$
17 $(0\cdot0081)^{-0\cdot25}$
18 $1296^{0\cdot75}$
19 $(2^0 - 2^{-1})^{-2}$
20 $\dfrac{9^{-1/2}}{9^{-1} - 9^{-1\frac{1}{2}}}$

21 Given that $f(x) = (0\cdot25)^x$, work out the values of
 a $f(0)$ **b** $f(-1)$ **c** $f(\frac{1}{2})$ **d** $f(-1\frac{1}{2})$

22 Given that $f(x) = x^{-1\cdot5}$, work out the values of
 a $f(1)$ **b** $f(9)$ **c** $f(0\cdot04)$

23 Solve the equations
 a $4^x = 32$ **b** $x^{2/3} = 100$ **c** $(0\cdot125)^x = 2$

Use the index laws to simplify the following quantities, then work out their values:

24 $2^{2\cdot4} \times 2^{3\cdot6}$

25 $9^{1/6}/9^{2/3}$

26 $(3^{2/5})^{10}$

27 $(32^{0\cdot25})^{0\cdot8}$

28 For a certain period the velocity of a decelerating body is given by the formula $v = 40 \times 2^{-t}$, where $v\,\mathrm{m\,s}^{-1}$ is the velocity of the body after t seconds. Work out
 a the initial velocity of the body,
 b the velocities after 1 s, 2 s and 3 s,
 c the decrease in the velocity in the third second of the motion,
 d the time at which the velocity is $20\sqrt{2}\,\mathrm{m\,s}^{-1}$.

Set Theory

Note: *The whole of this section is Level 3.*

Language and notation

Exercise 11A

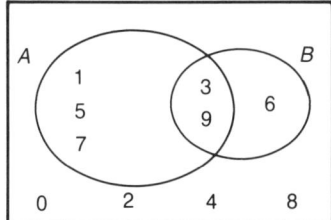

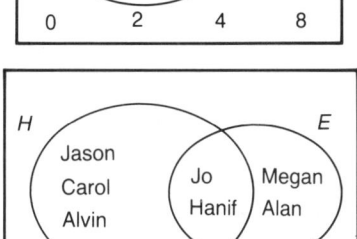

1. In the Venn diagram on the left A is the set {odd numbers} and B is the set {multiples of 3}. Give brief descriptions of the following sets:
   a. the universal set
   b. $A \cap B$
   c. $A \cup B$
   d. A'
   e. $(A \cup B)'$

2. The Venn diagram on the left shows the students in a sixth form tutor group. H is the set of students who study history and E is the set of students who study economics. List the students who
   a. study both subjects,
   b. study history but not economics,
   c. study either history or economics,
   d. do not study economics.

   List also the members of the following sets:
   e. $(H \cup E)'$
   f. $H' \cap E$
   g. $H \cup E'$

3. $\mathscr{E}$ is the set {letters of the alphabet up to and including h}, $A = $ {vowels} and B is the set {d, e, f, g}. Work out the values of
   a. $n(\mathscr{E})$
   b. $n(A')$
   c. $n(A \cap B)$
   d. $n(A \cup B)$
   e. $n(A' \cap B')$

4. In each of the Venn diagrams below, S is the set of students in a class who like strawberries and B is the set of those in the class who like blackberries.

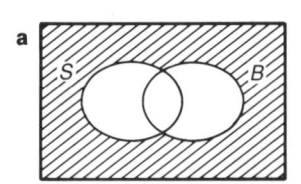

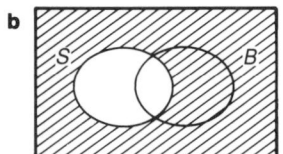

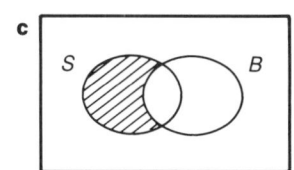

   Describe, both in words and in set notation, the sets represented by the shaded areas.

35

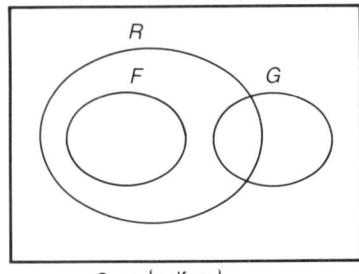

G = {golfers}
F = {people who fish}
R = {ramblers}

5 The Venn diagram on the left shows the results of a survey in which all the members of a club are asked whether they play golf, go fishing or enjoy rambling. Given that each region of the Venn diagram contains some members, say whether the following statements are true or false:
   a All the ramblers fish.
   b $F \cap G = \emptyset$.
   c R and G are disjoint sets.
   d $F \subset G'$.
   e $R' \cap G \subset F'$.
   f G' and F' are disjoint sets.
   g $F \cap R = F$.
   h All those who do not ramble do not fish.
   i All those who neither play golf nor fish are ramblers.
   j $R \cup F \cup G = R \cup G$.

6 $\mathscr{E} = \{$natural numbers from 3 to 12 inclusive$\}$, $P = \{$prime numbers$\}$ and $Q = \{4, 6, 7, 9, 11\}$. List the following sets:
   a Q'
   b $P \cap Q$
   c $P \cup Q$
   d $P \cap Q'$
   e $P' \cup Q$

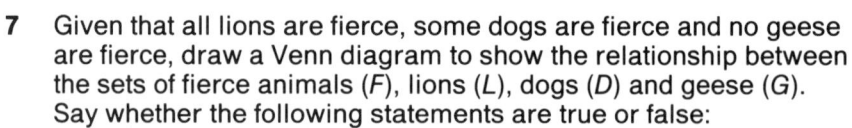

7 Given that all lions are fierce, some dogs are fierce and no geese are fierce, draw a Venn diagram to show the relationship between the sets of fierce animals (F), lions (L), dogs (D) and geese (G). Say whether the following statements are true or false:
   a The sets D and G are disjoint.
   b F is a subset of G'.
   c $L' \subset F$.
   d $L \cap D' = L$.
   e $F \cap D \cap G = F \cap D$.
   f $F' \cap L = \emptyset$.
   g $F \cup L = F$.
   h $D' \subset F'$.

8 It is found that all the staff in an office have at least one of the skills of typing, using a word processor and doing shorthand. While, however, some of the typists can use the word processor and there are also some typists who can do shorthand, none of the staff can both use the word processor and do shorthand. Draw a Venn diagram to show the relationship between the sets of people who can type (T), use a word processor (W) and do shorthand (S).

What can you say about the following sets:
   a $T \cap W \cap S$?
   b $T \cup W \cup S$?
   c $T' \cup W' \cup S'$?
   d $T' \cap W' \cap S'$?

9 Letting the set of people in a room who have blue eyes be B, the set of people over six feet tall be T and the set of those who have ginger hair be G, express each of the following statements in ordinary English:

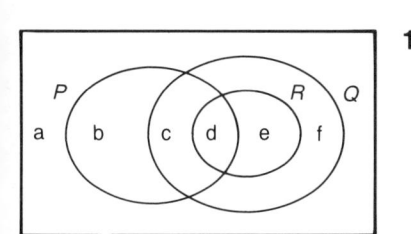

a $G \subset T$
b $B \cap G = \emptyset$
c $n(B \cup T) = 8$
d $n(G \cap B') = 3$
e $T \cap G \subset B'$

10 From the Venn diagram on the left list the small letters which represent each of the following sets:
a $P \cup R$
b P'
c $P \cap Q \cap R$
d $(P \cup Q \cup R)'$
e $P \cap Q'$
f $P' \cap Q \cap R'$
g $P' \cap Q'$
h $P \cup R'$

11 $\mathscr{E} = \{\text{natural numbers}\}$, $P = \{\text{prime numbers}\}$, $S = \{\text{square numbers}\}$, $O = \{\text{odd numbers}\}$. Say whether the following statements are true or false:
a $221 \in P$.
b $P \cap S = \emptyset$.
c P is a subset of O.
d $256 \in S \cap O$.
e $S \subset P'$.
f $169 \in P \cup S$.
(Note that 1 is not a prime number.)

Exercise 11B

Level 3

1 $P = \{a, c, f, g, j\}$ and $Q = \{b, c, d, f, h, j\}$. List the sets
a $P \cap Q$
b $P \cup Q$

2 Given that $\mathscr{E} = \{\text{natural numbers}\}$, $A = \{\text{even numbers}\}$ and $B = \{\text{multiples of 5}\}$, give brief descriptions of the following sets:
a $A \cap B$
b $A \cup B$
c A'
d $A' \cap B$

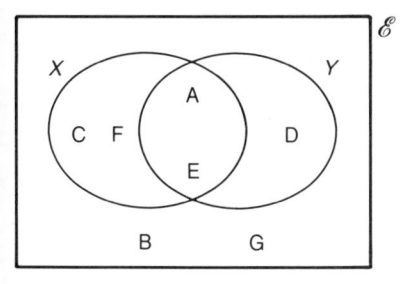

3 In the Venn diagram on the left, $\mathscr{E} = \{\text{letters of the alphabet from A to G}\}$, $X = \{\text{letters of the word FACE}\}$, $Y = \{\text{letters of the word DEAD}\}$. List the letters which are members of
a both sets,
b either of the sets,
c X',
d $(X \cup Y)'$,
e $X \cap Y'$,
f $X' \cup Y'$.

4 $\mathscr{E} = \{$natural numbers from 10 to 20 inclusive$\}$, $P = \{$prime numbers$\}$, $Q = \{13, 14, 15, 16, 17, 18\}$. Work out the values of
   a $n(\mathscr{E})$
   b $n(P)$
   c $n(Q')$
   d $n(P \cap Q)$
   e $n(P \cup Q)$
   f $n(P' \cap Q)$
   g $n(P \cup Q')$

5 In each of the Venn diagrams **a**, **b** and **c** on the left, S is the set of people in a club who like snooker and H is the set of those who like hockey. Describe, both in words and in set notation, the sets represented by the shaded areas.

6 Letting T be the set of students who watched television last night, R the set of those who listened to the radio and M the set of those who played records, express each of the following statements in ordinary English:
   a $M \cap R = \emptyset$
   b $n(T \cup M) = 15$
   c $R \subset T$
   d $n(T \cup M)' = 3$
   e $n(R' \cap T \cap M') = 7$

7 $\mathscr{E} = \{$natural numbers from 1 to 10 inclusive$\}$, $P = \{$primes$\}$, $Q = \{2, 3, 5, 6, 10\}$, $R = \{3, 4, 5, 6\}$. List the sets
   a $P \cap Q \cap R$
   b $P \cup Q \cup R$
   c $R \cap (P \cup Q)$
   d $P \cup (R \cap Q)$

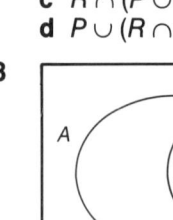

8

Assuming that each region in the above Venn diagram contains members, say whether the following statements are true or false:
   a A and C are disjoint.
   b C is a subset of B.
   c $B \cap C = C$.
   d $A \cap C \subset A \cap B$.
   e $A \subset C'$.
   f $A \cup B \cup C = A \cup B$.
   g $(A \cup B)'$ and C are disjoint.

9 Letting the sets of teenagers who like hamburgers, like chips and like milk shakes be H, C and M, respectively, draw Venn diagrams to illustrate each of the following statements:
   a All the teenagers who like hamburgers like both chips and milk shakes.
   b All the teenagers who like either hamburgers or milk shakes like chips.
   c None of the teenagers who like hamburgers like chips, but some teenagers like both hamburgers and milk shakes and some like both chips and milk shakes.

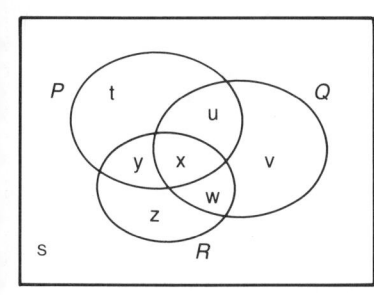

10 From the Venn diagram on the left, list the small letters which represent each of the following sets:
 a $P \cap Q \cap R$
 b $Q \cup R$
 c $P \cap R$
 d $P \cap Q'$
 e $(P \cup Q)'$
 f $(Q \cup R) \cap P$

11 $\mathscr{E}$ = {triangles}, E = {equilateral triangles}, I = {triangles with two or more equal sides}, R = {right-angled triangles}, S = {triangles with no equal sides}. Draw a Venn diagram to show the relationship between these sets, and say whether the following statements are true or false:
 a $E \cap S = \emptyset$.
 b $I \subset R'$.
 c $I \cap E = I$.
 d S and R are disjoint sets.
 e $I \cap R \subset E'$.
 f All subsets of E are subsets of I.
 g $S' \cup I' = \mathscr{E}$.

Numerical problems

Exercise 12A

1 In the Venn diagram on the left, $\mathscr{E}$ is the set of all the pupils in a class, and C and B are the sets of pupils who play chess and bridge, respectively. Write down the number of pupils who play
 a chess,
 b bridge,
 c both games,
 d bridge but not chess,
 e either (or both) of the games,
 f exactly one of the games.

Given, further, that there are 29 pupils in the class, work out the number who
 g play neither game (x, in the diagram),
 h do not play chess.

2 a $n(A) = 20$, $n(B) = 15$ and $n(A \cap B) = 12$. Find $n(A \cup B)$.
 b $n(A) = 35$, $n(B) = 40$ and $n(A \cup B) = 60$. Find $n(A \cap B)$.
 c $n(A) = 50$, $n(A \cup B) = 120$ and A, B are disjoint sets. Find $n(B)$.
 d $n(A \cup B) = 47$, $n(A \cap B) = 21$ and $n(A) = n(B)$. Find $n(A)$.
 e $n(A \cup B) = 32$, $n(A \cap B) = 8$ and $n(A \cap B') = 10$. Find $n(A)$ and $n(B)$.

3 In a group of 30 people, 10 drink lager but not beer, 5 drink beer but not lager and 13 drink neither lager nor beer. How many drink both lager and beer?

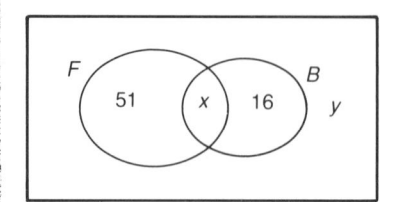

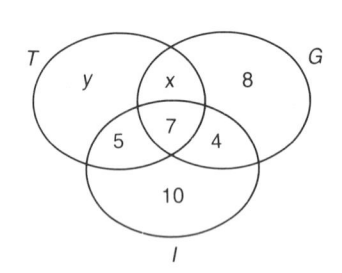

4 As part of a keep-fit programme, 28 members of a health club can opt to attend classes on aerobics, weight training or both of these activities. There is, however, an upper limit of 20 students for the aerobics classes. Given that five students opt for both classes, and more opt for aerobics than for weight training, find the maximum and minimum possible numbers of weight training students.

5 In a survey it is found that 38 families have either a washing machine, a dishwasher or both of these, that 29 have a washing machine, 15 have both types of machine and 26 do not have a dishwasher. Work out the number who
   a have only a washing machine,
   b have a dishwasher,
   c took part in the survey.

6 The Venn diagram on the left shows the percentages of people in a certain town who have fair hair (F) and who have blue eyes (B). Given that twice as many have fair hair as have blue eyes, form an equation in x and solve it, then deduce the value of y.

7 The Venn diagram on the left shows some of the results of a survey to determine the numbers of people who read the Times (T), the Guardian (G) and the Independent (I). All the people surveyed read at least one of these newspapers.

Write down the number of people who read
   a the Independent,
   b both the Independent and the Times,
   c the Independent and the Guardian but not the Times.

Given that 22 people read the Guardian and 36 read either the Times, the Guardian or both, work out
   d x,
   e y,
   f the number of people who read exactly one of the newspapers,
   g the number of people surveyed.

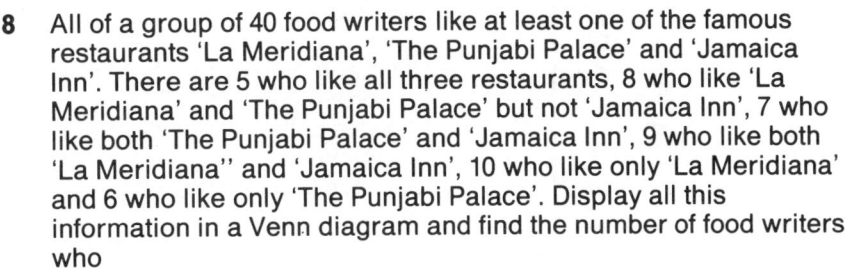

8   All of a group of 40 food writers like at least one of the famous restaurants 'La Meridiana', 'The Punjabi Palace' and 'Jamaica Inn'. There are 5 who like all three restaurants, 8 who like 'La Meridiana' and 'The Punjabi Palace' but not 'Jamaica Inn', 7 who like both 'The Punjabi Palace' and 'Jamaica Inn', 9 who like both 'La Meridiana'' and 'Jamaica Inn', 10 who like only 'La Meridiana' and 6 who like only 'The Punjabi Palace'. Display all this information in a Venn diagram and find the number of food writers who
   a like only 'Jamaica Inn',
   b do not like 'The Punjabi Palace',
   c like exactly two of the restaurants.

9   All of a group of 30 men smoke cigarettes, cigars or a pipe. None of the men smoke both cigarettes and a pipe, but all the cigarette smokers and 3 of the 13 pipe smokers sometimes smoke cigars. The number who smoke only a pipe is twice the number who smoke only cigars. Work out the number of men who smoke
   a cigarettes,
   b cigars but not cigarettes.

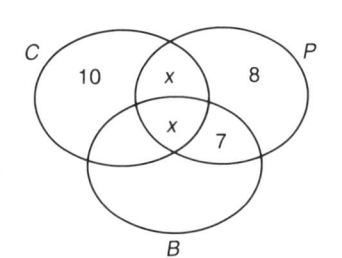

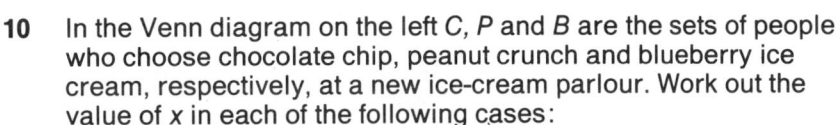

10 In the Venn diagram on the left C, P and B are the sets of people who choose chocolate chip, peanut crunch and blueberry ice cream, respectively, at a new ice-cream parlour. Work out the value of x in each of the following cases:
   a 12 people choose both chocolate chip and peanut crunch.
   b 33 people choose peanut crunch.
   c 30 people choose chocolate chip, and 16 of these also choose blueberry.
   d 75 people choose peanut crunch, blueberry or both, and 50 of these choose blueberry.
   e $n(B \cup C \cup P) = 90$ and $n(B) = 61$.

11 P, Q and R are three sets in which Q is a subset of P, $n(P \cup Q \cup R) = 50$, $n(P) = 35$, $n(Q) = 22$, $n(R) = 25$ and $n(P \cap Q' \cap R) = 6$. Draw a Venn diagram showing the relationship between the three sets and put the correct numbers into each separate region.

12 All the 26 guests at a party can choose anything from a table containing portions of lasagne, pizza and quiche. There are 10 guests who are not hungry and take nothing, while 6 guests take all three of the types of food and 5 guests take two of the three. The quiche is chosen by 7 of the guests, and no one chooses only quiche; while pizza is chosen by 11 guests, only one of whom chooses only pizza.

   Letting the sets of guests who choose lasagne, pizza and quiche be L, P and Q, respectively, draw a Venn diagram and put the correct numbers into each separate region. State also the values of
   a $n(L \cap Q)$
   b $n(L \cap Q' \cap P)$
   c $n(L' \cup Q \cup P)$

Exercise 12B

1 In the Venn diagram below, $\mathscr{E}$ is the set of all the employees in a certain company, C is the set of those who have a car and M is the set of those who have a motorcycle. Write down the number of employees who
 a have both a car and a motorcycle,
 b have a car,
 c have neither a car nor a motorcycle,
 d do not have a motorcycle.

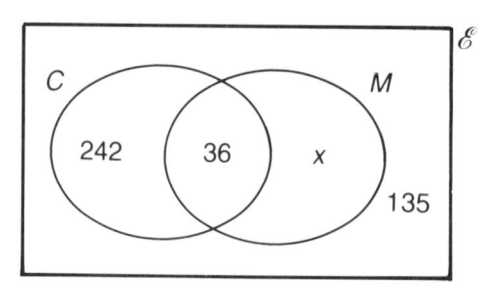

[Venn diagram: Universe $\mathscr{E}$ contains two overlapping circles labelled C and M. C-only region: 242; intersection: 36; M-only region: x; outside both: 135.]

Given, further, that 209 of the employees do not have a car, work out
 e the value of x,
 f the number of employees who have either a car or a motorcycle but not both of these.

2 **a** $n(P) = 12$, $n(Q) = 14$ and $n(P \cap Q) = 11$. Find $n(P \cup Q)$.
 b $n(P) = n(Q) = 52$ and $n(P \cup Q) = 60$. Find $n(P \cap Q)$ and $n(P \cap Q')$.
 c $n(P \cup Q) = 50$, $n(P \cap Q) = 13$ and $n(P) = 21$. Find $n(Q)$.
 d $n(P) = 18$, $n(P' \cap Q) = 20$ and P is a subset of Q. Find $n(Q)$, $n(P \cap Q)$ and $n(P \cup Q)$.
 e $n(P \cap Q') = n(P' \cap Q) = 12$ and $n(P \cup Q) = 5 \times n(P \cap Q)$. Find $n(P \cap Q)$.

3 Out of 50 families questioned, 23 have a dog, 17 have a cat and 18 have neither a cat nor a dog. How many have both a cat and a dog?

4 A repair firm decides to engage 20 skilled workers, all of whom must be able to repair refrigerators, washing machines or both of these. At least 5 of these employees must be able to repair both machines, and there must be 10, 11 or 12 employees who can repair refrigerators. Work out the maximum and minimum possible numbers of employees who can repair washing machines.

5 An opinion poll among television viewers shows that 48% of the viewers dislike snooker, and 22% like snooker but dislike golf. A quarter of the viewers dislike both these sports. Work out the percentage of the viewers who
 a like golf,
 b like one but not both of the two sports.

6 In a group of people questioned there are 70 who like rock music and dislike soul, while 16 like soul and dislike rock music. Given that the number who like rock music is 3 times the number who like soul, form an equation and solve it to find the number of people who like both types of music.

7 In the Venn diagram below L, G and F are the sets of travel agents at a conference who have visited Lisbon, Gothenburg and Florence, respectively. Write down the number of travel agents who have visited
   a Gothenburg,
   b Gothenburg and Florence,
   c Gothenburg and Lisbon but not Florence,
   d only Lisbon.

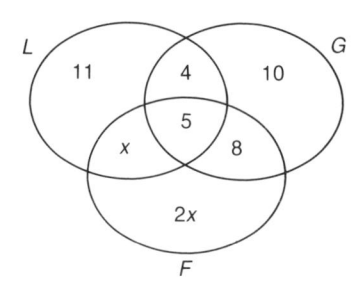

Given that $n(L \cup G \cup F) = 59$, work out
   e the value of x,
   f the number of travel agents who have visited exactly two of the three cities,
   g $n(L' \cap G' \cap F)$.

8 In a certain town there are three shops which sell both milk and frozen vegetables and two shops which sell both bread and milk. There are no shops, however, which sell both bread and frozen vegetables.

   Letting the sets of shops which sell frozen vegetables, milk and bread be F, M and B, respectively, draw a Venn diagram to show the relationship between the three sets. Given that $n(M) = 6$, $n(F \cup M \cup B) = 13$ and $n(F \cap M') = 4$, fill in the numbers in each separate region.

9 It is found that 15% of the pupils at a school do not jog or swim or cycle, that 8% do all three of these activities, that 25% swim and cycle but do not jog, 15% both jog and swim, 20% swim only, 18% cycle only and 42% do two or more of the activities. Work out the percentage of pupils who
   a both jog and cycle,
   b swim or cycle,
   c do not swim,
   d do not both jog and swim.

10 A, B and C are three sets within a universal set which contains 60 members. Given that $C \subset A \cap B$, that $n(A') = 38$, $n(B) = 25$, $n(A \cup B) = 35$ and $n(C') = 52$, draw a Venn diagram and show the numbers in each separate region.

11 In connection with a criminal investigation, the police question 54 men, all of whom are tall, slim or bald. There are 32 tall men, 20 who are tall and slim, 23 who are tall and bald, 24 who are slim and bald, 6 who are slim but not tall or bald and 4 who are tall but not slim or bald.

Letting x be the number of men who have all three characteristics, draw a Venn diagram and fill in as many regions as possible, using expressions in terms of x where appropriate. By first obtaining an equation in x, work out
 a the number of men questioned who have all three characteristics,
 b the number of slim men,
 c the number who are bald but not tall or slim.

12 A survey of the employees of an advertising agency shows that 70% of them own their homes, 53% have cars and 17% neither own their homes nor have cars. There are 30% who are classed as well paid, all of whom have cars, and only one sixth of these people do not own their homes. Of those who own their homes but are not well paid, two thirds do not have cars. Work out the percentage of employees who
 a are well paid and own their homes,
 b own their homes but do not have cars,
 c have cars but neither are well paid nor own their homes.

Statistics

Note: *The last four questions in Exercises 13A and 13B are Level 3 only, and the topics they cover are not required by all the examining groups.*

Exercise 13A

1. One evening Kevin spends 35% of his time gardening, 30% cooking, 20% chatting to his flatmate and 15% reading a novel. Display this information in the form of a pie chart, stating the angles at the centre.

2. A street contains five families with no children, six families with one child, eight families with two children and two families with three children. Find the mode, median and mean of the number of children per family.

3. In each of the following cases say which of the three averages (mean, median, mode) would be the most appropriate to use as a representative of the whole set of values:
   a the numbers 2, 2·8, 3, 3·5, 3·7, 4, 4·5, 5, 27, 27, 43,
   b a cricketer's scores throughout a season,
   c the glove sizes of all the women in Britain.

4. The following are the numbers of lectures missed in one term by a class of 20 students:

   3, 6, 11, 0, 4, 9, 0, 4, 7, 16,
   4, 12, 5, 2, 5, 8, 6, 1, 5, 9

   a Copy the table below and use the above data to complete it.

Lectures missed	Tally	Frequency
Fewer than 4	⊬⊬⊦	5
4–6		
7–9		
10–12		
More than 12		

   b Display the data in the form of a bar chart, letting 2 cm represent each division on the horizontal axis and 1 cm represent 1 unit of frequency on the vertical axis.
   c Display the same data in the form of a pie chart, stating the angles at the centre.

   If the college to which the students belong contains 1460 students altogether, and the class considered above is fairly typical regarding lectures missed, how many students in the whole college would be likely to miss
   d fewer than 4 lectures?
   e 7, 8 or 9 lectures?

5. Find the mode, median, mean and range of the following sets of numbers:
   a 5, −2, −1, 1, −2, −1, 0, −1, 2, 9, 1, 7
   b 25, 41, 20, 70, 41, 55, 25, 23, 41, 29

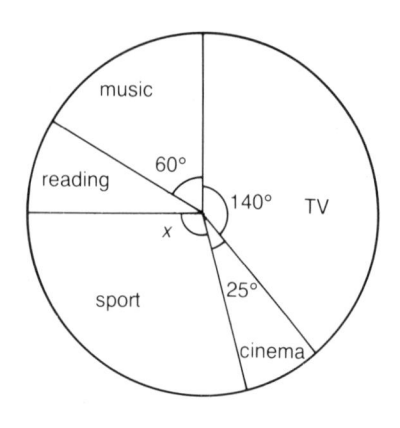

6 In a survey, 144 people are asked to choose their favourite activity from watching television, playing a sport, reading, going to the cinema and listening to music. Some of the results are shown in the pie chart on the left.

Work out the number of people who choose
a listening to music,
b watching television,
c going to the cinema.

Given that 42 people choose sport, work out
d the angle x,
e the number of people who choose reading.

7 Each pupil in a class is asked how many sisters he or she has. The results are shown in the following frequency table.

Number of sisters	0	1	2	3
Frequency	10	8	5	2

Work out
a the modal number of sisters,
b the median number of sisters,
c the number of pupils in the class,
d the total number of sisters,
e the mean number of sisters per pupil.

8 Find the mode, median and mean of the sets of numbers indicated by the following frequency tables:

a
Number	0	1	2	3
Frequency	5	4	4	2

b
Number	−5	−3	−1	1	3
Frequency	4	5	2	7	2

c
Number	1	2	3	4	5
Frequency	12	28	21	10	9

9 The weights of a set of articles are as shown in the following frequency table:

Weight (kg)	20–22	23–25	26–28	29–31	32–34
Frequency	25	34	40	35	26

a State the width of the class interval.
b State the modal class.
c Draw a histogram to represent the data, letting 4 cm represent 5 kg on the horizontal axis and 1 cm represent 5 units of frequency on the vertical axis. (Note that the bars should extend from 19·5 kg to 22·5 kg, from 22·5 kg to 25·5 kg, etc.)

d Estimate the mean weight of an article, using mid-interval values. (For example, assume that all the articles in the first class have weights of 21 kg.)

10 a Kumar takes three mathematics tests and obtains a mean mark of 62%. What mark must he get at his next test to bring his mean mark up to 70%?

b A cricketer has a mean score of 38 after seven innings. After three more innings his mean score has become 36·5. Work out his mean score for these last three innings.

11 A golfer's scores in 30 rounds are as follows:
70, 73, 78, 84, 76, 75, 83, 80, 72, 74, 77, 71,
75, 68, 75, 82, 73, 81, 84, 71, 80, 74, 69, 79,
75, 78, 67, 79, 81, 80

a Copy and complete the following table:

Score	65–68	69–72	73–76	77–80	81–84
Frequency					

b State the width of the class interval and the modal class.
c Draw a histogram to represent the data.
d Estimate the mean score using mid-interval values, and work out the correct mean score using the original data. (Give each of these answers to one decimal place.)

12 The lengths of a set of 25 articles, in centimetres, are as follows:
16·6, 19·0, 15·6, 18·2, 16·7, 17·7, 19·1, 17·9, 17·6,
16·9, 18·4, 17·2, 16·2, 16·4, 16·6, 18·8, 20·2, 19·2,
17·0, 19·9, 17·6, 15·9, 17·3, 15·8, 17·4

a Copy and complete the following table:

Length (cm)	15·5–	16·5–	17·5–	18·5–	19·5–20·5
Frequency					

b Draw a histogram to represent the data.
c Estimate the mean length, using mid-interval values.
d Assuming that the above set is a typical sample of a certain type of article, work out the number of these articles in a set of 12 000 which would be likely to have lengths between 17·5 cm and 19·5 cm.

13 a The first table below gives the frequency distribution of the marks obtained by a set of students in a test. Copy the second table and use the data in the first table to complete it.

Mark	0–2	3–4	5	6	7–8	9–10
Frequency	3	6	8	10	9	4

Mark	≤ 2	≤ 4	≤ 5	≤ 6	≤ 8	≤ 10
Cumulative frequency						

b The first table below gives the cumulative frequencies of a set of men's heights. Copy the second table and use the data in the first table to complete it.

Height (cm)	<165	<172	<178	<182	<186	<192	<198
Cumulative frequency	0	28	63	103	140	169	187

Height (cm)	165–	172–	178–	182–	186–	192–198
Frequency						

14 The following cumulative frequency table gives the distribution of wages of the 92 employees of a certain firm:

Wage (£)	⩽50	⩽70	⩽90	⩽100	⩽110	⩽120	⩽130	⩽140	⩽150	⩽180	⩽200
Cumulative frequency	2	6	22	34	50	64	74	80	84	90	92

Draw a cumulative frequency curve and use it to estimate

a the median wage and the lower and upper quartiles,
b the semi-interquartile range,
c the number of employees who earn more than £125.

15 When the same piece of work is undertaken by 440 different women, the distribution of the times they take is as follows:

Time (min)	0–	5–	10–	11–	12–	14–	17–	20–	22–25
Frequency	30	72	49	50	73	67	51	28	20

Make a cumulative frequency table and draw a cumulative frequency curve. Use the curve to estimate
a the median time and the lower and upper quartiles,
b the semi-interquartile range,
c the number of women who take between 8 minutes and 23 minutes.

16 The temperature of a loft is recorded at 12 noon on 80 successive days, with the following results:

Temperature (°C)	7–	10–	12–	13–	14–	16–20
Frequency	18	15	8	7	12	20

a Draw a histogram to represent this information, using class boundaries of 7°C, 10°C, 12°C, etc., as in the table. Let 1 cm represent 1°C on the horizontal axis and let 1 cm represent 1 unit of frequency **density** (frequency per degree) on the vertical axis.
b Estimate the mean temperature, to one decimal place, using mid-interval values.

Exercise 13B

1. In a local election 9800 people vote Conservative, 7000 vote Labour, 5600 vote Liberal and 1600 vote for other parties. Display this information in a pie chart, stating the angles at the centre.

2. The following table gives a record of the numbers of cigarettes smoked by a woman over a period of 30 days:

Cigarettes per day	9	10	11	12
Frequency	7	9	12	2

   Find the modal, median and mean numbers of cigarettes smoked per day.

3. A sixth former has classes in mathematics (M), physics (P), economics (E), liberal studies (L) and games (G). Her timetable for each week is as follows:

Monday	M	M	E	P	G	G
Tuesday	P	M	M	L	E	E
Wednesday	M	M	P	P	L	E
Thursday	E	L	P	M	M	M
Friday	E	E	M	P	P	P

   a Copy and complete the following frequency table:

Subject	Maths	Physics	Econ.	Lib. Studies	Games
Periods per week					

   b Draw a bar chart to display this information.
   c Display the information in a pie chart, stating the angles at the centre.
   d Work out the number of physics classes the student will attend in 36 school weeks.
   e Work out the number of school weeks in which she will attend 175 economics classes.

4. The following questions refer to the relative merits of the three averages (mean, median, mode) as representative of a whole set of values.
   a Which average is usually the least appropriate to use when the total number of values is small?
   b Which average should be used if all the values are to be given equal weight?
   c Which average gives the value which is most likely to occur if one particular value is chosen at random?
   d Which average is the most liable to distortion owing to the presence of extreme values?

5. Find the mode, median, mean and range of the following sets of numbers:
   a 5, 20, 0, 7, 5, 0, 2, 7, 3, 10, 7
   b 4, −3, 6, 0, −3, 6, −5, −8, 6, 8

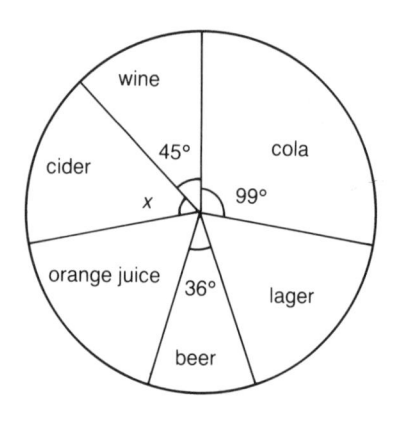

6 All the 80 guests at a party are offered a drink when they arrive. The pie chart on the left indicates their choices.

Work out the number of guests who choose
a wine,
b beer,
c cola.

Given that 12 people choose cider, and equal numbers of people choose orange juice and lager, work out
d the angle x,
e the number who choose orange juice.

7 A survey is carried out to find out how many bedrooms the houses in Sandhill Road have. The results are shown in the following frequency table:

Number of bedrooms	2	3	4	5	6
Frequency	4	20	14	7	5

Work out
a the modal number of bedrooms,
b the median number of bedrooms,
c the mean number of bedrooms.

If 10 more three-bedroom houses are built in Sandhill Road, work out
d the new modal, median and mean numbers of bedrooms.

8 Find the mode, median and mean of the sets of numbers indicated by the following frequency tables:

a
Number	−4	−3	−2	−1	0	1	2
Frequency	9	6	3	3	2	1	1

b
Number	10	15	20	25	30
Frequency	7	8	3	5	7

If the data of part **b** were displayed in a pie chart, work out
c the number corresponding to a sector angle of 96°.

9 The following frequency table indicates the distribution of weights of a set of articles:

Weight (lb)	110–114	116–120	122–126	128–132	134–138
Frequency	12	16	19	14	9

a State the width of the class interval.
b State the modal class.
c Draw a histogram to represent the data, using scales of 2 cm to 5 lb on the horizontal axis and 2 cm to 5 units of frequency on the vertical axis.
d Estimate the mean weight of the articles, to one decimal place, using mid-interval values.

10 **a** The mean age of 12 men, 8 of whom are married, is 37·4. The mean age of the men and their wives (i.e. 20 people) is 35·8. Find the mean age of the wives.
b From the following table, showing the goals scored by a netball team in a series of matches, it is possible to find just two of the three averages.

Goals	Fewer than 3	3	4	5	More than 5
Frequency	8	12	10	7	4

State the averages that can be found, and give their values.

11 A woman buys 17 items in the January sales, the prices of which are as follows:

£7·20   £11   £20·40   £27·10   £8·25   £36·50
£18·99   £15·40   £25   £38   £19·50   £9
£29·60   £12·99   £20   £13·06   £21·30

a Copy and complete the following frequency table:

Price (£)	5–10	11–16	17–22	23–28	29–34	35–40
Frequency						

b State the width of the class interval.
c Draw a histogram to represent the data, using scales of 2 cm to £5 on the horizontal axis and 2 cm to 1 unit of frequency on the vertical axis.
d Comment briefly on the suitability of these ways of presenting the data.

12 The populations of 60 small towns are shown in the following table:

Population	0–	2000–	4000–	6000–	8000–10 000
Frequency	16	10	13	12	9

a Draw a histogram to represent the data.
b Estimate the mean population using mid-interval values.
c Assuming that the above towns form a typical sample from a region of the country which contains 744 such towns altogether, work out the number of towns in this region which would be likely to contain between 4000 and 8000 people.

13 Each of a group of children is asked how many coins he or she is carrying. The results are shown in the following cumulative frequency table:

Number of coins	⩽2	⩽4	⩽5	⩽7	⩽10
Cumulative frequency	7	12	15	21	25

a How many children have 5 coins?
b Given that one child has 3 coins, how many children have 4 coins?
c How many children have more than 5 coins but fewer than 11 coins?
d What is the maximum possible number of children with 6 coins?

14 The percentage marks obtained by 200 students in an examination are shown in the following cumulative frequency table:

Mark (%)	⩽20	⩽30	⩽40	⩽46	⩽50	⩽54	⩽60
Cumulative frequency	10	24	48	74	110	134	158

Mark (%)	⩽70	⩽80	⩽90	⩽94
Cumulative frequency	182	192	198	200

Draw a cumulative frequency curve and use it to estimate
a the median mark and the lower and upper quartiles,
b the semi-interquartile range,
c the number of students who pass the examination, given that the pass mark is 42%.

15 The following frequency table shows the distances travelled per week by a group of commuters in travelling to and from work:

Distance (miles)	0–	20–	40–	60–	80–	100–	120–	140–160
Frequency	5	9	11	14	10	6	3	2

Make a cumulative frequency table and draw a cumulative frequency curve. Use the curve to estimate
a the median distance and the lower and upper quartiles,
b the semi-interquartile range,
c the number of commuters who travel between 30 miles and 110 miles.

16 In a survey to test fitness, a group of volunteers are timed over an 80 metre sprint. The results are shown in the following frequency table:

Time (seconds)	9·5–	10·0–	10·3–	10·5–	10·6–	10·8–11·1
Frequency	50	36	40	18	30	33

a Draw a histogram to represent this data, using the class boundaries indicated in the table. On the horizontal axis let 8 cm represent 1 second, and on the vertical axis let 1 cm represent the frequency in an interval of 0·1 seconds.
b Estimate the mean time, to one decimal place, using mid-interval values.

Probability

Elementary techniques

Exercise 14A

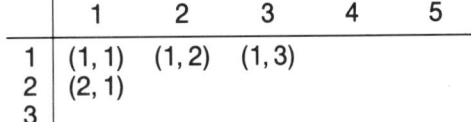

1. A fair die is tossed once. Find the probability that it gives
   a an even number,
   b a 5 or a 6.

   Two fair dice are then tossed together. Find the probability of
   c two odd numbers,
   d two numbers of 3 or over.

2. When Simon fires a shot at a target his probability of a hit is $\frac{2}{5}$, and when Mandy fires her probability of a hit is $\frac{5}{8}$.

   If Simon fires twice, find the probability that he gets
   a two hits,
   b two misses.

   If Simon and Mandy both fire one shot, find the probability that
   c Simon misses and Mandy hits,
   d they both miss.

3. Five children are arranged in a line at random, including Jacob and his sister. Find the probability that Jacob stands next to his sister, given that
   a Jacob is at one of the end positions,
   b Jacob is not at one of the end positions.

4. A biased coin is tossed 2000 times and gives a head 1374 times.
   a Estimate the probability, to one decimal place, that the coin gives a head on any single throw.

   The coin is then tossed three times. On the basis of the above estimate, work out the probability that
   b three tails occur,
   c the sequence of results is head, tail, head, in that order.

5. The diagram shows two spinners, each of which is divided into equal sectors. Copy and complete the following table, showing all the possible results when both pointers are spun once:

	1	2	3	4	5
1	(1, 1)	(1, 2)	(1, 3)		
2	(2, 1)				
3					

   Use the table to find the probability that
   a both spinners give the same number,
   b the sum of the two numbers is more than 5,
   c the difference between the two numbers is 2.

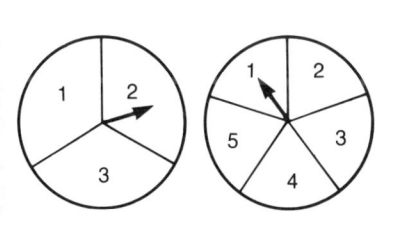

6 One number is chosen at random from the whole numbers between 3 and 30 inclusive. Find the probability that the number
   a has two digits,
   b is prime,
   c is a perfect square.

7 a One ball is chosen at random from a bag containing 15 blue balls and some red balls. The probability that the ball selected is red is $\frac{4}{7}$. How many balls does the bag contain altogether?
   b A hall contains 60 men and some women and children. When one person is selected from the hall at random, the probability that it is a man is $\frac{3}{10}$ and the probability that it is a woman is $\frac{9}{20}$. How many children are in the hall?

8 A group of students take a test and each is given a mark out of 10. The results are shown in the following frequency table:

Mark	0–3	4	5	6	7–8	9–10
Frequency	3	6	10	8	9	4

One student is selected from the group at random. Find the probability that he or she gets
   a 4 marks,
   b the modal mark,
   c more than 4 marks but less than 9,
   d the median mark.

9 In a certain country 75% of the men and 80% of the women have blue eyes. If one married couple is selected at random, find the probability, as a fraction in its lowest terms, that
   a both partners have blue eyes,
   b the woman has blue eyes and the man does not.

Given that the country contains 6 million married couples altogether, work out
   c the approximate number of couples in which both partners do not have blue eyes.

10 In the quarter-final of the FA cup competition, Arsenal, Manchester United, Manchester City and five other teams are left. When the draw is made for the quarter-final, find the probability that
   a Arsenal is drawn to play Manchester United,
   b Arsenal is **not** drawn to play a Manchester club,
   c the two Manchester clubs are **not** drawn to play each other.

11 The diagram represents a network of roads. A man goes for a walk, starting as shown. When he comes to a junction the probability that he takes the left fork is $\frac{2}{3}$, and if he does not take the left fork he is equally likely to take any of the other roads available. He never retraces his steps. Find the probability that he eventually reaches
   a the point P,   **c** the point R,
   b the point Q,   **d** the point S.

12 I drive to work, on average, on three days out of every five and I go by bus on the other days. When I drive, my probability of getting to

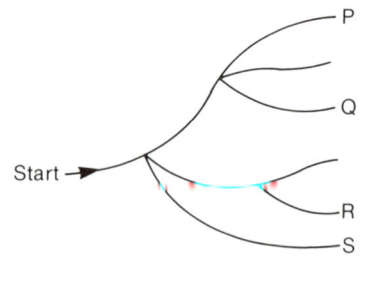

work on time is $\frac{2}{3}$, and when I go by bus it is $\frac{5}{7}$. Find the probability that, on any particular day,
a I go to work by bus,
b I drive and am late for work,
c I go by bus and arrive on time.

13 Find the probability that
a two people chosen at random,
b three people chosen at random,
were born on different days of the week.

14 A 2p coin, a 5p coin and a 10p coin are tossed together. Copy and complete the table below, showing all the possible outcomes. ('H' stands for 'heads' and 'T' stands for 'tails'.)

2p coin	5p coin	10p coin
H	H	H
H	H	T
H	T	H

a How many possible outcomes are there altogether?
b What is the probability that exactly two heads are obtained?
c What is the probability that all the three coins give the same result?

15 Assuming that any baby born is equally likely to be a boy or a girl, find the probability that a family of four children are all boys. Deduce the probability that a family of four children contains at least one girl.

16 If the probability that it rains on any particular day is $\frac{1}{3}$, what is the probability that, on three successive days,
a it does not rain at all?
b it rains at least once?

17 I play two games of darts with a friend. Given that my probability of winning any particular game is x, write down expressions for the probability that
a I win both games,
b I lose both games,
c I lose at least one game.

18 Patrick and Mohammed play a game with a die. Patrick throws first and wins the game if he gets a 5 or a 6. Otherwise Mohammed throws and wins the game if he gets a 4, 5 or 6. If neither boy wins they play the game again, with Mohammed throwing first. Find the probability that
a Patrick wins the first game,
b Mohammed wins the first game,
c neither boy wins the first game, then Mohammed wins the second.

State also
d whether the game is fair, giving the reason for your answer.

Exercise 14B

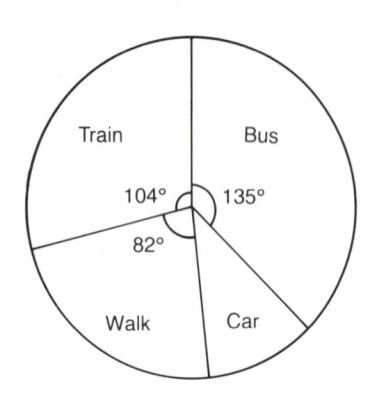

1 Rob and Kylie are both about to take their driving test. If Rob's probability of passing is $\frac{3}{4}$ and Kylie's is $\frac{2}{3}$, find the probability that
 a they both pass,
 b Rob passes and Kylie fails,
 c they both fail.

2 At a celebration dinner eight chairs are spaced evenly around a circular table, and eight guests including Sunil and his friend Lisa, are seated on the chairs at random. Find the probability that
 a Sunil sits directly opposite Lisa,
 b Sunil does not sit next to Lisa.

3 The pie chart shows how some children travel to and from school. Find the probability that a child chosen at random travels
 a by bus, **b** by train, **c** by car.

4 A biased dice is thrown 6000 times and gives a six 2487 times.
 a Estimate the probability, to one decimal place, that the dice gives a six on any single throw.

The die is thrown three times. On the basis of the above estimate, work out the probability that
 b no sixes occur,
 c a six occurs on the last throw only.

5 Two numbers, not necessarily different, are selected from the whole numbers between 4 and 13 inclusive. Find the probability that
 a both numbers are multiples of 3,
 b the first number has two digits and the second has one digit,
 c neither number is a perfect square.

6 When two fair dice are thrown, one way to list all the possible outcomes is to make a table as shown on the left.
 a If the table were completed, how many outcomes would it display altogether?

By making tables for each of the following events, work out their probabilities.
 b The sum of the numbers on the dice is 7.
 c The numbers on the dice differ by 2.
 d At least one of the numbers is more than 3.

7 In a certain country the probability that any baby born is a boy is 0·5 and the probability that any particular boy will grow to over 6 feet tall is 0·2. Given that the country has 2 million families of two children, work out the approximate number of these families in which
 a both children are girls,
 b both children are boys, each of whom grows to over 6 feet tall,
 c both children are boys, neither of whom grows to over 6 feet tall.

8 I am one of 12 people at a tennis club who are waiting to be divided, in a random way, into six teams of two who will be paired

1st die	2nd die
1	1
1	2
1	3

off against each other to play doubles. Among the other 11 people are Ian and Beverly Wilson and their daughter Carolyn. Find the probability that
a Ian and Beverly Wilson partner each other,
b Carolyn is one of my two opponents,
c one of the Wilson family is my partner,
d Carolyn and I play in different matches.

9 a In a group of people there are six who have ginger hair. When one person is selected from the group at random, the probability that he or she has ginger hair is $\frac{2}{9}$. How many people are there in the group?
b My pocket contains eight 10p coins, some 20p coins and some £1 coins. When I select one coin at random, the probability that it is a 20p coin is $\frac{1}{6}$ and the probability that it is a £1 coin is $\frac{1}{2}$. How many coins are in my pocket altogether?

10 When Sunita plays tennis with her friend, her probability of winning any particlar set is $\frac{1}{3}$. One day they play three sets.
a Work out the probability that Sunita loses all three sets.
b Deduce the probability that Sunita wins at least one set.

11 Work out the probability that
a when a coin is tossed three times, at least one head occurs;
b when a fair die is tossed twice, at least one six occurs.

12 The diagram represents a network of roads. A car starts as shown and never retraces its path. When it comes to a junction the probability that it takes the left fork is 0·7. Find the probability that the car reaches
a the point X,   b the point Y.

From your answers to **a** and **b**, deduce
c the probability that the car reaches the point Z.

13 The probability that a certain man will get married is $\frac{2}{3}$, and if he gets married the probability that he will buy a house is $\frac{3}{4}$. If he does not get married the probability that he will buy a house is $\frac{1}{4}$. Find the probability that
a the man marries and does not buy a house,
b he does not marry and buys a house.

14 Lancashire, Sussex, Middlesex and Gloucestershire reach the semi-final of a cricket knockout competition. Assuming that the teams are equally likely to win any particular game, and the draw for the semi-final is random, find the probability that
a Sussex reach the final,
b Middlesex play Lancashire in the semi-final and lose the match,
c Gloucestershire win the competition,
d Lancashire and Gloucestershire both reach the final.

15 The probability that a woman watches television on any particular day is x. Write down expressions for the probability that
a she watches on Monday and Tuesday but not on Wednesday,
b she does not watch on any of these three days,
c there is at least one of these three days on which she does not watch.

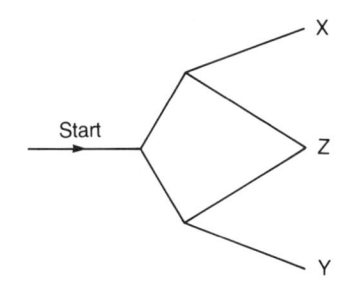

16 Two girls play a game using just the aces, kings and queens from an ordinary pack of cards. One of the girls draws a card at random, and wins the game if she gets a diamond. If she fails, the card is replaced, the second girl draws, and she wins if she gets an ace. If neither girl wins, the game is repeated. Work out whether the game is fair, explaining your answer.

Harder problems

Exercise 15A

1 The aces, kings and queens are taken from a pack of cards and two cards are drawn at random, without replacement, from these twelve cards. Find the probability that
  a both cards are aces,
  b the first card is a club and the second is a heart,
  c one of the cards is a king and the other is a queen,
  d at least one of the cards is red.

2 Three balls are drawn at random, without replacement, from a box containing four red balls and three black balls. Copy and complete the tree diagram below, showing all the possible outcomes and their probabilities. (The fraction on the extreme right is the product of the probabilities on the three branches leading to it.)

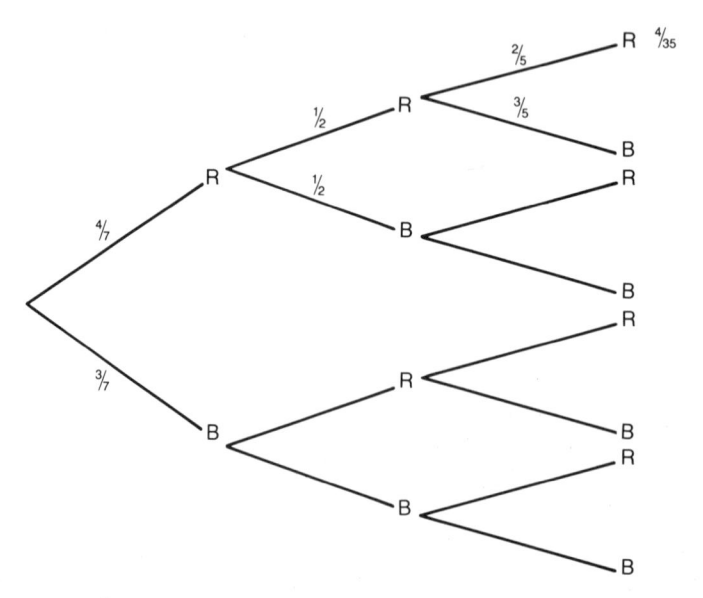

Use the tree diagram to find the probability that
  a exactly two red balls are drawn,
  b the last ball drawn is the same colour as the first.

3   Five equally matched children, including Andrea and Hamdi, run a race. Find the probability that
    a Andrea wins and Hamdi is second,
    b Hamdi is in one of the first two places and Andrea is in the last three,
    c Andrea and Hamdi occupy the last two places (in either order).

4   I toss a coin to decide whether to go to work by train or bus. If I go by train my probability of arriving on time is $\frac{9}{10}$ and if I go by bus it is $\frac{4}{5}$. Find my overall probability of arriving on time.

5   In the Venn diagram on the left, T is the set of girls in a class who like tennis and H is the set of girls who like hockey.

    If one girl is selected from the class at random, find the probability that
    a she likes tennis,
    b she does not like hockey,
    c she likes at least one of the two sports.

    If two girls are selected from the class at random, find the probability that
    d they both like only tennis,
    e they both like neither of the sports.

6   A man has the following coins in his pockets.

    Left pocket: three £1 coins   Right pocket: one £1 coin
                 two 20p coins   one 20p coin
                 one 10p coin   two 10p coins

    The man takes one coin at random from his left pocket and places it in his right pocket. A little later he takes one coin at random from his right pocket. Draw a tree diagram to show all the possible outcomes and their probabilities, and use it to find the probability that
    a the second coin selected is a £1 coin,
    b the second coin selected has the same value as the first coin.

7   When I play snooker with my friend my probability of winning any particular frame is $\frac{1}{8}$. Find the probability, to two decimal places, that
    a I lose the first four games we play,
    b I win at least one of the first four games we play.

    Similarly, work out the probability that
    c I win at least one of the first five games we play,
    d I win at least one of the first six games we play.

    Deduce from these answers
    e the minimum number of games I need to play to make it more likely than not that I will win a frame.

8   The probability of obtaining a head when a biased coin is tossed is 0·6. When the coin is tossed twice, find the probability that
    a at least one tail is obtained,
    b exactly one tail is obtained.

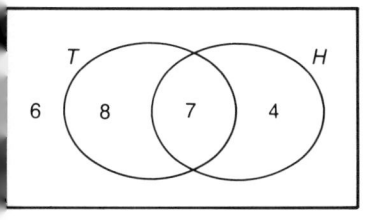

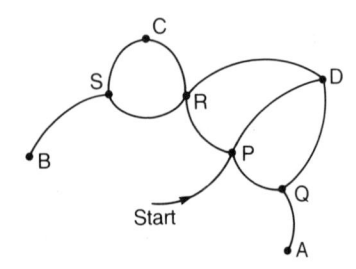

9 The diagram on the left represents a network of paths. A hiker starts as shown and never retraces her steps. At the junctions P, Q, R, S she makes a random choice between all the paths available, and when she reaches A, B, C or D she stops for a snack. Find the probability that she has her snack
 a at A,   c at C,
 b at B,   d at D.

10 In a 400 metre race between ten girls, Fatima rates her probability of winning to be $\frac{1}{2}$ if she is drawn in lanes 1 or 2, and $\frac{3}{8}$ if she is drawn in one of the other lanes. If her estimate is correct, what is Fatima's overall probability of winning the race?

11 All days are classed as 'fine' or 'wet'. If one day is fine the probability that the next day is fine is $\frac{3}{4}$, while if one day is wet the probability that the next day is wet is $\frac{1}{2}$. Given that Sunday is wet, draw a tree diagram for Monday, Tuesday and Wednesday, and use it to find the probability that
 a Wednesday is fine,
 b Wednesday's weather is the same as Monday's,
 c two or more of these three days are wet.

12 Three boxes, A, B and C, contain the following counters.

 Box A: 1 black counter and 5 white counters
 Box B: 2 black counters and 2 white counters
 Box C: 2 black counters and 1 white counter

One counter is drawn from a box at random, the box being chosen by throwing a die and applying the following rule.

 1, 2, or 3: Box A
 4 or 5:   Box B
 6:           Box C

If a black counter is obtained, a prize of £5 is given. To play the game, however, one has to pay a fee of £1·50.
 a By drawing a tree diagram, or otherwise, work out the probability of winning the £5 prize.
 b Say whether it is worthwhile to pay the fee and play the game, explaining your answer.

Exercise 15B

1 Two children make one random draw each from a box containing 12 sweets and 10 chocolates. Find the probability that
 a two sweets are drawn,
 b a sweet is drawn first and a chocolate is drawn second,
 c at least one chocolate is drawn,
 d a sweet and a chocolate, in either order, are drawn.

2 Michael estimates his probability of passing a qualifying examination to be $\frac{3}{5}$. He knows that if he passes his probability of a salary increase is $\frac{2}{3}$, while if he fails the probability of an increase is only $\frac{1}{4}$. Work out Michael's overall probability of getting a salary increase.

3 Three coins are drawn at random, without replacement, from a purse containing six 20p coins and four 10p coins. Draw a tree diagram and use it to find the probability that
a the third coin drawn differs in value from the first,
b less than 50p is drawn altogether.

4 Three brothers, Joe, Derek and Richard, all want to borrow their father's car. Joe proposes the following method for deciding who shall have it.

> 'If we throw two coins, three things can happen. We can get two heads, two tails or a head and a tail. I suggest that two heads should mean that Richard gets the car, two tails that Derek gets it and a head and a tail that I get it.'

Comment on the fairness, or otherwise, of this procedure.

5 Tania and her two sisters, with five other children, are seated at random along one side of a straight table. Given that she does not sit at one of the end positions, work out the probability that Tania has one sister on her immediate left and one on her immediate right.

6 Jill and Hannah play three games of draughts in their lunch hour at work. They are equally likely to win the first game, but when Jill wins a game her probability of winning the next game rises to $\frac{3}{4}$, while when Hannah wins her probability of winning the next game is simply $\frac{1}{2}$. Draw a tree diagram for the three games and use it to find the probability that
a Hannah wins the last game,
b the women win alternate games,
c Jill wins two or more games.

7 On average, one egg in every twelve supplied to a grocer is cracked. If the grocer selects two eggs at random, find the probability that
a both are uncracked,
b at least one is cracked,
c exactly one is cracked.

If the grocer selects three eggs at random, find
d the probability, as a decimal to two places, that exactly one of them is cracked.

8 Neville and Melissa toss a coin to decide who shall have a ticket to a rock concert. Melissa wins, then their brother Sylvester appears and suggests that Melissa should toss the coin with him for the ticket. Melissa claims that this is unfair, but offers to decide between herself and Sylvester on the basis of a throw of a die, provided that Sylvester has to get a 5 or a 6 to win. Investigate the fairness, or otherwise, of the procedures suggested by Sylvester and Melissa.

9 A town has 12 hotels, each of which is chosen at random by a series of visitors to the town. Find the probability, as a decimal to two places, that the visitors all stay at different hotels when the number of visitors is
a 2 **b** 3 **c** 4 **d** 5 **e** 6

Deduce from these answers
f the minimum number of visitors needed to make it more likely than not that there is an hotel with more than one visitor.

10 In a quiz show, 50 questions are provided of which 10 are classed as difficult. A particular contestant has a probability of $\frac{1}{3}$ of answering a difficult question correctly and a probability of $\frac{3}{4}$ of answering one of the other questions correctly. If one question is selected from the 50 questions at random, what is the contestant's probability of answering it correctly?

11 A box initially contains one black counter and three white counters. When a counter is drawn from the box it is replaced by two counters of the same colour. Draw a tree diagram to show all the possible results of three random draws, and use it to find the probability that
a alternating colours are obtained,
b two or more black counters are obtained.

12 When Michelle plays Eric at table-tennis, her probability of winning any particular point is $\frac{3}{5}$. One of their games reaches a score of 19-all. Find the probability that
a Eric wins the game 21-19,
b the score reaches 20-all,
c Michelle wins the game 22-20.

Algebra

Some basic techniques

Note: *In Exercises 16A and 16B, question 7 is Level 3 with most examining groups.*

Exercise 16A

1. Given that $x = 1$, $y = 2$ and $w = 5$, work out the values of the following expressions:
   a. $3xyw$
   b. yw^2
   c. $xy - w + 4y$
   d. $y(w - 2x)$
   e. $w(y - w)^2$
   f. $(xy)^3 - y^2w$
   g. $\dfrac{w - x - y}{w - x - 4y}$
   h. $\dfrac{y(2w - 3y)}{x - 5w}$

2. Given that $p = -1$, $q = 2$ and $r = -3$, work out the values of the following expressions:
   a. $q - 2p$
   b. r^3
   c. $p^4q^2r^2$
   d. $q - (qr + p)$
   e. $-(q - r)^2$
   f. $5p^5q^4 + q^3r^2$
   g. $\dfrac{4pr}{p - q + r}$
   h. $-\dfrac{8p - 2q}{3qr}$

3. Simplify:
   a. $5x + 7 - 2x - 9$
   b. $-3y + 2s - 4y - s + 3$
   c. $abc - bc + 2acb - ab + 5cb - 3ba$
   d. $x^2 - 4x^3 + 2x - 3x^2 - x^3 + 2x^2$
   e. $5 - p - 2 + 4p^2 + 3p - 3 + p^3 - 2p - 5p^2$

4. Remove the brackets:
   a. $5(x - 4y)$
   b. $-(a - 2b + c)$
   c. $-4(6 - 3y - 7w)$
   d. $t(3t + 2s - t^2)$
   e. $3y(2x + 5y - 6xy)$
   f. $-2p(3 - 5p + 7p^2)$
   g. $8wx(-2w + 3x^2 - 5w^2x^3)$
   h. $-7r^2s(2r^2 - 5 - 3s^3 + 4r^3s^4)$

5. Remove the brackets and simplify:
   a. $2x - x(2 - 3x)$
   b. $3(x - 2y) + 4(y - 2x)$
   c. $5x(1 - 6p) - 2(3 - x - 15xp)$
   d. $-4w(1 - 2w + 3w^2) + 6w^2(2w - 1)$

6. Factorise:
   a. $12y - 36$
   b. $7 - 14r - 21s$
   c. $16y - 24xy$
   d. $20x^2 - 15xy + 25x$
   e. $xz - xyz$
   f. $22abcd + 11bcd - 33acd + 44cd$
   g. $2x^3 - 4x^4y + 6x^5y^2$
   h. $6p^2q^5r^2 - 9pq^4r^3 + 12p^5q^6r^2$

7 Remove the brackets and simplify:
 a $(x + 2)(x + 5)$
 b $(t - 1)(t + 3)$
 c $(m - 9)(m - 7)$
 d $(2y - 3r)(5y + 2r)$
 e $(8x - 11y)(3x - y)$
 f $(4 - 3w)(2 + 9w)$
 g $(9 - 5s)(8 - 2s)$
 h $(ab - 3c)(2c - 7ab)$
 i $(x + 6)^2$
 j $(1 - 3y)^2$
 k $(4p - 5r)^2$
 l $(7rs - 2t)^2$

Exercise 16B

1 Given that $v = 2$, $w = 5$ and $x = 10$, work out the values of the following expressions:
 a $vx - 3w$
 b wx^2
 c $(wx)^2$
 d $w(x - 7v)$
 e $w - (v - w)^2$
 f $\dfrac{6vx^2}{8w - x}$
 g $\dfrac{3v - w - x}{w - 2x}$
 h $\dfrac{5}{v}\left(v - \dfrac{1}{w}\right)$

2 Given that $m = -2$, $p = 3$ and $t = -5$, work out the values of the following expressions:
 a $p - t + m$
 b m^p
 c mt^2p
 d $t - (m - p)$
 e $p^2 - m^2$
 f $\dfrac{(p - m)^2}{pt}$
 g $m^4p^2 + mpt^2$
 h $\dfrac{p}{t}\left(t - \dfrac{10}{p}\right)$

3 Simplify:
 a $12 - 4r + 7r - 16$
 b $4m - 9p - 11m + 2m - 5p + 8m$
 c $xy - 5x + 5yx + 3x$
 d $3t^2 - 4t - 5t^2 - 7t^3 + 2t^2 + 5t$
 e $a^2b - ba + 2ab - 3a + ba^2 + b - ab$

4 Remove the brackets:
 a $6(2w - 7x)$
 b $-(3 - x + 5y)$
 c $-5(2y - 4z - 9)$
 d $p^2(5 + 3p - 4pq - 2p^2)$
 e $-2xy(5x - 12y^2 + 3x^2y)$
 f $9ac^3(2abc - 3a^2 + a^4b^2c^2)$

5 Remove the brackets and simplify:
 a $x(3 - 4x) - 4x + 2x^2$
 b $2x - (5 - x) + 2(x - 1)$
 c $3rt(t - 6r) - 2r(t - 9rt - 5t^2)$
 d $5(x - xy + 3y) - 4y(2 + x)$

6 Factorise:
 a $4x - xy + 3xyz$
 b $27p - 45q$
 c $4xy - 6wy - 2y$
 d $35rt - 56r^2$
 e $150m + 75m^2 - 225m^3$
 f $10abcd + 5abc^2d^2 - 15ac^2d + 20a^2bc$
 g $12pyt^2 - 15tp^2x + 27x^2pyt$
 h $60w^2x^5y^4 + 45wx^2y^3 + 30w^4x^3y^6$

7 Remove the brackets and simplify:
  a $(y + 4)(y + 3)$
  b $(r - 5)(r + 2)$
  c $(x - 8)(x - 3)$
  d $(2f - 7g)(4f + 2g)$
  e $(9w - 5z)(9w + 5z)$
  f $(10 - 2x)(5 - x)$
  g $(4 - 25y)(2 + 15y)$
  h $(2ac - 7d)(7d - 3ac)$
  i $(p + 10)^2$
  j $(7 - y)^2$
  k $(5x - 8y)^2$
  l $(3x^2 - 2x)^2$

Linear equations and inequalities

Note: *The solution of linear inequalities is a Level 3 topic.*

Exercise 17A

Solve the following equations:

1. $5x + 4 = 39$
2. $3x - 8 = 22$
3. $7 - 2x = -4$
4. $12 = -5x + 2$
5. $7x + 2 = 5x + 14$
6. $11x - 8 = 8x + 2$
7. $3x - 2 = 12x + 4$
8. $7 - 2x = -8 + 4x$
9. $2 - 4x - 5 + 6x = 0$
10. $5(x + 3) = 4(2x - 5)$
11. $3(7 - 2x) = 2(5 - 4x)$
12. $10(x - 3) - 3(x + 2) = 2(2x - 15)$
13. $\dfrac{x}{3} = 4$
14. $\dfrac{2x}{5} = 6$
15. $\dfrac{x}{5} - 1 = -3$
16. $\dfrac{2x - 3}{4} = 5$
17. $\dfrac{2}{x} = \dfrac{4}{5}$
18. $\dfrac{3}{2x - 1} = 2$
19. $\dfrac{x}{x - 2} = \dfrac{1}{5}$
20. $3 = \dfrac{5x}{5x - 2}$
21. $\dfrac{x}{3} + \dfrac{x - 1}{2} = 2$
22. $\dfrac{3x + 5}{4} - \dfrac{x + 3}{2} = 4$
23. $\tfrac{1}{2}(3x - 4) = 5x + 12$
24. $\dfrac{x}{6} - \tfrac{1}{3}(x - 2) = \dfrac{x}{2} + 1\tfrac{1}{2}$

Solve the following inequalities:

25. $3x - 7 < 5$
26. $2 > -4x$
27. $5 - 2x \geqslant 3x - 10$
28. $4(x - 2) > 2(1 - x)$
29. $-\dfrac{3x}{4} > -9$
30. $\dfrac{x}{3} + 4 \leqslant 6 + 2x$
31. $\tfrac{2}{3}(5x - 3) - 2(3x - 2) > 0$

In each of the following questions, find all the natural numbers which satisfy both of the given inequalities:

32. $5x > 10$, $2x - 3 < 9$
33. $12 - x > x - 9$, $4x - 15 \geqslant x + 9$
34. $3x - 5 < 7 < 6x - 2$
35. $14 - x \leqslant 12 \leqslant 5(8 - x)$

In each of the following questions, find the complete set of values which satisfy both of the given inequalities:

36. $7x < 35$, $3x + 2 > 5$
37. $6 \geqslant 2 - x$, $\dfrac{x}{3} + 2 < 3$
38. $5x - 1 > 9 > x - 4$
39. $4x \leqslant 26 \leqslant 8x + 14$

Exercise 17B

Solve the following equations:

1. $8x - 3 = 13$
2. $4x + 7 = -11$
3. $15 = 14 - x$
4. $-3x + 12 = -3$
5. $9x + 2 = 6x + 20$
6. $4 - 3x = 2x + 4$
7. $20 - 2x = 13 - 5x$
8. $12 - x - 6 = x + 4 - 3x$
9. $4\tfrac{1}{2}x + 7 - 1\tfrac{1}{2}x - 5 = 0$
10. $4(2x - 3) = 2(x + 9)$
11. $2x - (3 - x) = 3 - 2(2 - x)$
12. $7(2 - 3x) - 5(4 - x) = 6(5 - 4x)$
13. $\dfrac{x}{2} = \dfrac{1}{4}$
14. $-6 = \dfrac{3x}{7}$
15. $\dfrac{2x}{3} + 4 = 8$
16. $6 = \dfrac{3x + 2}{2}$
17. $\dfrac{5}{x} = \dfrac{10}{13}$
18. $1\tfrac{1}{2} = \dfrac{1}{2 + x}$
19. $\dfrac{x - 3}{x + 4} = 5$
20. $1\tfrac{1}{3} = \dfrac{2x}{4 + 3x}$
21. $-2 = \dfrac{3(1 - 3x)}{2x - 7}$
22. $\dfrac{x}{2} + \dfrac{x - 2}{5} = 8$
23. $\dfrac{2x - 3}{3} - \dfrac{x - 2}{6} = 2$
24. $1\tfrac{1}{2}(x - 3) = 1\tfrac{1}{4}(2x - 5)$
25. $\tfrac{1}{2}(2x + 7) - \dfrac{3x}{10} = -\tfrac{1}{5}(4x + 5)$

Solve the following inequalities:

26 $8 - x > 3x$

27 $-6x < -9$

28 $11 - 3x \geqslant 3 - 5x$

29 $4x - 3(4x - 5) > 3(10 - x)$

30 $2 - \dfrac{x}{5} \geqslant \dfrac{3}{5}$

31 $2(3x - 4) > \tfrac{1}{2}(8x + 3)$

32 $\tfrac{1}{4}(x - 2) - \tfrac{3}{8}(2 - x) < \tfrac{1}{2}$

In each of the following questions, list the integers for which all the given statements are true:

33 $2x > -8$, $-8 < x < 2$

34 $10 \geqslant 3 - x$, $x + 2 < -1$

35 $5 < 4x + 1 < 2x + 9$

36 $2 \geqslant x \geqslant -5$, $-3 \leqslant x \leqslant 7$

In each of the following questions, find the complete set of values which satisfy both the given inequalities:

37 $2x > 12$, $2x + 5 < 25$

38 $4 - x < 7$, $-3 > -x$

39 $4x - 3 > 17 \geqslant 2x - 11$

40 $\dfrac{x}{2} < \dfrac{6-x}{4}$, $\dfrac{2-x}{6} < \dfrac{7-x}{9}$

Construction and solution of linear equations from given data

Note: *In these exercises all algebraic expressions should be put in the simplest possible form.*

Exercise 18A

1 A hiker walks x km on Monday, $(x + 7)$ km on Tuesday and $(x - 3)$ km on Wednesday.
   a Write down an expression for the total distance she walks in the three days.
   b Given that in fact she walks 88 km in the three days, form an equation and solve it to find x.

2 A woman buys an article for £$(x + 10)$ and sells it for £$3x$.
   a Write down an expression for the profit she makes.
   b Given that in fact she makes a profit of £6, form an equation, solve it, and hence find the prices the woman paid and received for the article.

3 Darren is x years old and his sister Carmel is 3 years younger.
   a Write down expressions for the ages the children will be in 10 years' time.
   b Given that their total age in 10 years will be 35 years, form an equation, solve it, and hence find the children's present ages.

67

4 **a** Write down an expression for the cost of *N* postcards at 8p each and (*N* + 2) biros at 10p each.
   b Given that the postcards and biros cost £2 altogether, form an equation and solve it to find *N*.

5 Three angles have values of $(2p + 30)°$, $(p + 12)°$ and $(p - 18)°$. Find the values of *p* and the three angles, given that
   a the first angle is 68° more than the second,
   b the three angles could form the angles of a triangle.

6 **a** Write down expressions for five consecutive even numbers, the smallest of which is *n*.
   b Given that the sum of five consecutive even numbers is 620, form an equation, solve it, and hence find the five numbers.

7 Mr Maxwell leaves £8700 in his will to be divided among his wife and two children, Paul and Eileen. Paul receives £*x*, Eileen gets £100 more than Paul, and their mother gets twice as much as Eileen.
   a Write down expressions for the amounts that Eileen and Mrs Maxwell get.
   b Form an equation, solve it, and hence work out how much Mrs Maxwell gets.

8 The length and width of a rectangular field are $(2x - 10)$ m and $(x + 30)$ m, respectively.
   a Obtain an expression for the perimeter of the field.
   b Find the perimeter if $x = 50$.
   c Find *x* and the perimeter if the length of the field is 130 m.
   d Given that the perimeter is 550 m, find *x* and the width of the field.

9 A girl has *y* 2p coins, $(10 - y)$ 5p coins and $(y + 3)$ 10p coins.
   a Obtain an expression for the total amount of money she has.
   b Given that in fact she has £1·36, form an equation and solve it to find the value of *y*.

10 All the angles in the figure on the left are right angles.
   a Obtain expressions for the perimeter and the area of the figure.
   b Find *x*, given that the perimeter and the area are numerically equal.

11 **a** Write down a formula for the distance, *x* km, covered by a body which moves at a speed of *v* km/h for *t* hours.
   b A body travels at a speed of *v* km/h for 4 hours, then travels 5 km/h faster for 2 hours. Obtain an expression for the total distance it covers.
   c Given that in fact the total distance covered is 400 km, form an equation and solve it to find the value of *v*.

12 A job takes 40 hours altogether. One woman works at it for *t* hours, then another woman spends $(2t + 5)$ hours on it.
   a Obtain an expression for the time that remains to be spent on the job.
   b Given that a worker completes the third stage in 1 hour less than the first woman spent on the job, form an equation and solve it to find the value of *t*.

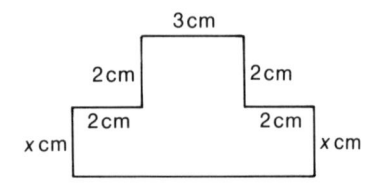

13 The rule for obtaining each term of the following sequence is 'double the last term and subtract 1':
$$2, 3, 5, 9, 17, \ldots$$
  a Letting any term of the sequence be x, write down expressions for the next two terms.
  b Obtain an expression for the sum of x and the two terms which follow x.
  c Given that the sum obtained in b is 451, form an equation, solve it, and hence find the three terms.

Exercise 18B

1 Joe earns £x per week, Salim earns twice as much as Joe, and Richard earns £20 less than Joe.
  a Write down expressions for the amounts that Salim and Richard earn.
  b If Salim earns £240, how much do Joe and Richard earn?
  c Given that Joe, Salim and Richard together earn a total of £340, form an equation, solve it, and hence find the amount that each man earns.

2 I need to study for 60 hours altogether in three weeks.
  a If I study for $3x$ hours in the first week and for $4x$ hours in the second, write down an expression for the number of hours I need to study in the third week.
  b Given that in fact I need to study for 11 hours in the third week, form an equation and solve it to find the value of x.

3 Three numbers can be expressed as y, $2y + 6$ and $4y + 20$. Find y, given that
  a the second number is 15 more than the first,
  b the second number and the third have a sum of 104,
  c the third number is 30 more than the second.

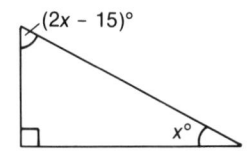

4 Find the values of x, y and p in diagrams 1 to 3.

5 a Write down an expression for the total cost of n articles at 12p each and $(n - 3)$ articles at 6p each.
  b Given that the total cost of these articles is £3·78, form an equation and solve it to find n.

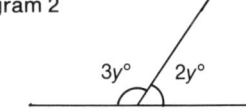

6 The following is a simple sequence of numbers:
$$2, 5, 8, 11, 14, \ldots$$
  a Letting any number in the sequence be x, write down expressions for the number just before this number and the two numbers just after it.
  b Write down an expression for the sum of these four numbers.
  c Given that the sum of the four numbers is 134, form an equation and solve it to find x.

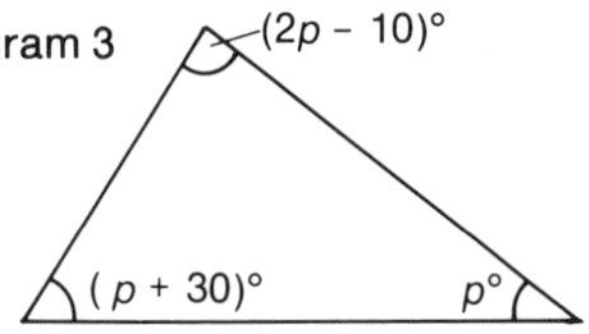

7 A textbook contains p pages, a novel has 30 pages fewer than the textbook, and a dictionary has three times as many pages as the novel.
  a Write down expressions for the numbers of pages that the novel and the dictionary have.

diagram 1: triangle with angles $(2x - 15)°$, $x°$, and a right angle

diagram 2: angles $3y°$ and $2y°$ on a straight line

diagram 3: triangle with angles $(2p - 10)°$, $(p + 30)°$, and $p°$

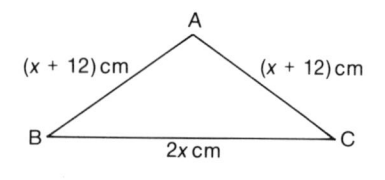

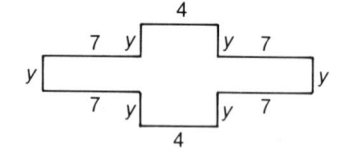

b Given that the total number of pages in the three books is 1230, form an equation, solve it, and hence find the number of pages in the dictionary.

8 Find x, in the figure on the left, given that
  a the perimeter of the triangle is 68 cm,
  b BC exceeds AB by 5 cm.

9 A man has $2y$ 10p coins and $(3y - 8)$ 20p coins. Find y, given that
  a the man has the same amount of money in 10p coins and 20p coins,
  b the total amount he has is £8.

10 In the figure on the left all the angles are right angles and the distances shown are in centimetres. Find y if
  a the perimeter is 45 cm,
  b the perimeter is numerically equal to the area.

11 A train travels at 80 km h^{-1} for t hours, then at 100 km h^{-1} for $(t + 2)$ hours. Given that the total distance covered by the train is 470 km, find the value of t.

12 The rule for obtaining the terms of a certain type of sequence, given the first two terms, is 'add the two terms just before the term required'. For example, a sequence of this type is
$$1, 3, 4, 7, 11, \ldots$$
  a Given that the first two terms of such a sequence are 2, x, write down expressions for the third, fourth and fifth terms.
  b Given that the sum of the first five terms of this sequence is 73, form an equation, solve it, and hence find the five terms.

Further factorisation

Level 3

Exercise 19A

Factorise the following expressions:

1. $x^2 - 4$
2. $9 - y^2$
3. $4p^2 - 49$
4. $1 - 16a^2$
5. $m^2n^2 - r^2$
6. $100 - t^4$
7. $w^6 - 25z^6$
8. $81a^{16} - 64b^{10}$
9. $36x^2y^4 - 121$
10. $1 - 9p^6q^8r^{10}$

Factorise the following expressions, starting by taking out a common factor:

11. $2x^2 - 18$
12. $5 - 5y^2$
13. $m^3 - m$
14. $2p^3 - 32p$
15. $3xy - 12x^3y^3$
16. $45y^2 - 5y^8$
17. $50t^5y^3 - 8ty^5$

Factorise the following quadratic expressions:

18. $x^2 + 6x + 8$
19. $y^2 + 15y + 36$
24. $f^2 - 20f + 51$
21. $w^2 + 19w + 60$
22. $t^2 - 2t - 3$
23. $x^2 + 3x - 10$
24. $y^2 - 18y + 32$
25. $v^2 - 5v - 6$
26. $r^2 - 10r + 24$
27. $s^2 - 12s + 36$
28. $20 + x - x^2$
29. $15 - 14y - y^2$
30. $36 - 13a + a^2$
31. $12p^2 - 11p - 1$
32. $1 + 3f - 40f^2$
37. $3t^2 - 11t + 6$
34. $2x^2 + 7x + 3$
35. $2m^2 - 3m - 5$
36. $3p^2 - 10p + 7$
37. $2y^2 + y - 6$
38. $3r^2 + 11r - 4$
39. $6x^2 - 11x + 4$
40. $8w^2 - 6w - 9$
41. $8 - 18t - 5t^2$
42. $10 - 23y + 12y^2$

Factorise the following expressions by grouping the terms in pairs:

43. $2x + 4y + ax + 2ay$
44. $xt - 3t + 5x - 15$
45. $4m - 5n + 8m^2 - 10mn$
46. $3pr - p^2 + 3r - p$
47. $4a^2 + 6ab - 6a - 9b$
48. $5x + 2 - 15xy - 6y$
49. $t^2 - 4vt - 3t + 12v$
50. $14wxy - 2w^2 - 21x^2y + 3xw$

Exercise 19B

Factorise the following expressions:

1. $p^2 - 25$
2. $64 - a^2$
3. $100y^2 - 9$
4. $1 - 4r^2s^2$
5. $144 - m^4$
6. $t^8 - 196v^6$
7. $49p^{12}q^{10} - 1$
8. $256x^{20} - 169y^{16}w^{18}$

Factorise the following expressions, starting by taking out a common factor:

9. $3x^2 - 3$
10. $7 - 28y^2$
11. $8w - 2w^3$
12. $5x^3 - 125x$
13. $18y^3 - 2y^7$
14. $a^2b^2 - b^2c^2d^2$
15. $147xy - 48xy^9$
16. $90p^5s - 1000pr^2s^3$

Factorise the following quadratic expressions:

17 $x^2 + 12x + 20$
18 $w^2 + 14w + 33$
19 $y^2 + 48 + 19y$
20 $80 + p^2 + 24p$
21 $t^2 - 12t - 28$
22 $r^2 + 2r - 35$
23 $a^2 - 15a + 54$
24 $f^2 - 20f + 51$
25 $64 - 16p + p^2$
26 $100 - m^2$
27 $90 + 9v - v^2$
28 $y^2 - 14y + 49$
29 $w - w^2 + 30$

30 $-24x + 63 + x^2$
31 $8p^2 - 7p - 1$
32 $1 - 2r - 24r^2$
33 $16w^2 - 8w + 1$
34 $2x^2 + 9x + 7$
35 $3y^2 + 16y + 5$
36 $5a^2 + 3a - 2$
37 $3t^2 - 11t + 6$
38 $5p^2 - 11p - 12$
39 $6g^2 + 5g - 4$
40 $8 - 11m - 10m^2$
41 $6 - 17s + 12s^2$
42 $21x - 18 + 4x^2$

Factorise the following expressions by grouping the terms in pairs:

43 $4x + 8 + xy + 2y$
44 $5p - p^2 + 10r - 2pr$
45 $3w - 2x + 3wx - 2x^2$
46 $a^2r^2 - 3arw + ar - 3w$

47 $xy + 4y - 3x - 12$
48 $4m^2n + 6m - 10mn^2 - 15n$
49 $3t^2 - 4t - 3tv + 4v$
50 $12x^2ry - 10xrp - 18xyp + 15p^2$

Level 3

Quadratic equations

Exercise 20A

Solve the following quadratic equations by the factor method:

1 $x^2 + 6x + 5 = 0$
2 $x^2 + 9x + 20 = 0$
3 $x^2 + 7x - 18 = 0$
4 $x^2 - 5x = 24$
5 $x^2 - 13x + 42 = 0$
6 $x^2 + 30 = 17x$
7 $x^2 - 5x = 0$
8 $3x = 4x^2$

9 $8x - x^2 = 16$
10 $48 - 8x = x^2$
11 $6x^2 - 1 = 5x$
12 $6x - 1 = 8x^2$
13 $2x^2 + x = 3$
14 $6x^2 + 3 = 9x$
15 $4x = 15 - 4x^2$
16 $(x - 2)(x - 3) = 20$

17. $2x(x - 2) = 3(x + 10)$
18. $6(x^2 + x) - 2x(x - 3) = 0$
19. $(3x - 1)(x + 4) = 16$
20. $(2x - 3)(3x + 2) = 4(3x - 4)$

Use the formula $x = \dfrac{-b \pm \sqrt{b^2 - 4ac}}{2a}$ to solve the following quadratic equations to two decimal places:

21. $x^2 + 4x + 2 = 0$
22. $x^2 + 5x - 7 = 0$
23. $x^2 - 6x = 8$
24. $x^2 + 11 = 14x$
25. $2x^2 + 9x + 1 = 0$
26. $5x^2 - 13x = 12$
27. $8 - 12x^2 = 7x$
28. $15x - 6 = 7x^2$

In each of the remaining questions the given information should be used to form a quadratic equation.

29. The distance travelled by a moving body in t seconds is $(5t + t^2)$ metres. Find the time the body takes to travel 36 m.

30. The product of two whole numbers which differ by 8 is 884. Find the numbers.

31. The sides of a rectangle of area 120 cm² are $(x - 4)$ cm and $(2x - 9)$ cm. Find the value of x.

32. The sides of a right-angled triangle are $(x - 2)$ cm, $(x + 2)$ cm and $(x + 6)$ cm. Use Pythagoras' theorem to find x, and deduce the lengths of the three sides.

Exercise 20B

Level 3

1. $x^2 + 10x + 16 = 0$
2. $x^2 - 14x + 40 = 0$
3. $x^2 + x - 30 = 0$
4. $x^2 - 8x = 65$
5. $x^2 + 54 = 21x$
6. $x^2 + 9x = 0$
7. $4x = 6x^2$
8. $x^2 - 100 = 21x$
9. $48 - 2x = x^2$
10. $2x^2 - 4x = x^2 - 4$
11. $12x^2 - 2 = x - 1$
12. $60 = 16x - x^2$
13. $3x^2 + 22x + 7 = 0$
14. $20x^2 = 90x - 40$
15. $25x = 6x^2 - 14$
16. $(x - 7)(x + 6) = -40$
17. $(2x - 5)(x - 2) = 15$
18. $5(x - 6) - 2(x^2 - 15) = 0$
19. $2x(x - 5) = (x - 8)(x - 2)$
20. $(3x - 4)(5x + 1) = 3x(x - 10)$

Use the quadratic formula (see Exercise 20A) to solve the following equations to two decimal places:

21. $x^2 + 6x + 4 = 0$
22. $x^2 + 3x - 5 = 0$
23. $x^2 + 10 = 8x$
24. $x^2 = x + 3$
25. $3x^2 + 13x + 6 = 0$
26. $11 - 7x = 6x^2$
27. $4(1 - 2x) = 5x(3x + 2)$

Solve the following problems by using the given information to obtain quadratic equations:

28 It can be shown that the sum of the first n whole numbers is $\frac{n}{2}(n+1)$. For what value of n do the first n whole numbers have a sum of 120?

29 A ball which is thrown upwards at 60 m s^{-1} has a height of $(60t - 5t^2)$ metres after t seconds. Find the two times at which the height of the ball is 135 m.

30 The area of a right-angled triangle is 62.5 cm^2. Given that the two sides which meet at right angles differ in length by 2.5 cm, work out the lengths of these two sides.

31 In the figure on the left, all the angles are right angles and the distances are in centimetres. Find the two values of x for which the area of the figure is 125 cm^2.

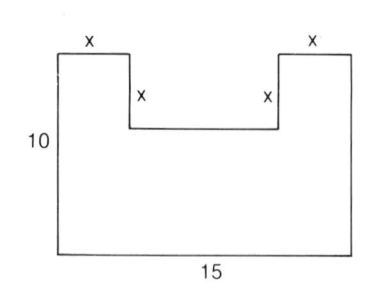

Transformation of formulae — new subject in one term only

Exercise 21A

In questions 1–26, make the letter given in brackets the subject of the formula.

1. $a + x = 2y$ (x)
2. $7x - y = 3x$ (y)
3. $pt = 5$ (t)
4. $4as = 6aw$ (s)
5. $\dfrac{x}{y} = 3y$ (x)
6. $\dfrac{2wr}{s} = r^2 s$ (w)
7. $ay - w - l$ (a)
8. $5a - 9pr = 20a$ (p)
9. $2x(3y - w) = 5w$ (y)
10. $4y(p - 2q) = p(y - 3r)$ (r)
11. $\dfrac{3}{x} = \dfrac{6}{y}$ (x)
12. $2rs = \dfrac{4r}{5t}$ (t)
13. $\dfrac{2p}{r} - r = s$ (p)
14. $s = (u + v)\dfrac{t}{2}$ (v)
15. $2m = \dfrac{y}{m}(ax + 3)$ (x)
16. $\dfrac{x}{x + y} = 3$ (y)
17. $\dfrac{2a + y}{ap - 3y} = \dfrac{1}{2}$ (p)

18   $\dfrac{2a}{x+a} = \dfrac{5w}{t+w}$ (t)

19   $y - \dfrac{3y}{p} = ax$ (p)

20   $\dfrac{av}{3x} - m\dfrac{1}{6}$ (a)

21   $\dfrac{2x}{w} + \dfrac{y}{w^2} = w$ (x)

22   $\sqrt{y - 2x} = 3$ (x)

23   $2\sqrt{\dfrac{p}{m}} = r$ (m)

24   $a\sqrt{\dfrac{3+y}{x}} = \dfrac{2}{x}$ (y)

25   $px^2 - y = 3y + p$ (x)

26   $w^2 - a^2y^2 = x^2$ (a)

27   **a** Write down a formula for p, where p cm is the perimeter of a rectangle of length l cm and breadth b cm.
      b Make l the subject of this formula.
      c Find the length of a rectangle of perimeter 84 cm and breadth 18 cm.

28   A salesperson is paid according to the formula

$$P = 400x + 25y$$

where £P is the pay she receives for working x months and selling y articles.
      a Make y the subject of the formula.
      b Find the number of articles the salesperson sells in 8 months if she earns £8650 in that time.

29   The area of a circle is given by the formula $A = \pi r^2$.
      a Express r in terms of A and π.
      b Taking π to be 3, find the radius of a circle of area 48 cm².
      c Using the value of π given by a calculator, find, to two decimal places, the radius of a circle of area 20 cm².

30   In the figure on the left all the angles are right angles and the distances are in centimetres.
      a Write down a formula for p, where p cm is the perimeter of the figure.
      b Make y the subject of this formula.
      c Find y when the perimeter of the figure is 73 cm and its total height is 12·5 cm.
      d Write down a formula for A, where A cm² is the area of the figure.
      e Make x the subject of this formula.
      f Find x when the area of the figure is 346 cm² and its total width is 32 cm.

Exercise 21B

In questions 1–26, make the letter given in brackets the subject of the formula.

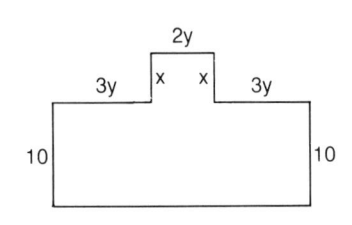

1   $5 + x = 2 + y$ (y)

2   $at - v = 7$ (v)

3   $4ax = y$ (a)

4   $6xw = 3px$ (w)

5. $2f = \dfrac{g}{4h}$ (g)

6. $\dfrac{5ar}{x} = 10a^2$ (r)

7. $2 + xy = 7 + z$ (x)

8. $3ab - 5am = 9ab - 2c$ (m)

9. $4w(aw - 3) = 2x$ (a)

10. $2z(x - 3) = 3x(2y - z)$ (y)

11. $\dfrac{a}{c} = \dfrac{b}{d}$ (d)

12. $\dfrac{x}{3p} = \dfrac{y}{6x}$ (p)

13. $7m - \dfrac{mv}{r} = r$ (v)

14. $\dfrac{2}{x}(y - z) = 4$ (x)

15. $\dfrac{1}{x}(xy - 5p) = 3y$ (p)

16. $\dfrac{a + 2b}{d - b} = 2$ (d)

17. $\dfrac{3f}{f + gh} = -\dfrac{1}{2}$ (h)

18. $\dfrac{3x}{x - 2y} = \dfrac{z}{2z - w}$ (w)

19. $\dfrac{m}{2} + \dfrac{3}{4} = \dfrac{m + n}{4}$ (n)

20. $a - \dfrac{2x}{v} = \dfrac{3x}{v} - xy$ (y)

21. $\dfrac{x}{2s} - wy = \dfrac{w}{4s^2}$ (y)

22. $2x = \sqrt{x^2 - 3y}$ (y)

23. $x\sqrt{3rt} = r$ (t)

24. $\sqrt{\dfrac{x}{y + xz}} = \dfrac{1}{2}$ (z)

25. $2a - mg^2 = 5a - m$ (g)

26. $4x^2y^2 - x^2 = 9w^2$ (y)

27. Mr Jacobs buys n digital watches for £x each and sells them on his market stall for a total price of £y.
    a Write down a formula for p, where £p is the profit Mr Jacobs makes.
    b Make x the subject of this formula.
    c Given that Mr Jacobs makes a profit of £35 by selling 24 watches for a total of £395, find the price for each watch.

28. The volume of a cone is given by the formula
    $$V = \tfrac{1}{3}\pi r^2 h$$
    where r is the radius of the base and h is the height of the cone.
    a Make h the subject of the formula.
    b Make r the subject of the formula.

    Using the value of π given by a calculator, work out, to two decimal places
    c the height of a cone of volume 50 cm³ and radius 2·4 cm,
    d the radius of a cone of volume 240 cm³ and height 11 cm.

29. A group of x boys and y girls contribute to a charity. The boys give an average of n pence each, and the girls give a total of £14.
    a Write down a formula for A, where A pence is the average amount contributed by all the children.
    b Make y the subject of this formula.
    c Given that the group contains 26 boys, who contribute an average of 50p each, and the average amount contributed by all the children is 54p, find the number of girls in the group.

30 A body travels at a speed of 20 m s^{-1} for t seconds and then at a speed of $v \text{ m s}^{-1}$ for T seconds.
   a Write down a formula for d, where d metres is the total distance the body travels.
   b Make T the subject of this formula.
   c Given that the body travels 680 m altogether, that its second speed is twice its first and that it travels at its lower speed for 8 seconds, work out the value of T.

Level 3

Transformation of formulae — harder problems

Exercise 22A

Make the letter given in brackets the subject of the formula.

1. $2x = wx + y$ (x)
2. $ab - 3c + d = cd$ (c)
3. $2pr - 4 = ap - 5p$ (p)
4. $x(p - 2r) = r(p - 3x)$ (r)
5. $\dfrac{tv + m}{v} = 2m$ (v)
6. $\dfrac{x + y}{x - y} = \dfrac{2}{5}$ (x)
7. $\dfrac{x}{y} = \tfrac{1}{2}(y - x)$ (x)
8. $\dfrac{3af + 2fg}{ag - 3f} = \dfrac{2}{3}$ (g)
9. $\dfrac{7p}{r + ps} = \dfrac{3}{s - rp}$ (s)
10. $\dfrac{x}{2} - \dfrac{y}{4} = x + \dfrac{xy}{4}$ (y)
11. $\dfrac{1}{x} - \dfrac{1}{y} = \dfrac{1}{w}$ (y)
12. $\dfrac{r}{6t} - \dfrac{2}{3} = r$ (t)
13. $\dfrac{b}{2a} = \dfrac{3}{4} + \dfrac{b}{a^2}$ (b)
14. $\dfrac{a}{2}(v - 3u) = \dfrac{u}{4}$ (u)
15. $\sqrt{\dfrac{y - x}{x}} = 2$ (x)
16. $\dfrac{r}{2} = \sqrt{\dfrac{r^2 - s}{2s - 3}}$ (s)
17. $ap^2 - q = 2p^2$ (p)
18. $y = x\sqrt{4 - y^2}$ (y)
19. $4 - \dfrac{y^2}{x^2} = w^2$ (x)
20. $\dfrac{r - s^3}{s^2} = \dfrac{s}{r}$ (s)

Exercise 22B

Make the letter given in brackets the subject of the formula.

1. $3y - z = xy$ (y)
2. $2pr - s = 4s - 3p$ (p)
3. $abc = b - c - bd$ (b)
4. $2x(y - w) = y(5x + w)$ (w)
5. $\dfrac{r - 3m}{mr} = 4$ (m)
6. $\dfrac{2a - 3b}{a + 2b} = \dfrac{1}{2}$ (a)
7. $\dfrac{w}{y}(py - x) = x$ (y)
8. $-\dfrac{1}{2} = \dfrac{tv - w}{3t - wv}$ (w)
9. $\dfrac{a}{a - f} = \dfrac{a - d}{f - d}$ (f)
10. $1\tfrac{1}{3} = \dfrac{mp}{6} - m$ (m)
11. $\dfrac{3y}{4x} = \tfrac{1}{2}(y - x)$ (y)
12. $\dfrac{1}{u} - \dfrac{1}{2v} = \dfrac{3u + v}{4uv}$ (u)
13. $\dfrac{2a - b}{a^2} = \dfrac{b}{a} - 2$ (b)
14. $\dfrac{8p}{q} = \dfrac{q}{2p}$ (p)
15. $x\sqrt{\dfrac{p}{y}} = \dfrac{w}{y}$ (y)
16. $\sqrt{\dfrac{a + 2b}{a - 3f}} = \dfrac{k}{2}$ (a)
17. $3m^2 - x = 2x - am^2$ (m)
18. $x^2y^2 - y^2r^2 = r^2x^2$ (x)
19. $x\sqrt{\dfrac{r^2 - 2}{x^2 + w^2}} = \dfrac{r}{2}$ (x)
20. $\dfrac{m^2}{v^2} = \dfrac{u^2}{m^2} - \dfrac{2}{v^2}$ (v)

Simultaneous equations

Exercise 23A

Solve the following pairs of simultaneous equations:

1. $5x - y = 9$
   $2x + y = 5$
2. $p + 8q = 21$
   $p + 5q = 15$
3. $4a - b = 13$
   $2a - b = 7$
4. $3v + w = 17$
   $4v - 2w = 36$
5. $5f + 3g = 24$
   $f + 5g = -4$
6. $4x - y = -2$
   $3x - 2y = 1$
7. $7a - 3b = 18$
   $5a + 2b = 17$
8. $3r + 7s = 130$
   $2r + 3s = 70$
9. $8t - 4v = 3$
   $7t - 3v = 4\tfrac{1}{4}$

10 $5x = 2 + 3y$
    $2y = 8 + x$

12 $2x = 20 - y = 5y + 8x$

11 $2r + 1 = -4s$
    $s - 3r + 9 = 0$

13 $1\tfrac{1}{2}p = 1\tfrac{1}{4}q$
    $4p + 8q = 8\tfrac{1}{2}$

14 $x - 6y - 10 = 4y - 3x + 3 = 3x - 2y + 6$

15 $2a + b + 6 = 3a + 4b + 2 = 15b - 5a - 8$

16 A man has 54p in his pocket, all in 2p coins and 5p coins. There are 15 coins altogether in his pocket. Letting the numbers of 2p coins and 5p coins be x and y, respectively, write down two simultaneous equations in x and y. Solve these equations to find how many of each type of coin the man has.

17 At the school canteen Avril buys three doughnuts and two hamburgers for a total cost of £1·30. Simon buys one doughnut and three hamburgers for a total cost of £1·25. Form two simultaneous equations and solve them to find the price of a doughnut and the price of a hamburger.

18 A woman is now $2\tfrac{1}{2}$ times the age of her daughter. In eight years' time she will be only twice her daughter's age. Write down two simultaneous equations and use them to find the woman's present age.

19 In a triangle ABC the lengths of the sides AB, BC and CA are $3x$ cm, $2y$ cm and $(x + y)$ cm, respectively. Given that the perimeter of the triangle is 96 cm, and that AB exceeds CA by 8 cm, form two simultaneous equations and solve them to find the values of x and y.

20 One day a man covers 7 km by jogging for 30 minutes and walking for 20 minutes. The next day he jogs for 12 minutes and walks for 30 minutes, thereby covering 5 km. Assuming that the man always walks and jogs at the same speeds, form two simultaneous equations and solve them to find these speeds in km h^{-1}.

Exercise 23B

Solve the following pairs of simultaneous equations:

1   $7a + b = 18$
    $3a - b = 2$

4   $5t - 3v = 19$
    $3t + v = 3$

2   $x + 3y = 10$
    $x + 8y = 15$

5   $r + 3s = 2$
    $7r + 15s = -10$

3   $9p - 2q = 7$
    $6p - 2q = -2$

6   $9x - 4y = -23$
    $6x - y = -2$

7 $10a + 4b = -7$
   $8a + 3b = -5$

8 $4v - 2w = 1$
   $5v + 3w = 15$

9 $5f - 4g = -1$
   $8f - 7g = 2$

10 $3y = 2x$
   $3x - 5y - 4 = 0$

11 $2x = 3y + \frac{3}{4}$
   $5y = 4\frac{1}{4} - 4x$

12 $12a - 15b = 8a - 9b = 4$

13 $\dfrac{p}{5} = \dfrac{q}{10}$
   $11p + 50 = 13q$

14 $x + 2y + 6 = 3x - y - 5 = 2x + 3y + 3$

15 $2v - 3w + 4 = 4v + 2w - 8 = 8v - 6w -$

16 A record and four blank cassettes cost £6·50 altogether. Given that the record costs £2·75 more than each of the cassettes, form two simultaneous equations and solve them to find the price of the record and the price of each cassette.

17 The graph of $y = Ax^2 + Bx$ passes through the points (2, 8) and $(-1, 5)$. Find the values of A and B.

18 In the two figures on the left all the angles are right angles and the distances are in centimetres. Given that the areas of the figures are 45 cm² and 25 cm², find the values of x and y.

19 Three years ago Anita was five times the age of her brother Patrick. In 6 years' time she will be twice Patrick's age. Letting the present ages of Anita and Patrick be x years and y years, respectively, write down two simultaneous equations in x and y. Solve these equations to find Anita's and Patrick's present ages.

20 By travelling at a certain speed for 2 hours, then at a higher speed for 3 hours, a train covers a distance of 540 km altogether. The following day the train makes the return journey, covering the same distance by travelling at the lower speed for 4 hours and at the higher speed for $1\frac{1}{2}$ hours. Work out the two speeds at which the train travels.

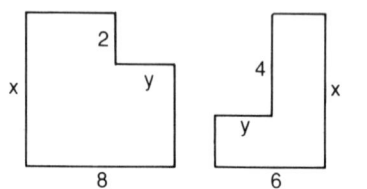

Level 3

Variation

Exercise 24A

1 a Express the statement 'y is directly proportional to x' in the form of an equation containing a constant of proportionality, k.
   b Find the value of k, given that $y = 20$ when $x = 5$.

   With this value of k, find
   c the value of y when $x = 7.5$,
   d the value of x when $y = 5.6$.

2 a Express the statement $y \propto x^2$ in the form of an equation containing a constant of proportionality, k.
   b Find the value of k, given that $y = 8$ when $x = 4$.

   With this value of k, find the values of
   c y when $x = 6$,
   d y when $x = 12{\cdot}4$,
   e x when $y = 50$,
   f x when $y = 3{\cdot}7$, to two decimal places.

3 a Express the statement 'p is inversely proportional to q' in the form of an equation containing a constant of proportionality, k.
   b Find the value of k, given that $p = 0{\cdot}5$ when $q = 12$.

   With this value of k, find the values of
   c p when $q = 3$,
   d p when $q = 0{\cdot}25$,
   e q when $p = 4{\cdot}8$.

4 Given that $w \propto x^3$, and $w = 24$ when $x = 2$, find the values of
   a w when $x = 4$,
   b w when $x = 0{\cdot}3$.

5 Given that t varies inversely as v^2, and $t = 14$ when $v = 0{\cdot}5$, find the values of
   a t when $v = 2$,
   b t when $v = 0{\cdot}1$,
   c v when $t = 2{\cdot}6$, to two decimal places.

6 Given that z varies directly as the square of p, and $z = 0{\cdot}72$ when $p = 0{\cdot}2$, find the values of
   a z when $p = \frac{1}{6}$,
   b z when $p = 3{\cdot}5$,
   c p when $z = 162$,
   d p when $z = 4{\cdot}5$.

7 The time a gardener takes to mow a lawn is directly proportional to the area of the lawn. If the gardener takes 40 minutes to mow a lawn of area $180\,m^2$, work out
   a how long she will take to mow a lawn of area $126\,m^2$,
   b the area of lawn she can mow in an hour,
   c how long she will take to mow a lawn of area $72\,m^2$.

8 The resistance to the motion of a certain body is directly proportional to the square of its speed. By what factor is the resistance multiplied when the speed is
   a doubled?
   b halved?
   c multiplied by 5?
   d divided by 10?

9 The time a train takes to complete a journey of definite length is inversely proportional to the average speed of the train. If the train takes $2\frac{1}{2}$ hours when its average speed is 80 km h^{-1}, work out
   a the time the train takes when its average speed is 50 km h^{-1},
   b the average speed at which the train takes 2 hours,
   c the time the train takes when its average speed is 120 km h^{-1}.

10 The electrical resistance of a piece of wire of definite length varies inversely as the square of its radius. Given that the resistance is 4 ohms when the radius is 0·2 mm, work out, to two decimal places,
   b the radius at which the resistance is 3·7 ohms,
   c the resistance when the radius is 0·43 mm,
   d the radius at which the resistance is 6·4 ohms.

Exercise 24B

1 Write down equations, in terms of y, x and a constant of proportionality k, which express the following relationships:
   a y is directly proportional to x^2,
   b $y \propto \dfrac{1}{x^2}$,
   c y varies inversely as x,
   d $y \propto x^3$.

2 Given that $r \propto s$, and $r = 0.5$ when $s = 0.2$, find the values of
   a r when $s = 6$,
   b s when $r = 350$.

3 Given that t is inversely proportional to w, and $t = 40$ when $w = 0.25$, find the values of
   a t when $w = 20$,
   b w when $t = 1.25$.

4 If m is directly proportional to n, state
   a the factor by which m is multiplied when n is multiplied by 10,
   b the factor by which n is multiplied when m is divided by 2.

5 Given that z varies inversely as the square of x, and $z = \frac{1}{16}$ when $x = 6$, find the values of
   a z when $x = 0.25$,
   b x when $z = 4$,
   c z when $x = \frac{2}{16}$,
   d x when $z = 0.36$.

6 Given that $u \propto v^3$, and $u = 16$ when $v = 4$, find the values of
  a u when $v = 2$,
  b u when $v = 0.5$,
  c v when $u = 3$, to two decimal places.

7 The weight of any body is inversely proportional to the square of its distance from the centre of the Earth. By what factor is the weight of a body multiplied when
  a the body is moved to twice its distance from the centre of the Earth?
  b the body is moved to a quarter of its distance from the centre of the Earth?
  c the body is moved to five times its distance from the centre of the Earth?
  d the body is moved to one tenth of its distance from the centre of the Earth?

8 The mass of a hollow copper sphere varies directly as the square of its radius. Given that a sphere of radius 5 cm has a mass of 480 g, work out
  a the mass of a sphere of radius 7 cm, to three significant figures,
  b the radius of a sphere of mass 700 g, to two decimal places.

9 When a wire is connected to the terminals of a battery, the current flowing in the wire is inversely proportional to the wire's resistance. Given that the current in a wire of resistance 5 ohms is 1.2 amps, find
  a the current in a wire of resistance 4 ohms,
  b the resistance of a wire in which the current is 0.3 amps,
  c the current in a wire of resistance 0.8 ohms.

10

x	0.5	0.8	1	2	4
y	8	3.125	2	0.5	0.125

  a Use the data in the above table to obtain a relationship between x and y, given that it is one of the following:

$$y \propto x, \quad y \propto \frac{1}{x}, \quad y \propto x^2, \quad y \propto \frac{1}{x^2}$$

  b Write down the equation relating x and y.
  c Find the value of y when $x = 0.2$.
  d Find the value of x when $y = 12.5$, given that x is always positive.

Algebraic fractions

Exercise 25A

Simplify the following expressions:

1. $\dfrac{2a}{3} \times \dfrac{a}{5}$

2. $3x \times \dfrac{4xy}{3}$

3. $\dfrac{1}{5p} \times \dfrac{15p}{q}$

4. $\dfrac{3rt}{2} \times \dfrac{4t}{r}$

5. $\dfrac{9a}{2b} \times \dfrac{4b}{15}$

6. $\dfrac{st}{10v} \times \dfrac{25stv^2}{4}$

7. $\dfrac{m}{2} \div \dfrac{m}{6}$

8. $\dfrac{1}{4x} \div \dfrac{3x}{2}$

9. $\dfrac{5}{p} \div \dfrac{15}{pq}$

10. $\dfrac{2x^2}{y} \div \dfrac{4x}{y^2}$

11. $\dfrac{12rt}{u} \div \dfrac{3r^2}{2u}$

12. $\dfrac{15x^2y^2}{w^2} \div \dfrac{20x^3}{yw}$

13. $\dfrac{2}{a-3} \div \dfrac{4}{a+2}$

14. $\dfrac{9}{p+2} \div \dfrac{6(p+3)}{p+2}$

15. $\dfrac{8(x-4)}{5} \div \dfrac{6(x-4)}{15(x+4)}$

16. $\dfrac{a}{4} + \dfrac{a-2}{5}$

17. $\dfrac{2k}{3} - \dfrac{k+2}{2}$

18. $\dfrac{2m-3}{7} - \dfrac{m-4}{5}$

19. $\dfrac{2(x+2)}{3} + \dfrac{3(x-3)}{4}$

20. $\dfrac{3x-2}{6} - \dfrac{2x+1}{3}$

21. $\dfrac{7(t-2)}{8} - \dfrac{5(t-3)}{6}$

22. $\dfrac{3x+y}{3x} - \dfrac{x+2y}{2y}$

23. $1 - \dfrac{a}{a+b}$

24. $\dfrac{r+6}{r-2} + 3$

25. $\dfrac{3}{2} - \dfrac{x-3}{x}$

26. $\dfrac{r-2s}{2r+s} - \dfrac{1}{2}$

27. $\dfrac{wy-3}{3y} + \dfrac{1}{y}$

28. $\dfrac{a+b}{2(a-b)} - \dfrac{b}{a-b}$

Level 3

Exercise 25B

Simplify the following expressions:

1. $\dfrac{3}{x} \times \dfrac{x}{6}$

2. $\dfrac{2}{a} \times \dfrac{1}{2a}$

3. $\dfrac{8xy}{3} \times \dfrac{6x}{y}$

4. $\dfrac{9}{4rt} \times \dfrac{2r}{3t}$

5. $\dfrac{x^2 y}{w} \times \dfrac{w^2}{xy}$

6. $\dfrac{2}{15a^2 b^3} \times \dfrac{9a^3 b^2}{4}$

7. $\dfrac{1}{3w} \div \dfrac{1}{2w}$

8. $\dfrac{r}{2} \div \dfrac{rp}{6}$

9. $\dfrac{21y}{x} \div \dfrac{14x}{3y}$

10. $\dfrac{m^3}{6v} \div \dfrac{m}{8v^3}$

11. $\dfrac{7a^2 bc}{10d^2} \div \dfrac{14ac^2}{15bd}$

12. $\dfrac{1}{3(x-6)} \div \dfrac{5}{6(x-6)}$

13. $\dfrac{m^2}{n+v} \div m(n+v)$

14. $\dfrac{r-s}{r+s} \div \dfrac{r-s}{r}$

15. $\dfrac{12(a-b)}{a+b} \div \dfrac{14(a-b)^2}{(a+b)^3}$

16. $\dfrac{x+3}{4} + \dfrac{x+2}{3}$

17. $\dfrac{3k-5}{6} - \dfrac{k}{2}$

18. $\dfrac{5-y}{3} - \dfrac{2-y}{2}$

19. $\dfrac{3(w+4)}{5} - \dfrac{4(w+3)}{7}$

20. $\dfrac{4-g}{10} + \dfrac{g-2}{5}$

21. $\dfrac{x-3y}{9} - \dfrac{x-5y}{15}$

22. $\dfrac{2x+3}{4x} - \dfrac{y-2}{2y}$

23. $\dfrac{a}{a+2b} - 1$

24. $2 - \dfrac{f+g}{f-g}$

25. $\dfrac{3}{5} + \dfrac{2y}{3y-2}$

26. $\dfrac{2ab + b^2}{3a - 2b} + \dfrac{b}{2}$

27. $\dfrac{6x+5}{9x} - \dfrac{4x+1}{6x}$

28. $\dfrac{x-y}{3(x+y)} + \dfrac{8y}{12(x+y)}$

Graphs of equations

Exercise 26A

1. Copy and complete the following table for the graph of $y = 2x + 3$.

x	−2	−1	0	1	2	4	6
y				5		11	

   Draw the graph, letting 2 cm = 1 unit on the x-axis and letting 1 cm = 1 unit on the y-axis. Find
   a the coordinates of the point where the graph meets the x-axis,
   b the gradient of the graph,
   c a solution of the equation $2x + 3 = 8.6$.

   Make a table for the equation $y = 10 - 3x$, letting x have the values 0, 1, 2, 3. Draw the graph of this equation on the same axes as the first graph and find
   d the gradient of the second graph,
   e the coordinates of the point of intersection of the graphs,
   f the solution of the simultaneous equations $y = 2x + 3$, $y = 10 - 3x$.

2. A train is travelling directly away from London. The following table shows how its distance from London varies with time:

Time (hours)	0	1	2	3	4
Distance (km)	50	135	220	305	390

   Draw a graph of distance from London against time, using scales of 4 cm to 1 hour and 2 cm to 50 km.
   a Read off, to the nearest 10 km, the train's distance from London after 1·3 h, 2·8 h and 3·4 h.
   b Write down the train's initial distance from London.
   c Work out the gradient of the graph, and say what this represents.
   d Write down the equation of the graph, letting d km be the distance from London and t seconds be the time.

3. Without drawing the graphs, work out the coordinates of the points at which the following graphs meet the x-axis and the y-axis:
   a $y + 2x = 6$
   b $3y - 2x = 12$
   c $4y = 6 - x$
   d $4x - 2y + 10 = 0$
   e $3 - 10x = 5y$

4. Copy and complete the following table for the graph of $y = 1·2x^2$.

x	−2	−1·5	−1	−0·5	0	0·5	1	1·5	2
y	4·8					0·3			

Draw the graph, taking 4 cm as 1 unit on the x-axis and 2 cm as 1 unit on the y-axis. Work out from the graph, to one decimal place
a the value of y when $x = 1.8$,
b the two solutions of the equation $1.2x^2 = 3.4$,
c the range of values of x for which $1 < y < 2$.

Draw a tangent to the graph at the point where $x = 0.7$, and hence
d estimate the gradient at this point.

5 Draw on the same axes the graph of $3x + y = 13$, letting $x = 2, 4, 6$, and the graph of $x + 2y = 8.5$, letting $x = 0.5, 2.5, 4.5$. (Choose appropriate scales yourself.) Hence work out the values of x and y at which the two equations are simultaneously true.

6 A rectangle has a fixed area of 10 m^2. Given that its width is x m, show that its length, y m, is given by the equation $y = 10/x$.

Make a table for the equation $y = 10/x$ for $0 < x \leqslant 10$. Taking the same scale on each axis, draw the graph of the equation and use it to estimate, to one decimal place,
a the length of the rectangle when its width is 1.7 m,
b the range of values of x for which the length lies between 4.2 m and 6.5 m,
c the value of x for which the rectangle becomes a square.

Draw the line of symmetry of the graph of $y = 10/x$, and
d write down the equation of this line.

7 Copy and complete the following table for the graph of $y = x^2 - 4x$.

x	−1	−0.5	0	0.5	1	1.5	2	2.5	3	3.5	4	4.5	5
y	5		0	−1.75			−4	−3.75				2.25	

Draw the graph, letting 2 cm = 1 unit on each axis. Use the graph to estimate, to one decimal place
a the value of y when $x = 1.3$,
b the two solutions of the equations $x^2 - 4x = 3.4$,
c the minimum value of y,
d the equation of the line of symmetry of the graph.

8 For a certain time the height of a growing plant is given by the formula $h = 8 + \frac{1}{2}t$, where h cm is the height of the plant after t days. Draw the graph of h against t for the range $0 \leqslant t \leqslant 6$.
a Work out the gradient of the graph and say what it represents.

Another plant has a height of 3 cm when $t = 0$, and grows at 2.3 cm per day.
b State the equation relating h and t for the second plant.

On the same axes as the first graph draw the graph of h against t for the second plant and use the graphs to estimate
c the time at which the plants have the same height, and the value of this height,
d the period of time for which the difference in the plants' heights is more than 1.4 cm.

9 Draw the graph of $y = 9 - x^2$ for the range $-3 \leq x \leq 3$, taking scales of 2 cm to 1 unit on the x-axis and 1 cm to 1 unit on the y-axis.
  a By drawing tangents, estimate the gradients at the points where $x = -2 \cdot 5$, $-0 \cdot 8$ and $0 \cdot 4$.
  b Draw the line $y = 7$, and state the coordinates of the points at which it intersects the first graph.
  c State the positive solution of the equation $9 - x^2 = 7$, to one decimal place.
  d Draw the line $y = x$, and hence find the coordinates of the point on the graph of $y = 9 - x^2$ at which x and y are equal.

Exercise 26B

1 Make tables for the equations $x + y = 0$ and $x + y = -2$, letting x vary from -2 to $+2$ in each case. Draw the graphs of the equations on the same axes and draw also the graph which passes through the points $(0, 2)$ and $(2, 0)$.
  a State the gradient of all the three graphs.
  b Write down the equation of the third graph.

On the same axes draw the graph of the equation $2y = 3x + 5$, letting x have the values $-1, 0$ and 1. Find
  c the gradient of this graph,
  d the solution of the simultaneous equations $2y = 3x + 5$, $x + y = -2$.

2 Without drawing the graphs, work out the coordinates of the points at which the following graphs meet the x-axis and the y-axis:
  a $3y + x = 12$ **d** $4x + 2y - 1 = 0$
  b $y = 2x - 4$ **e** $5x - 10y = 2$
  c $6x = y - 9$

3 A pyramid of height $7\frac{1}{2}$ m has a square base of side-length x m. Given that the volume of any pyramid is one third of the area of the base multiplied by the height, show that the volume of the pyramid on the left is given by the formula $V = 2 \cdot 5x^2$.

Copy and complete the following table for the formula $V = 2 \cdot 5x^2$.

x	0	0·5	1	1·5	2	2·5	3
V	0	0·6	2·5				

Draw the graph of V against x, using scales of 4 cm to 1 unit on the x-axis and 2 cm to 5 units on the V-axis. Read off, as accurately as possible
  a the volume of the pyramid when $x = 2 \cdot 2$,
  b the value of x for which the volume is 7 m^3.

A pyramid has to be made with a base area of at least 4 m^2 and with a volume that does not exceed 20 m^3. Work out
  c the range of possible values of x.

4 Draw on the same axes the graphs of $y = 3x - 1$ and $2y = x + 6$, letting x have the values $0, 1, 2$ in each case. Hence solve the simultaneous equations $y = 3x - 1$, $2y = x + 6$.

5   For a certain time the population of a country obeys the equation $N = 80 + 12t - t^2$, where N is the population in millions after t years. Draw a graph of N against t, letting t vary from 0 to 7 and starting the N-axis at $N = 70$. Work out
   a   the population, to the nearest million, after 2·6 years,
   b   the time in years, to one decimal place, at which the population is 110 million,
   c   the maximum population.

   Draw a tangent to the graph at the point where $t = 3$, and hence find
   d   the rate of growth of the population after 3 years.

6   Copy and complete the following table for the equation $y = x + \dfrac{1}{x}$.

x	0·25	0·5	0·75	1	1·5	2	2·5	3	4
y	4·25				2·17			3·33	

   Draw the graph of the equation, taking scales of 4 cm to 1 unit on the x-axis and 2 cm to 1 unit on the y-axis. Use the graph to estimate, as accurately as possible,
   a   the value of y when $x = 1·7$,
   b   the two solutions of the equations $x + \dfrac{1}{x} = 4$,
   c   the minimum value of y,
   d   the gradient at the point where $x = 0·5$.

7   The speed of a car is given by the formula $v = 7 + \dfrac{3t}{2}$, where v ms^{-1} is the speed after t seconds. Draw a graph of v against t for the range $0 \leqslant t \leqslant 8$.
   a   Another car is travelling at a steady speed of 12·4 ms^{-1}. After what time will the two cars have the same speed?
   b   Work out the gradient of the graph and say what it represents.

   A lorry has a speed of 14 ms^{-1} at $t = 0$, and it loses speed at $\frac{3}{4}$ ms^{-1} every second.
   c   Write down the equation which gives v in terms of t for the lorry.

   Draw, on the same axes as the first graph, the graph of v against t for the lorry, and work out
   d   the time, to one decimal place, at which the car and the lorry have the same speed.

8   The perimeter of a rectangle is 30 cm. Show that, if the width of the rectangle is x cm, its area is given by the formula $A = x(15 - x)$.

   Draw the graph of A against x for $0 \leqslant x \leqslant 15$, taking a scale of 1 cm to 1 unit on the x-axis and 2 cm to 5 units on the A-axis. Find, from the graph, as accurately as possible
   a   the maximum area of the rectangle,
   b   the area of the rectangle when $x = 2·8$,
   c   the values of x for which the area is 48 cm^2,
   d   the range of possible values of x, given that the area must be at least 40 cm^2.

Further graphical techniques

Exercise 27A

1. The following linear equations represent straight line graphs. In each case find the values of m (the gradient) and c (the intercept on the y-axis). Use this information to sketch each graph.

   a $y = 2x + 3$
   b $y = 5 - x$
   c $y = \dfrac{x}{2} - 4$
   d $2y + 3x - 4 = 0$
   e $9x - 12y = 16$
   f $1\tfrac{1}{2}x = 3\tfrac{3}{4}y - 3$

2. Find the values of m and c for each of the following graphs:

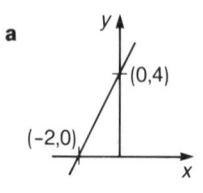

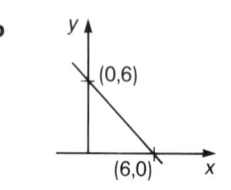

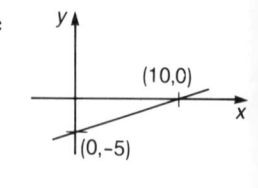

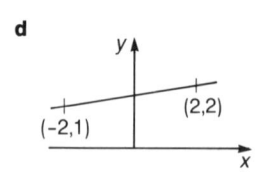

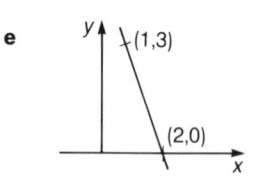

   a line through $(-2, 0)$ and $(0, 4)$
   b line through $(0, 6)$ and $(6, 0)$
   c line through $(10, 0)$ and $(0, -5)$
   d line through $(-2, 1)$ and $(2, 2)$
   e line through $(1, 3)$ and $(2, 0)$

3. A body moves with uniform acceleration for 25 seconds, its velocity varying with time as shown in the following table:

Time (s)	0	5	15	25
Velocity (m s^{-1})	0	1·6	4·8	8

   After this the body travels at constant speed for 15 seconds, and finally it decelerates to rest, its velocity during this last stage being given by the equation $v = 18 - \dfrac{t}{4}$, where v m s^{-1} is the velocity t seconds after the start of the first stage of the motion.

   a Represent the whole journey by a graph of velocity against time, taking scales of 1 cm to 5 seconds on the time axis and 1 cm to 1 m s^{-1} on the velocity axis.

   b State the accelerations of the body during the first and last stages of its journey.

   c By calculating areas, find the distances travelled by the body during each of the three stages of its journey.

4. Taking a scale of 2 cm to 1 unit on each axis and letting x vary from 0 to 4, draw on the same axes the graphs of $y = 2x + 2$, $2y + 2x = 7$ and $y = 6 - 2x$.

a State the coordinates of the three points of intersection of the graphs.
b Shade the *outer* boundary of the region defined by the inequalities $y \leqslant 2x + 2$, $2y + 2x \geqslant 7$ and $y \leqslant 6 - 2x$.

Within this region, state
c the maximum value of x, given that $y = 3.4$,
d the range of possible values of y, given that $x = 1.8$.

5 a Working to two decimal places where appropriate, copy and complete the following table for the equation $y = 6x^2 - 2x^3$:

x	0	0.25	0.5	1	1.5	1.75	2	2.25	2.5	2.75	3
y	0	0.34	1.25	4							0

b Draw the graph of the equation for the range $x = 0$ to $x = 3$, using the scales of 4 cm to 1 unit on the x-axis and 2 cm to 1 unit on the y-axis.
c Describe briefly how the gradient of the graph changes as x increases from 0 to 2.

By drawing certain straight lines to intersect the graph, obtain approximate solutions of
d the equation $6x^2 - 2x^3 = 6$,
e the simultaneous equations $y = 6x^2 - 2x^3$, $y = x + 2$.

6 The rate at which people enter a city increases uniformly from 50 per minute at 6 a.m. to 200 per minute at 8 a.m.

Sketch a graph of r against t, where r people per minute is the rate at which people enter the city at a time of t minutes after 6 a.m.
Work out
a the equation of the graph,
b the total number of people who enter the city between 6 a.m. and 8 a.m.

7 Using a scale of 2 cm to 1 unit on each axis, and taking the interval $0 \leqslant x \leqslant 5$, draw on the same axes the graphs of $y = x + 3$, $y + 2x = 9$ and $5y + 2x = 10$.
a Shade the outer boundary of the region defined by the inequalities $x > 0$, $y < x + 3$, $y + 2x < 9$ and $5y + 2x > 10$.
b List the points with integer coordinates within this region.
c Given that x and y are integers, find the maximum value of $5x + 3y$ and the minimum value of $x + 3y$ within the above region.

8 a Working to two decimal places where appropriate, copy and complete the following table for the equation $y = 5x^2 + \dfrac{1}{x} - 2$:

x	0.1	0.2	0.3	0.4	0.5	0.6	0.8	1	1.2
$5x^2$	0.05			0.8					7.2
$1/x$	10			2.5					0.83
-2	-2	-2		-2					-2
y	8.05			1.3					6.03

b Draw the graph of the equation for the range $x = 0.1$ to $x = 1.2$, using scales of 10 cm to 1 unit on the x-axis and 2 cm to 1 unit on the y-axis.
c Estimate the minimum value of y.
d By drawing a certain straight line to intersect the graph, obtain approximate solutions of the equation

$$5x^2 + \frac{1}{x} = x + 6$$

e Estimate the range of values of x for which

$$5x^2 + \frac{1}{x} < 5$$

f Show that when $y = 2$, the equation of the graph reduces to

$$5x^3 - 4x + 1 = 0$$

Hence obtain two approximate solutions of this equation.

Exercise 27B

1 The following linear equations represent straight line graphs. In each case find the values of m (the gradient) and c (the intercept on the y-axis). Use this information to sketch each graph.
  a $y = 5x + 2$
  b $y = x - 7$
  c $y = 3 - \frac{2x}{5}$
  d $3y - 2x = 12$
  e $15x = 20 - 6y$
  f $\frac{2y}{3} + \frac{5x}{6} + \frac{1}{3} = 0$

2 Find the equations of the graphs which pass through the following pairs of points:
  a (0, 0) and (2, 6)
  b (0, 8) and (4, 0)
  c (0, −6) and (9, 0)
  d (−12, 0) and (12, 12)
  e (−1, 5) and (1, 1)

3 The graph on the left shows how the velocity of a body changes over a period of 6 seconds:
  a Find the deceleration of the body, in m s^{-2}, over each of the three stages of its journey.
  b By calculating areas, find the total distance covered by the body.
  c Find the equation relating v (velocity in m s^{-1}) and t (time in seconds) for the first stage of the motion.

4 Taking a scale of 1 cm to 1 unit on each axis and letting x vary from 0 to 14, draw on the same axes the graphs of $y = x - 6$, $x = 12$, $4y = x + 24$ and $y = 8 - x$.
  a Shade the outer boundary of the region defined by the inequalities $y \geqslant x - 6$, $x \leqslant 12$, $4y \leqslant x + 24$ and $y \geqslant 8 - x$.

Within this region, state
  b the maximum value of y, given that $x = 5.6$,
  c the range of possible values of x, given that $y = 4.2$.

5 For 8 minutes the rate at which a pipe delivers water is given by the equation $r = 20 + \frac{t}{2}$, where r is the rate of delivery in litres per second and t is the time in minutes. After this period of 8 minutes the rate decreases uniformly, reaching zero 20 minutes after the delivery of water first began.
  a Sketch a graph of r against t for the range $t = 0$ to $t = 20$.
  b Obtain a formula for r in terms of t for the period $t = 8$ to $t = 20$.
  c Work out the area between the graph and the time axis for the complete period $t = 0$ to $t = 20$. Say what this area represents.

6 By drawing graphs for the range $x = -3$ to $x = 3$, display the region which is defined by the inequalities $y > 2 - x$, $y < 8 - 4x$ and $y < 2x + 8$.
  a List the points with integer coordinates within this region.
  b Given that x and y are integers, find the maximum value of $7y + 26x$ and the minimum value of $15y + 16x$ within the region.

7 The 'rate of inflation' may be defined as the rate at which money is losing value. Each of the graphs on the left gives an example of how the value of money (represented on the vertical axis) is changing with time (represented on the horizontal axis).

  Say in each of the following cases which graph fits the given description:
  a Inflation is rapidly increasing.
  b Inflation is steady.
  c Inflation is being gradually reduced.
  d Inflation is zero.

8 Working to two decimal places where appropriate, copy and complete the following table for the equation $y = 8 - 2x - \frac{3}{x}$:

x	0·4	0·5	0·7	1	1·2	1·4	1·6	2	2·5	3	3·7
	8	8			8		8				8
$-2x$		$-0·8$			$-2·4$		$-3·2$				$-7·4$
$-3/x$		$-7·5$			$-2·5$		$-1·88$				$-0·81$
y		$-0·3$			3·1		2·92				$-0·21$

  b Draw the graph of the equation for the range $x = 0·4$ to $x = 3·7$.
  c Use the graph to obtain approximate solutions of the equations
    (i) $8 - 2x - \frac{3}{x} = 0$ (ii) $8 - \frac{3}{x} = 3x$
  d Estimate the range of values of x for which
    $$8 - 2x - \frac{3}{x} > 2$$
  e Draw any line of gradient 3, and by 'translating' the line with the aid of a set square, obtain the tangent to the graph with this gradient. (A translation is a shift of a figure without any rotation.) Hence estimate the coordinates of the point on the graph at which the gradient is 3.

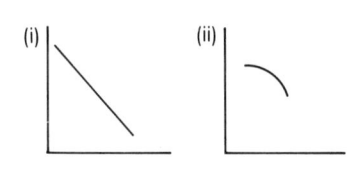

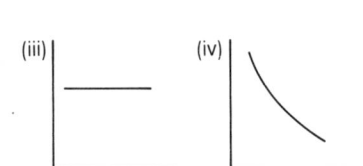

Geometry

Simple angle properties, symmetry, polygons

Exercise 28A

In questions 1–10, work out the angles indicated by letters:

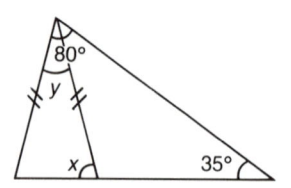

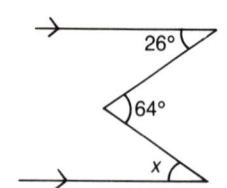

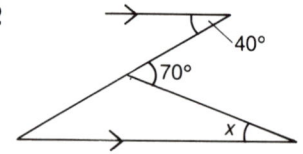

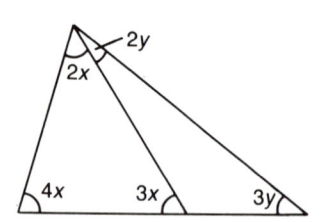

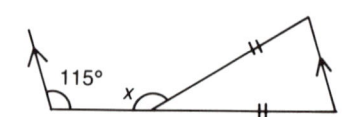

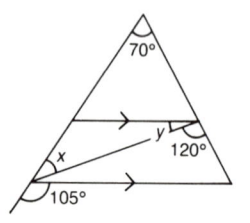

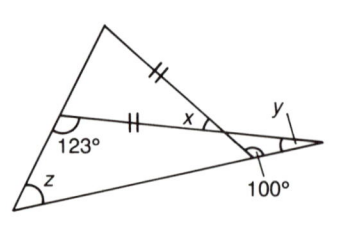

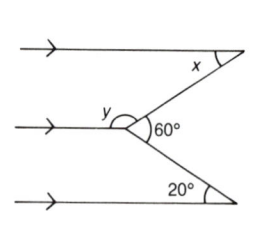

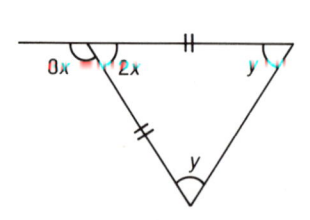

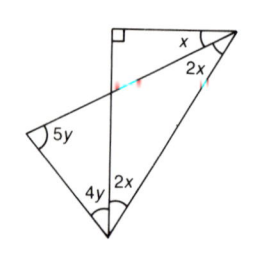

11 Sketch each of the following shapes and put in their axes of symmetry:

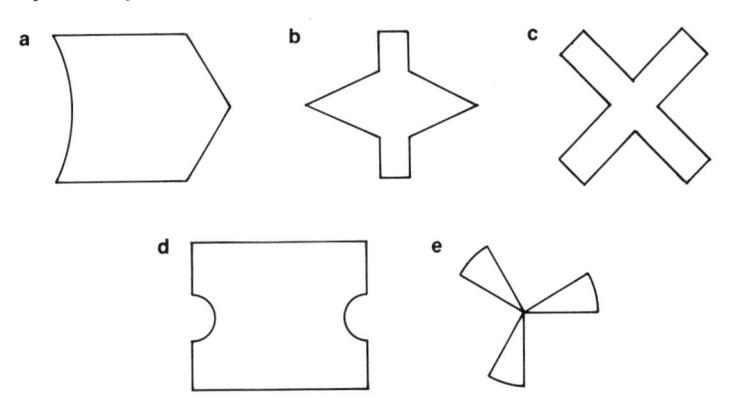

   a   b   c

   d   e

12 Each of the following figures has rotational symmetry. State the order of the symmetry in each case:

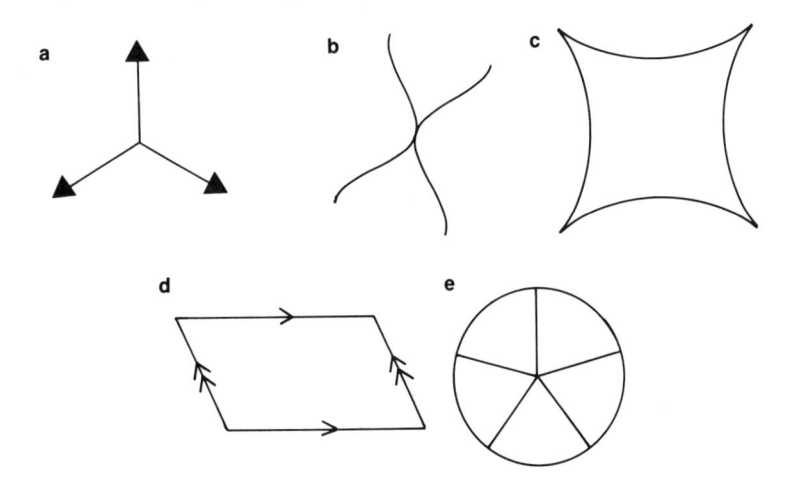

   a   b   c

   d   e

13 For each of the following capital letters state the number of axes of symmetry and also say whether or not the letter has rotational symmetry:

   a A   b P   c S   d H

14 State the number of axes of symmetry, and also the order of the rotational symmetry, if it exists, of
   a an isosceles trapezium,
   b a rhombus,
   c a kite,
   d a regular pentagon (five-sided polygon),
   e a regular hexagon (six-sided polygon).

15 a State the sum of the exterior angles of any polygon.

Use the answer to **a** to work out each exterior angle of
b a regular hexagon,
c a regular nine-sided polygon.

Deduce also the value of each interior angle of
d a regular hexagon,
e a regular nine-sided polygon.

16 In the figure (i) below, A, B, C, D are consecutive vertices of a regular hexagon. Work out angles BAC and ADC.

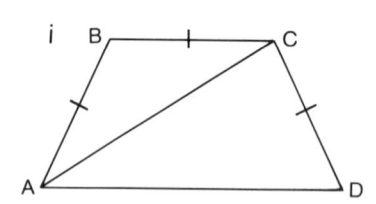

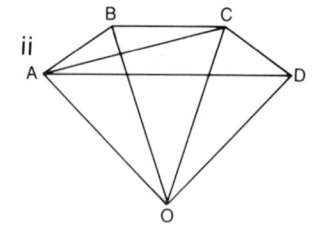

17 In the above figure (ii), A, B, C, D are consecutive vertices of a regular 12-sided polygon of centre O. Work out the angles AOB, ADO and CAD.

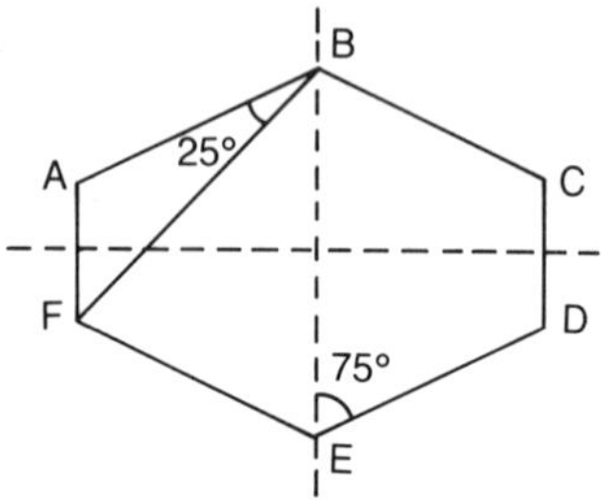

18 The hexagon on the left, which is not regular, has the two axes of symmetry indicated by the dotted lines. Work out angles BAF and BFE.

19 The non-regular pentagon on the left has the one axis of symmetry indicated by the dotted line, and BE is parallel to CD, as shown. Find angle BED.

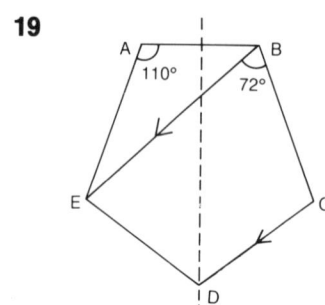

Exercise 28B

In questions 1–10, work out the angles indicated by letters:

1

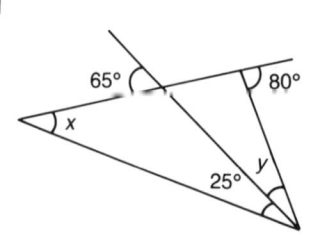

2

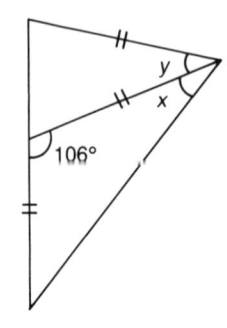

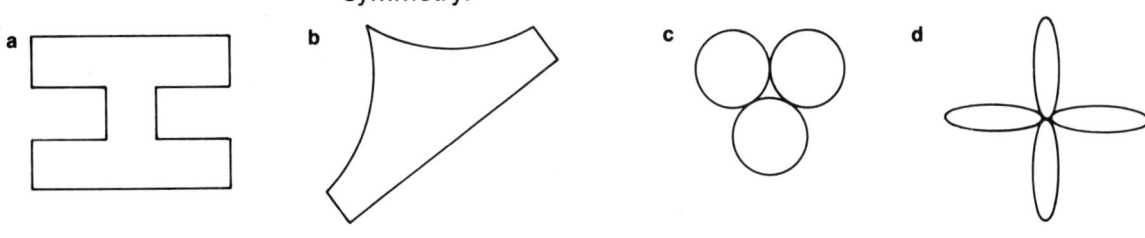

3 Triangle with angles 108°, 50° (on a parallel line), y, x, with arrows indicating parallel lines.

4 Two vertical parallel arrows connected by a zig-zag with a right angle at the top; angle x on the left, 140° on the right.

5 Quadrilateral with angles x, y at top, 88° at right, 2x at bottom; tick marks and arrows showing equal and parallel sides.

6 Rhombus with diagonals; angles y (top-left), z (centre), x (bottom-left), 78° (bottom-right exterior); tick marks on sides.

7 Kite with angles 8x (top), x and 2y (left interior), right angle (right), 6y and 4y (bottom).

8 Two triangles sharing a vertex; 84°, x, 40°, y; tick marks and parallel arrows.

9 Triangle split into two by a cevian; angles x and 2x at top; tick marks on two sides equal and another pair equal.

10 Triangle with 80° at top, 3y and 3x on an interior parallel line, y at right, x at bottom.

11 Sketch each of the following shapes and put in their axes of symmetry:

a **b** **c** **d**

12 Say for each of the cases below whether or not the figure has rotational symmetry. If it does, state the order of the symmetry.

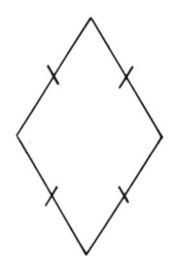

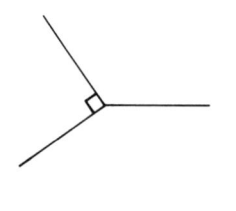

a   b   c

13 From the following set of capital letters list
 a the letters with one axis of symmetry,
 b the letters with more than one axis of symmetry,
 c the letters with rotational symmetry.

B X F N W O E

14 a Write down the equations of all the axes of symmetry of the square formed by the points $(0, 0)$, $(2, 2)$, $(0, 4)$, $(-2, 2)$.
 b State the order of rotational symmetry of a square.

15 Using the sum of the exterior angles of any polygon, work out
 a each exterior angle of a regular pentagon,
 b each interior angle of a regular pentagon,
 c each interior angle of a regular 10-sided polygon,
 d each interior angle of a regular 15-sided polygon.

16 The sum of the interior angles of any n-sided polygon (not necessarily regular) is $(n - 2)180°$. Use this formula to work out
 a the sum of the interior angles of a 13-sided polygon,
 b the number of sides in a polygon whose interior angles have a sum of $900°$,
 c the sum of the interior angles of an 18-sided polygon,
 d the number of sides in a polygon whose interior angles have a sum of $3960°$.

Either by using the above formula or by using the sum of the exterior angles, work out
 e the number of sides of a regular polygon in which each interior angle is $160°$,
 f the number of sides of a regular polygon in which each interior angle is $157·5°$.

17 In a regular pentagon ABCDE, the diagonals AC and BE meet at P. Find angle APE.

18 In the figure on the left, A, B, C, D are consecutive vertices of a regular nine-sided polygon of centre O. Work out angles AOC, ACD and APO.

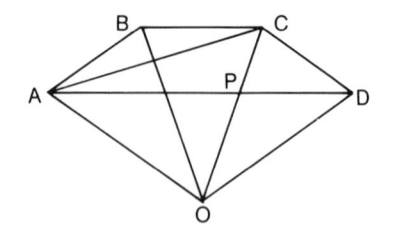

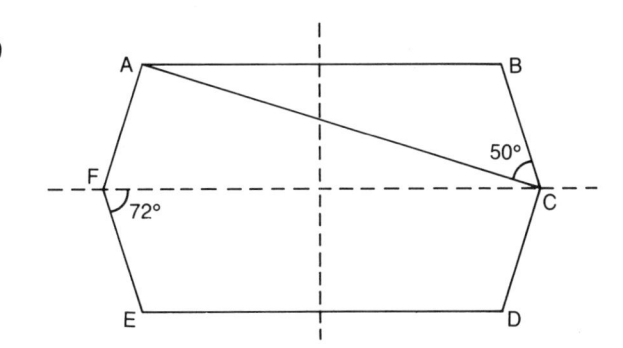

19 The above non-regular hexagon has the two axes of symmetry indicated by the dotted lines. Work out angles ABC and CAF.

20 The figure on the left has the one axis of symmetry shown by the dotted line. Work out angles GFE and BCD.

Congruence

Note: *In the questions requiring graph paper, use the same scale on the two axes.*

Exercise 29A

1

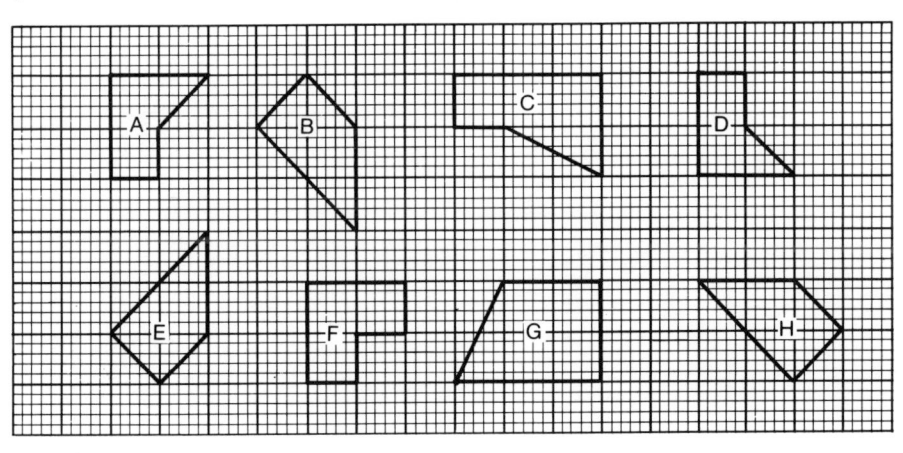

Say which of the above shapes are congruent to
a shape A,
b shape B.

diagram 1

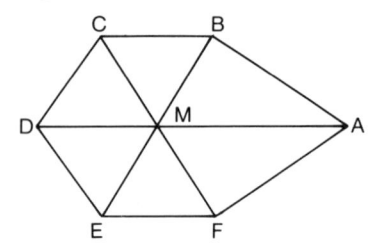

diagram 2

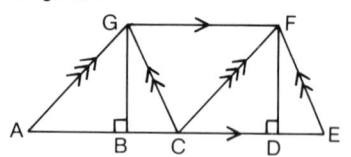

2 AD is an axis of symmetry of the figure in diagram 1. Name the figure which is congruent to
 a the triangle ABM,
 b the quadrilateral BCDM,
 c the quadrilateral ABCF.

3 In diagram 2 name
 a the triangle which is congruent to triangle ABG,
 b the two triangles which are congruent to triangle ACG.

4 Draw on graph paper the triangle formed by the points A(6, 0), B(0, 6), C(1, 1). State the coordinates of a point D such that the triangles ABC, ABD are congruent.

5 Draw on graph paper the triangle formed by the points A(1, 0), B(2, 0), C(2, 2). State the coordinates of three points, D, E, F, none of them below the x-axis, such that the triangles BAD, EBC and FCB are all congruent to triangle ABC.

6 Say in each of the following cases whether or not the triangles ABC, PQR are congruent.
 a A is (0, 0), B is (1, 0), C is (0, 3);
  P is (0, 0), Q is (0, 1), R is (3, 0).
 b A is (−1, 0), B is (1, 0), C is (0, 2);
  P is (0, −1), Q is (2, −1), R is (2, 1).
 c A is (2, 0), B is (1, 2), C is (−1, 1);
  P is (1, 0), Q is (3, 1), R is (2, 3).

7 Say in each of the following cases whether or not the two triangles shown are congruent:

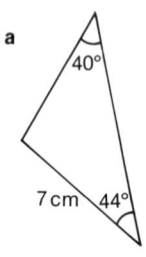

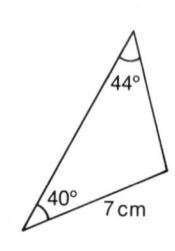

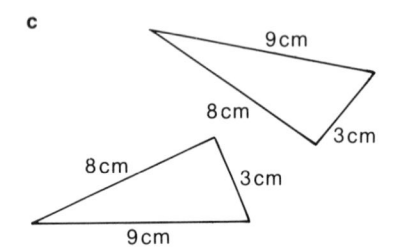

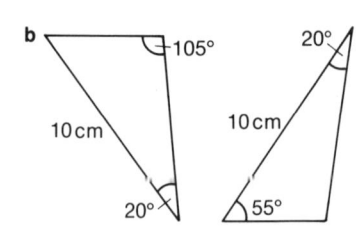

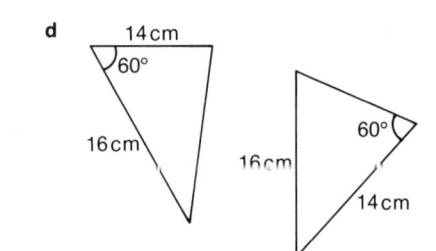

100

Exercise 29B

1.

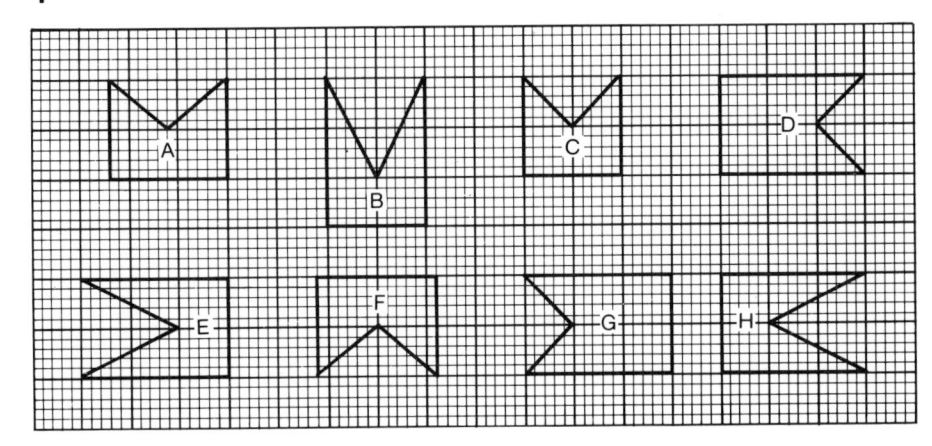

a From the above figure list three sets of congruent shapes.
b Name one shape which is not congruent to any of the others.

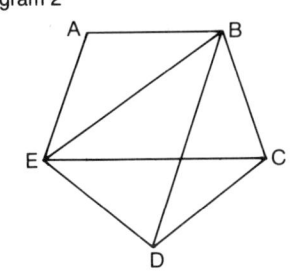

2 AD is an axis of symmetry of diagram 1. Name the figure which is congruent to
  a triangle AHC,
  b triangle ABE,
  c quadrilateral BCDE.

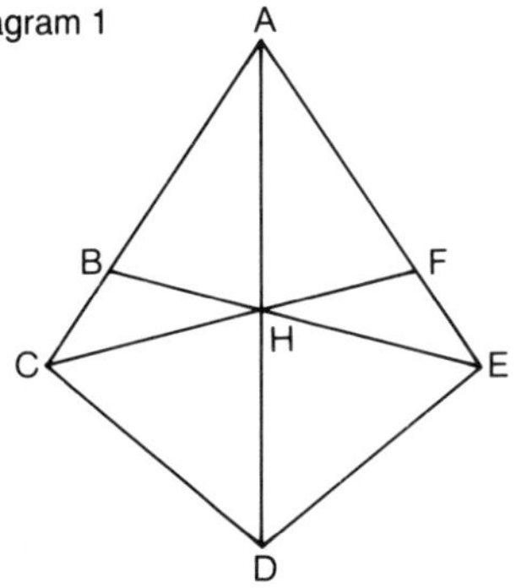

3 The figure ABCDE shown in diagram 2 is a regular pentagon. Name
  a two triangles which are congruent to triangle ABE,
  b one triangle which is congruent to triangle DEB.

4 Draw on graph paper the parallelogram whose vertices are A(4, 0), B(8, 0), C(12, 2), D(8, 2). The parallelogram PQRS is congruent to parallelogram ABCD. Given that P is the point (4, 6), Q is (4, 2) and R is (2, −2), find the coordinates of the point S.

5 Draw on graph paper the triangle whose vertices are A(2, 1), B(6, 1), C(1, 3).
  a State the coordinates of a point D, above the x-axis, such that triangle BAD is congruent to triangle ABC.
  b State the coordinates of two points, E and F, below the x-axis, such that triangles ABE and BAF are both congruent to triangle ABC.

6 Say in each of the following cases whether or not the triangles ABC, PQR are congruent.
  a A is (2, 0), B is (0, 0), C is (−2, 1);
     P is (0, 2), Q is (0, 4), R is (2, 7).
  b A is (1, 2), B is (4, 2), C is (2, 3);
     P is (0, 1), Q is (0, −2), R is (−1, 0).
  c A is (2, −1), B is (4, −4), C is (−2, −2);
     P is (4, −2), Q is (8, −2), R is (3, 2).

diagram 1

diagram 2

7 Say in each of the following cases whether or not the two triangles shown are congruent:

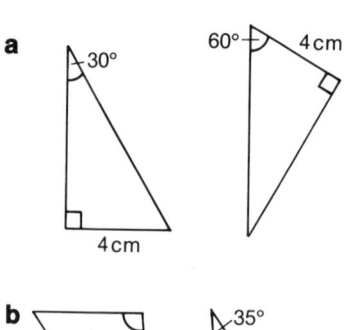

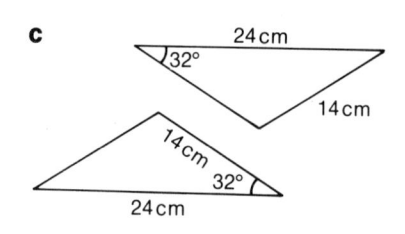

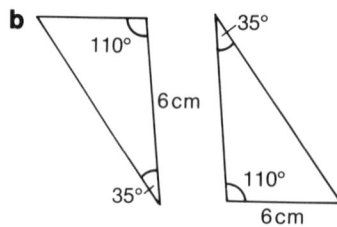

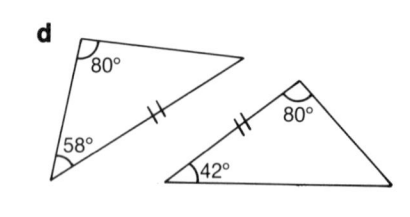

a, b, c, d

Similarity, enlargement

Notes: 1 *In each of the exercises on this topic, questions 9–12 are Level 3.* **2** *In all the questions requiring graph paper, use a scale of 1 cm to 1 unit on both axes.*

Exercise 30A

1 The triangles ABC, PQR shown on the left are similar.
   a Express the ratio BC:QR as simply as possible.
   b State the value of the ratio PQ:AB.
   c Given that PQ = 12 cm, find AB.
   d Given that AC = 25 cm, find PR.

2 Taking a range of 0 to 14 on the *x*-axis and a range of 0 to 10 on the *y*-axis, draw on graph paper the square whose vertices are A(3, 1), B(4, 1), C(4, 2), D(3, 2).
   a Draw the images of the square under enlargements of
      (i) centre the origin and scale factor 3,
      (ii) centre (4, 0) and scale factor 4.
   b State the coordinates of the images of B and D under each of these enlargements.
   c State the area of the square ABCD and the areas of its two images.
   d State the general relationship between the scale factor of an enlargement and the ratio *area of image : area of object*.

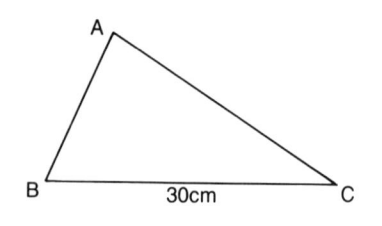

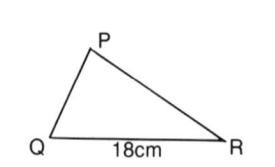

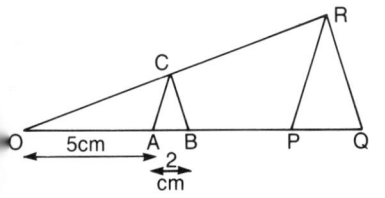

3 In the figure on the left, triangle PQR is an enlargement of triangle ABC. The centre of the enlargement is O and the scale factor is 2.
   a State two relationships between the lines QR, BC.
   b Work out the distances PQ, BP.
   c Given that the area of triangle PQR is 12 cm², work out the area of triangle ABC.
   d Name two pairs of similar triangles other than triangles ABC, PQR.

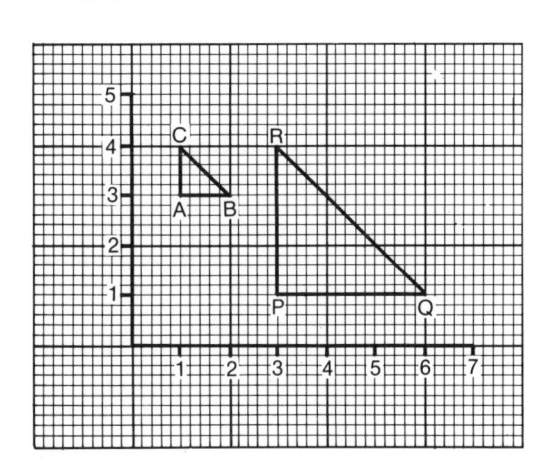

4 In the figure above, triangle PQR is an enlargement of triangle ABC. Work out the scale factor and the coordinates of the centre of the enlargement.

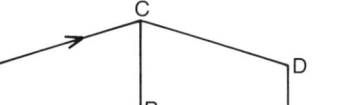

5 The line CW is an axis of symmetry of the figure on the left.
   a Given that AP = $1\frac{1}{2}$PW, state the ratio of any side in pentagon ABCDE to the corresponding side in pentagon PQRST.
   b Given that BC = 50 cm, find RS.
   c Given that WR = 18 cm, find RC.
   d Regarding the quadrilateral ABCW as an enlargement of the quadrilateral PQRW, state the centre and the scale factor of the enlargement.

6 Allowing a range of −2 to 8 on the x-axis and a range of 0 to 12 on the y-axis, draw on graph paper the triangle whose vertices are A(2, 4), B(4, 4), C(1, 5).
   a Draw the image A′B′C′ of triangle ABC under an enlargement of centre (0, 2) and scale factor 2. State the coordinates of A′, B′, C′.
   b Draw the image A″B″C″ of triangle A′B′C′ under an enlargement of centre (8, 2) and scale factor $1\frac{1}{2}$. State the coordinates of A″, B″, C″.
   c Find the scale factor and the coordinates of the centre of the enlargement which maps triangle ABC to triangle A″B″C″.

7 a Two spheres have radii of 4 cm and 12 cm. Find the ratio of
      (i) their surface areas,
      (ii) their volumes.
   b If four spheres of radius 12 cm are melted down and made into spheres of radius 4 cm, how many of these spheres will be obtained?

8 Two similar containers have base areas which are in the ratio 4:25. Find the ratio of
   a their heights,
   b their volumes.

   Given that the larger container can hold 2000 cm³ of liquid, work out
   c the volume of liquid that the smaller container can hold.

9 In the figure on the left, in which the distances are in centimetres, the quadrilateral PQRS is an enlargement with centre O of the quadrilateral ABCD. State the scale factor of the enlargement and work out the distances SR, BC and AO.

10 Allowing a range of −6 to 12 on the x-axis and a range of 0 to 10 on the y-axis, draw the quadrilateral whose vertices are A(8, 8), B(2, 8), C(2, 6), D(4, 4).
   a Draw the image A'B'C'D' of quadrilateral ABCD under an enlargement of centre (4, 7) and scale factor 2. State the coordinates of A' and C'.
   b Draw the image A"B"C"D" of quadrilateral ABCD under an enlargement of centre (0, 4) and scale factor $-\frac{1}{2}$. State the coordinates of B" and D".
   c Find the scale factor and the coordinates of the centre of the enlargement which maps quadrilateral A'B'C'D' to quadrilateral A"B"C"D".

Exercise 30B

1 The two figures shown on the left are similar, the ratio of corresponding sides being 1:2.
   a Which point in the smaller figure corresponds to the point L?
   b Which side in the larger figure corresponds to the side DC?
   c Given that BC = 5 cm, which side in the larger figure can be found and what is its length?
   d Given that PL = 21 cm, which side in the smaller figure can be found and what is its length?

2 Allowing a range of 0 to 10 on the x-axis and a range of −6 to 10 on the y-axis, draw on graph paper the triangle whose vertices are A(1, 1), B(2, 1), C(1, 2).
   a Draw the image FGH of triangle ABC under an enlargement of centre the origin and scale factor 3. State the coordinates of F, G, H and work the ratio area of triangle FGH : area of triangle ABC.
   b Draw the image JKL of triangle ABC under an enlargement of centre (0, 3) and scale factor 4. State the coordinates of J, K, L.
   c Draw the image PQR of triangle FGH under an enlargement of centre (4, 4) and scale factor 2. State the coordinates of P, Q, R.
   d State the scale factor of the enlargement which would map triangle JKL to triangle PQR.

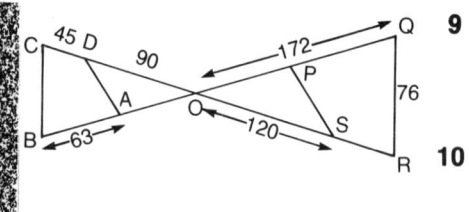

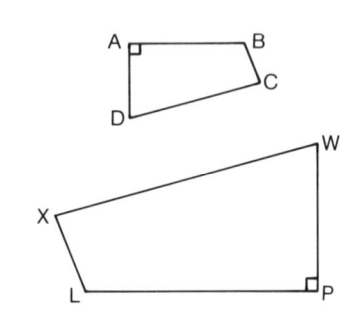

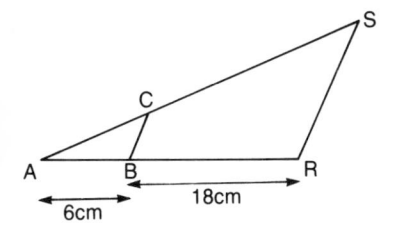

3 In the figure on the left, triangle ARS is an enlargement with centre A of triangle ABC.
   a State the scale factor of the enlargement.
   b State two relationships between the lines RS, BC.
   c Given that AS = 30 cm, work out CS.
   d Given that the area of triangle ABC is 11 cm^2, work out the areas of triangle ARS and trapezium BRSC.

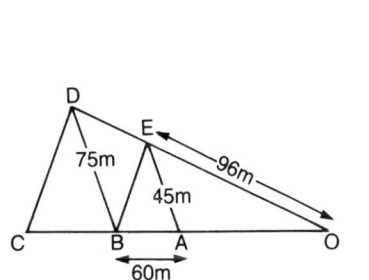

4 In the figure above, the larger triangle can be regarded as the image of the smaller under a certain enlargement. Work out the scale factor and the coordinates of the centre of the enlargement.

5 In the figure on the left, triangle BCD is an enlargement with centre O of triangle ABE. Work out
   a the scale factor of the enlargement,
   b BC,
   c DE,
   d OA.
   (For questions c and d, use the similar triangles OAE, OBD.)

6 Allowing a range of −2 to 16 on the x-axis and a range of 0 to 19 on the y-axis, draw on graph paper the triangle whose vertices are A(9, 2), B(11, 6), C(7, 4).
   a Draw the image A'B'C' of triangle ABC under an enlargement of centre (9, 0) and scale factor 3. State the coordinates of A', B', C'.
   b Draw the image A"B"C" of triangle A'B'C' under an enlargement of centre (3, 0) and scale factor $\frac{1}{6}$. State the coordinates of A", B", C".
   c Find the scale factor and the coordinates of the centre of the enlargement which maps triangle ABC to triangle A"B"C".

7 Two similar containers have heights which are in the ratio 5:3.
   a Find the ratio of their volumes.
   b Given that the smaller container holds 135 cm³ of liquid when half full, work out the volume of liquid which the larger container holds when full.

8 Four hundred lead cubes, each having a total surface area of 50 cm², are melted down. The lead obtained is then re-cast into larger cubes, each of which has a total surface area of 200 cm². How many of these cubes are obtained?

9 In the figure on the left, triangle PQR is an enlargement with centre O of triangle ABC. Given that OQ = 180 cm, AO = 40 cm, AB = 60 cm and BC = 50 cm, work out the scale factor of the enlargement and the distances PQ, QR.

10 Allowing a range of −4 to 14 on the x-axis and a range of 0 to 12 on the y-axis, draw on graph paper the parallelogram whose vertices are A(12, 1), B(13, 1), C(14, 2), D(13, 2).
   a Draw the image A′B′C′D′ of parallelogram ABCD under an enlargement of centre (11, 3) and scale factor −3. State the coordinates of A′ and C′.
   b Draw the image A″B″C″D″ of parallelogram ABCD under an enlargement of centre (12, 3) and scale factor −4. State the coordinates of B″ and D″.
   c Find the scale factor and the coordinates of the centre of the enlargement which maps parallelogram A′B′C′D′ to parallelogram A″B″C″D″.

Reflection, rotation, translation

Note: *In all the questions requiring graph paper, allow a range of −6 to +6 on both axes and use a scale of 1 cm to 1 unit.*

Exercise 31A

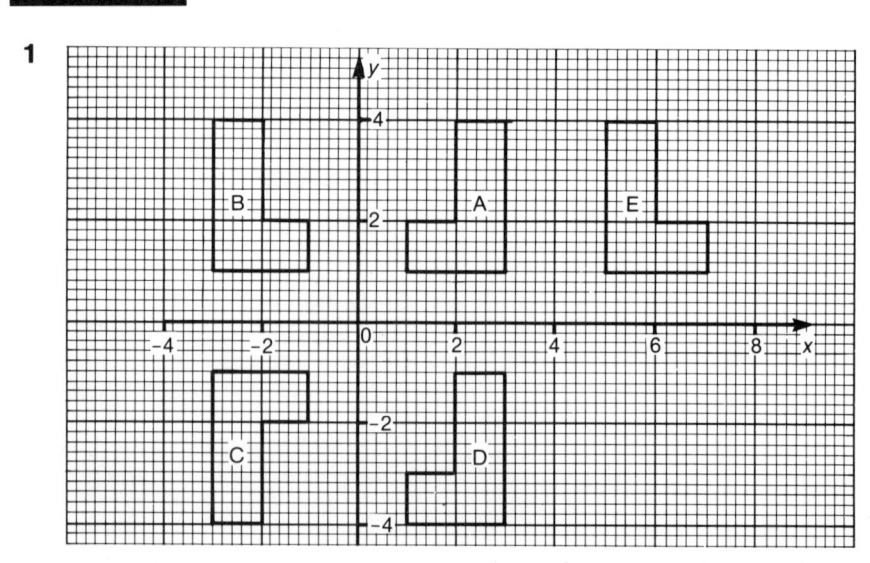

1

In the figure opposite, state the transformation which maps
a A to B   b B to C   c A to C   d A to D   e E to B

2 Draw the triangle whose vertices are A(1, 1), B(4, 1), C(4, 2).
   a Reflect triangle ABC in the y-axis, labelling the image PQR (where P is the image of A, Q is the image of B, and R is the image of C). State the coordinates of P, Q, R.
   b Rotate triangle ABC through a half-turn (a turn of 180°) about the origin. Label the image LMN and state the coordinates of L, M, N.
   c State the single transformation which maps PQR onto LMN.

3 a A certain translation maps the point (1, 3) to the point (4, 5). What is the image of the point (0, 1) under this translation?
   b Another translation maps the point (2, 4) to the point (3, 2). What is the image of the point (−3, 0) under this translation?

4 Draw the triangle OAB, where O is the origin, A is the point (4, 0) and B is the point (4, 1).
   a Rotate triangle OAB through an anticlockwise quarter-turn (a turn of 90°) about O. State the coordinates of the images of A and B.
   b Rotate triangle OAB through a clockwise quarter-turn about the point (5, 0). State the coordinates of the images of O, A and B.

5 The figure on the left is a square which is divided into identical right-angled triangles. Describe the transformation which maps
   a triangle ADN onto triangle MNC,
   b rectangle AMND onto rectangle BMNC,
   c triangle ADN onto triangle NMA.

6 Draw the triangle whose vertices are A(−2, 2), B(−2, 3), C(−4, 2).
   a Rotate triangle ABC through a clockwise quarter-turn about the origin, letting the image be PQR. State the coordinates of P, Q, R.
   b Rotate triangle ABC through an anticlockwise quarter-turn about the origin, letting the image be LMN. State the coordinates of L, M, N.
   c State the single transformation which maps PQR onto LMN.

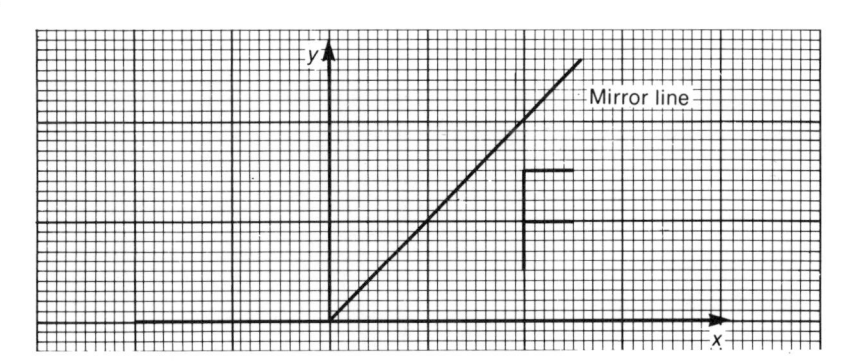

7 Copy the above diagram onto your own graph paper and reflect the F-shaped figure in the mirror line shown. Then reflect the image in the y-axis. By considering the original figure and the final image, state the single transformation which is equivalent to the two reflections you have performed.

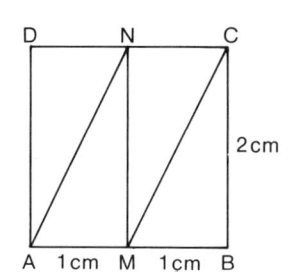

8 Draw the triangle whose vertices are A(4, −1), B(6, −1), C(6, −2). Reflect this triangle in the x-axis, then reflect the image in the line which is parallel to the x-axis and 3 units above it (the line y = 3). Label the final image PQR and
  a state the coordinates of P, Q, R,
  b describe the single transformation which maps ABC onto PQR.

9 Draw the triangle whose vertices are A(2, 2), B(5, 2), C(2, 3).
  a Draw the image PQR of triangle ABC under a half-turn about the origin, and state the coordinates of P, Q, R.
  b Draw the image LMN of triangle ABC under a translation of 6 units downwards and state the coordinates of L, M, N.
  c Describe the single transformation which maps PQR onto LMN.

Exercise 31B

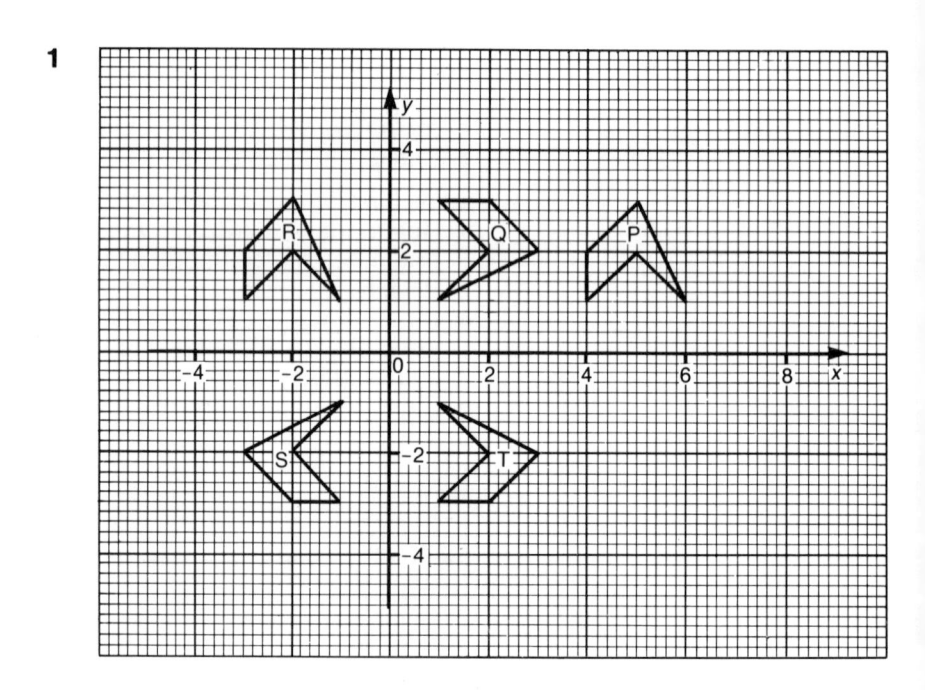

1

In the figure above, state the transformation which maps
  a Q to T
  b R to P
  c S to Q
  d T to S
  e Q to R
  f S to R

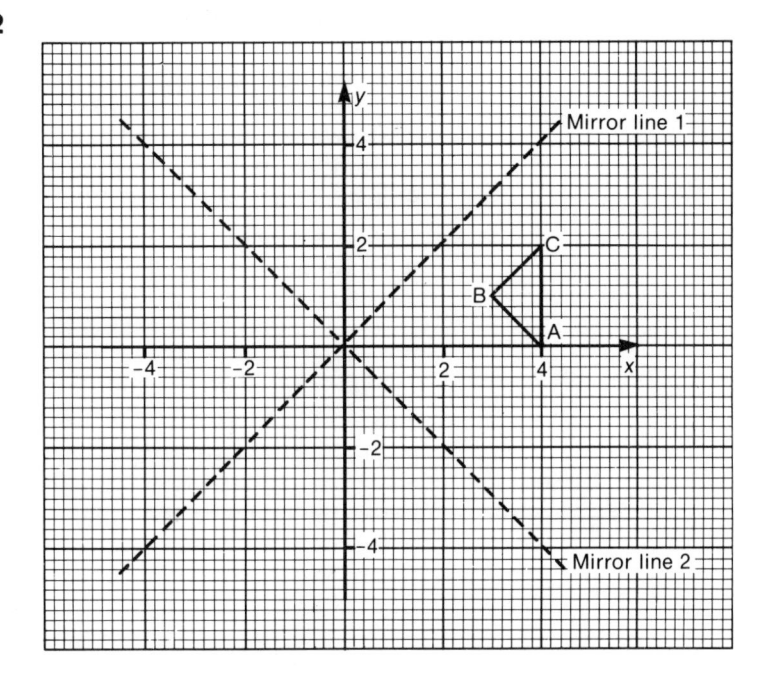

2   Copy the above diagram onto your own graph paper.
   a Reflect triangle ABC in mirror line 1, labelling the image PQR. State the coordinates of P, Q, R.
   b Reflect triangle ABC in mirror line 2, labelling the image LMN. State the coordinates of L, M, N.
   c State the single transformation which maps PQR onto LMN.

3 a A certain translation maps the point (0, 3) to the point (4, 5). What is the image of the point (1, 2) under this translation?
   b Another translation maps the point (3, −1) to the point (1, 0). What is the image of the point (0, −4) under this translation?

4 Draw the triangle whose vertices are A(2, 0), B(6, 0), C(6, 2).
   a Draw the image PQR of triangle ABC under a half-turn about the origin. State the coordinates of P, Q, R.
   b Draw the image AJK of triangle ABC under an anticlockwise quarter-turn about A. State the coordinates of J and K.
   c Draw the image of PMN of triangle PQR under a clockwise quarter-turn about P. State the coordinates of M and N.
   d State the single transformation which maps AJK onto PMN.

5 The figure on the left consists of identical right-angled triangles. Name the triangle or triangles onto which it is possible to map
   a triangle SPO by reflection in an axis.
   b triangle SDR by a translation.
   c triangle PBQ by reflection in an axis.

   Describe also the transformation which maps
   d triangle ROQ to triangle SAP.
   e triangle SOR to triangle QOR.
   f triangle APS to triangle DRS.
   g triangle APS to triangle OSP.

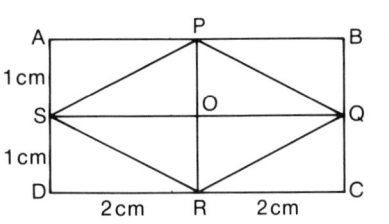

6 Draw the parallelogram whose vertices are A(2, 1), B(5, 1), C(6, 3), D(3, 3).
   a Draw the image PQRS of ABCD under a translation of 5 units to the left and 1 unit upwards. State the coordinates of P and R.
   b Draw the image JKLM of PQRS under a translation of 5 units downwards. State the coordinates of K and M.
   c State the single transformation which maps JKLM onto ABCD.

7 Draw the triangle whose vertices are A(6, 1), B(6, 2), C(4, 2).
   a Draw the image PQR of triangle ABC under reflection in the line which is parallel to the y-axis and 1 unit to the right of it (the line $x = 1$). State the coordinates of P, Q, R.
   b Draw the image JKL of triangle ABC under a translation of 2 units to the left. State the coordinates of J, K, L.
   c State the single transformation which maps PQR onto JKL.

8 Draw a pair of vertical lines 4 cm apart. Draw any simple figure slightly to the left of the left-hand line and reflect it in this line. Then reflect the image in the right-hand line.
   a By comparing your original figure and the final image state the single transformation which is equivalent to the pair of reflections you have performed.
   b What do you think the result would be if the two lines were 6 cm apart? (Check with a diagram if necessary.)
   c What would the result be if the lines were x cm apart?

9 Draw the triangle whose vertices are A(2, 1), B(4, 1), C(2, 2).
   a Draw the image PQR of triangle ABC under a half-turn about the point (0, 1). State the coordinates of P, Q, R.
   b Draw the image JKL of triangle PQR under a clockwise quarter-turn about the point (−1, 1). State the coordinates of J, K, L.
   c State the single transformation which maps ABC onto JKL.

Angle in a semicircle, angles made by tangents and radii

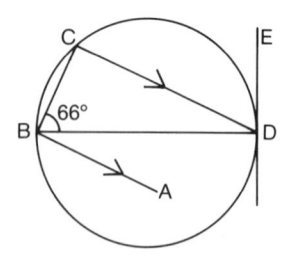

Exercise 32A

1 BD is a diameter of the circle on the left and DE is a tangent to it.
   a Write down the value of angle BCD.
   b Work out angle ABD.
   c Write down the value of angle BDE.
   d Work out angle CDE.

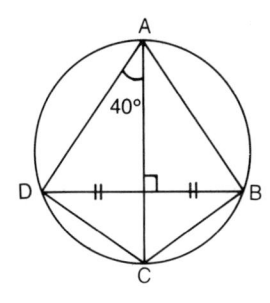

2 In the figure on the left AC is the perpendicular bisector of BD, as shown.
  a State one other fact about the line AC.
  b Work out angles BDC and BCD.

In questions **4–12**, find the angles denoted by letters. When a diagram contains the letter O, this denotes the centre of the circle.

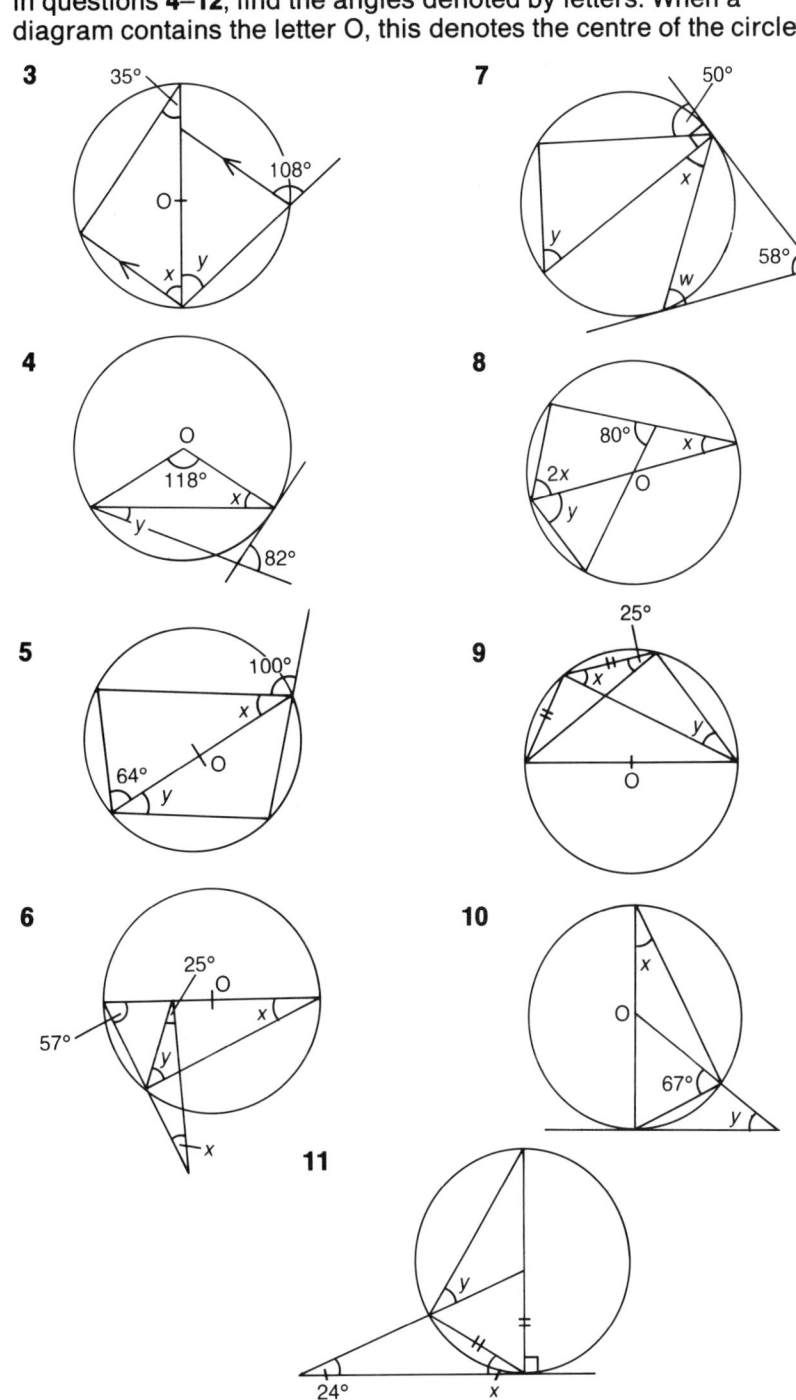

12 ABCDE is a regular pentagon inscribed in a circle and DX is a diameter of the circle. Work out angles EXD and BCX.

13 AB is a diameter of the circle ABCD and the perpendicular bisector of AD meets AB at P. Given that angles PBC, PAC are in the ratio 3:2, and that angle PAD = 61°, work out angles PCD and ADC.

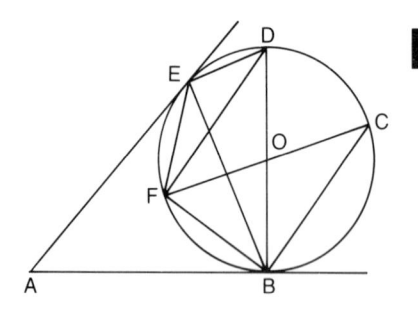

Exercise 32B

1 Given that AB and AE are tangents of the circle on the left, and O is the centre, name four right angles and four isosceles triangles.

In questions **2–10** find the values of x and y. The letter O denotes the centre of the given circle.

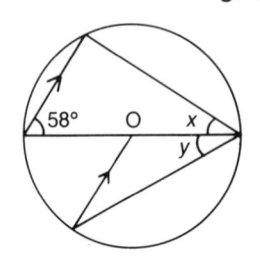

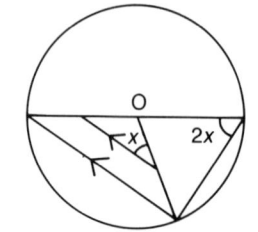

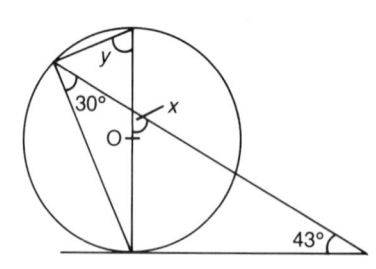

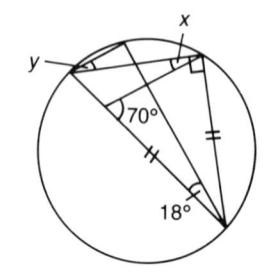

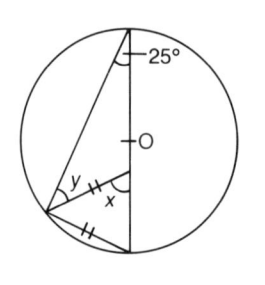

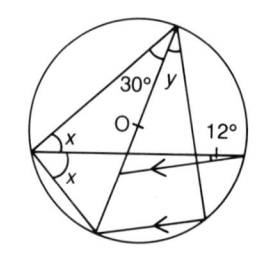

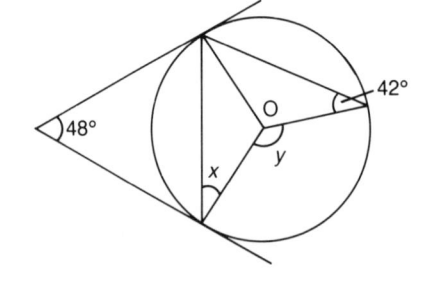

9 [diagram: triangle with inscribed circle, centre O, showing 57°, angles x, x, and y]

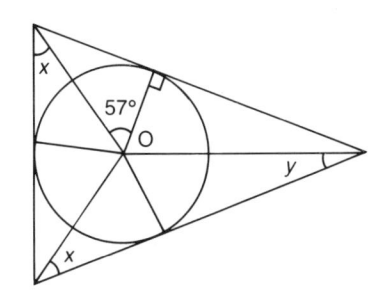

10 [diagram: circle with angles 27°, 35°, x, y and tick marks]

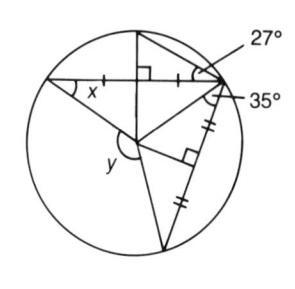

11 ABCDEF is a (non-regular) hexagon inscribed in a circle. The line AD and the perpendicular bisector of this line are axes of symmetry of the hexagon. Given that angle CAD = 34°, work out angles ACB, AFE and BAC.

12 In a circle ABCD of centre O, AC is a diameter and angle AOD = 90°. Given that angles CBD, OCB are in the ratio 3:4, work out angle ABO.

Further arc properties

Note: *In addition to the theorem that the angle in a semicircle is a right angle, these exercises cover the following theorems: (i) angles subtended by the same arc are equal; (ii) angle at the centre is twice the angle at the circumference; (iii) opposite angles of a cyclic quadrilateral add up to 180°.*

Exercise 33A

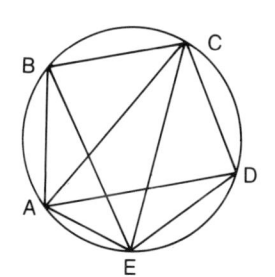

1 From the diagram on the left name
  a two angles which are equal to angle ABE,
  b an angle which is equal to angle AEC,
  c two angles, each of which is supplementary to angle ABC.

In questions **2** to **12**, find the angles denoted by letters. The letter O denotes the centre of the given circle.

2 [diagram: circle with centre O, angle 100° at centre, angles x and y]

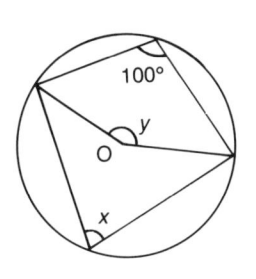

3 [diagram: circle with angles 35°, 112°, 52°, x and y]

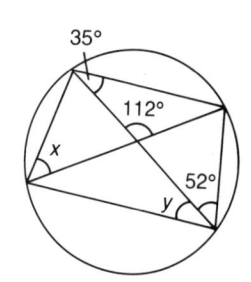

4 — 28°, 84°, x, y

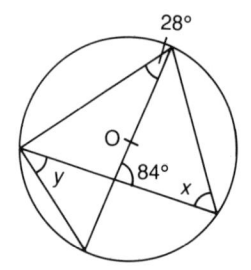

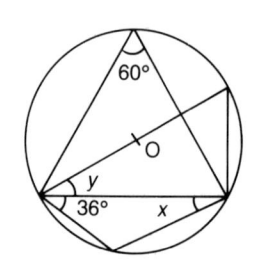

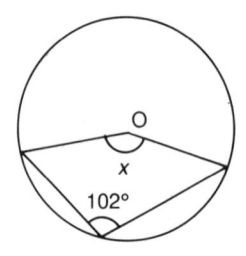

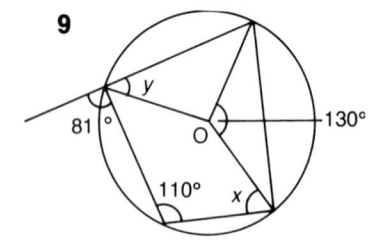

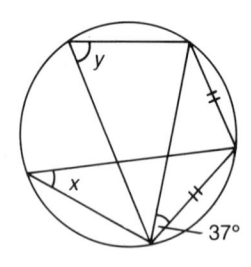

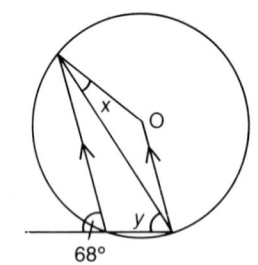

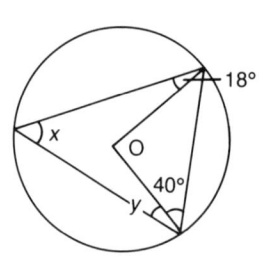

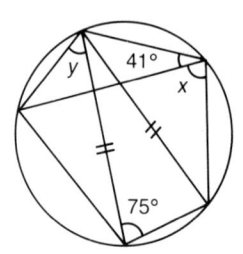

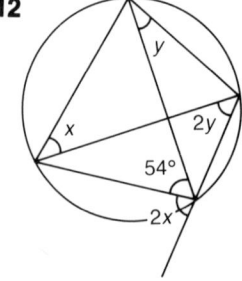

5 — 102°, x

6 — y, x, 37°

7 — 18°, x, 40°, y

8 — 60°, 36°, x, y

9 — 81°, y, 130°, 110°, x

10 — x, y, 68°

11 — 41°, y, x, 75°

12 — y, x, $2y$, 54°, $2x$

Exercise 33B

1 Given that O is the centre of the circle in diagram 1 on the left, name
  a an angle which is half the angle AOB,
  b an angle which is equal to angle OAB,
  c an angle which is supplementary to angle ADC,
  d an angle which is twice angle BAC.

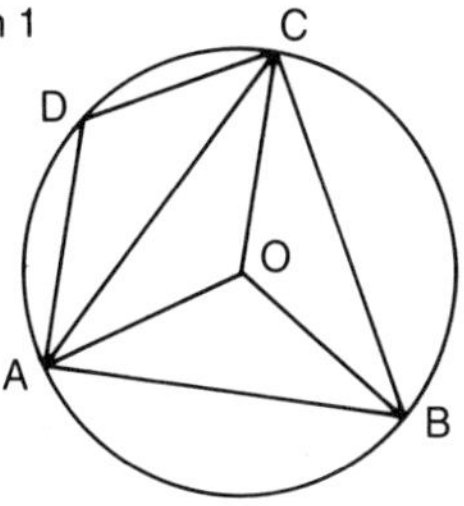

In questions **2–12**, find the angles denoted by letters. O is the centre of the given circle.

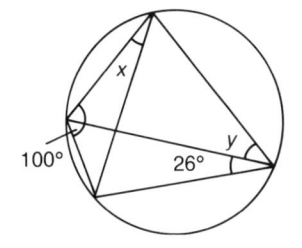

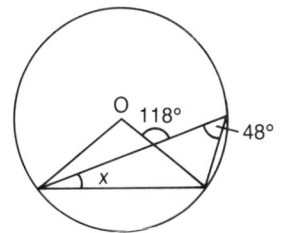

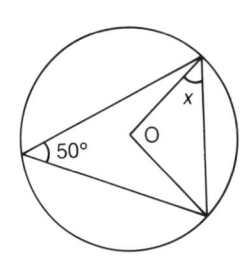

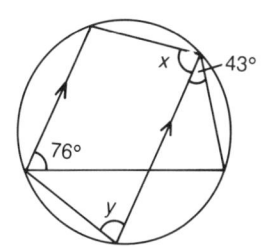

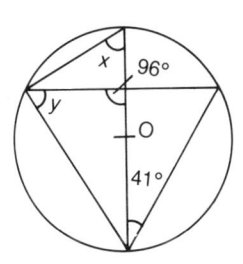

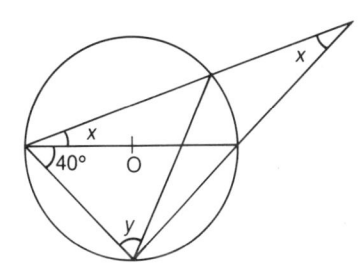

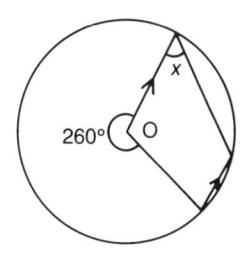

diagram 1

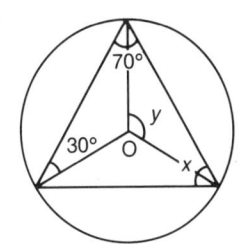

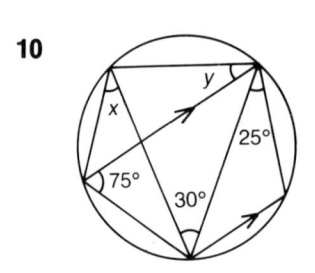

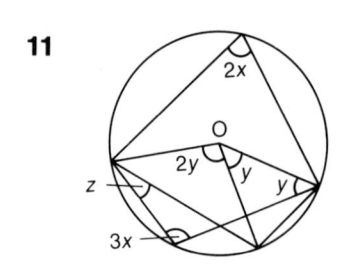

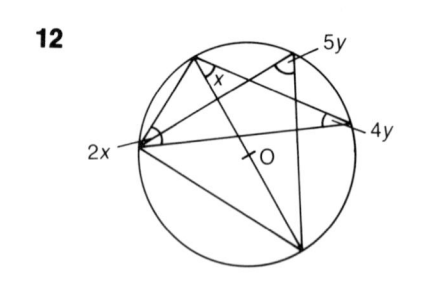

10

11

12

Trigonometry, Pythagoras' Theorem

Note: *When the answers in this section do not come out exactly, give angles other than bearings to one decimal place and lengths to three significant figures. Bearings should be given to the nearest degree.*

Quick revision exercise 34

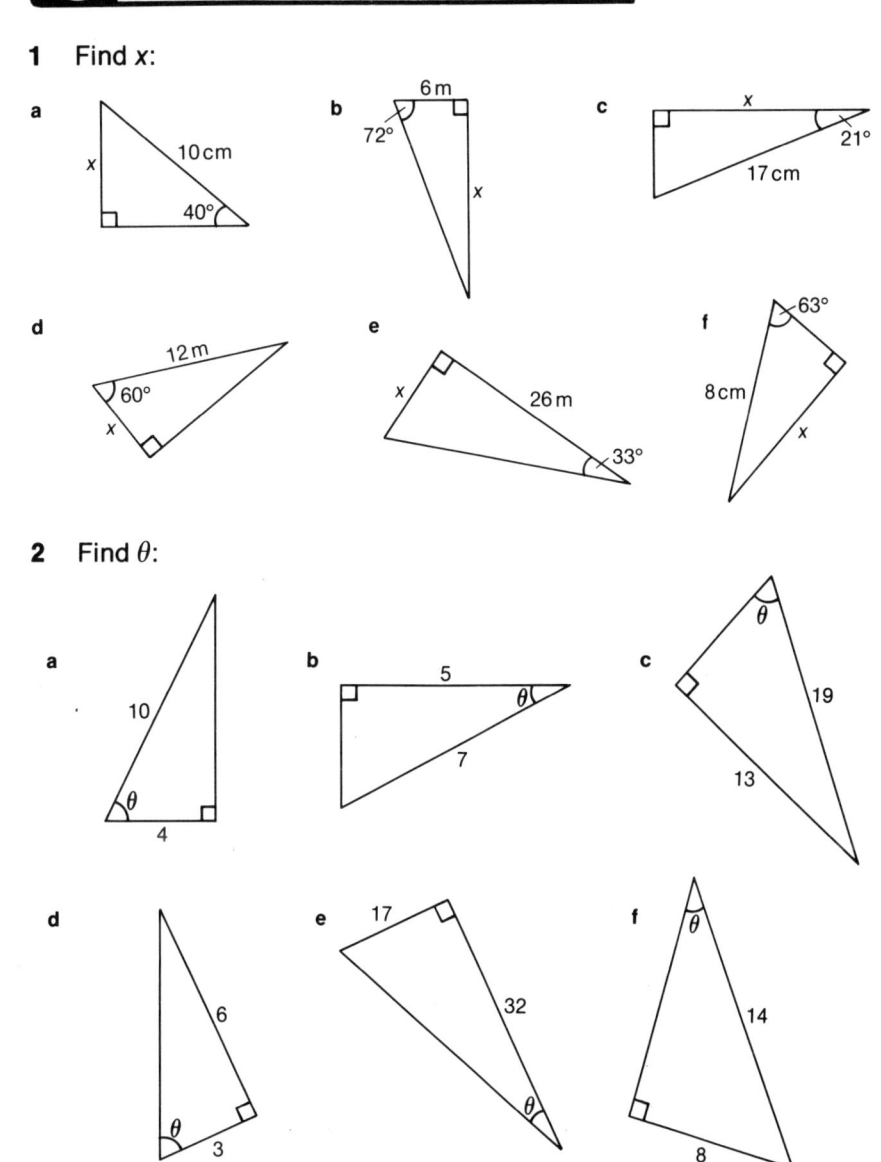

1 Find x:

a — right triangle, hypotenuse 10 cm, angle 40°, opposite side x

b — right triangle, top side 6 m, angle 72° at top left, x is the other leg

c — right triangle, angle 21°, hypotenuse 17 cm, x is adjacent side

d — right triangle, 12 m hypotenuse, angle 60°, x opposite

e — right triangle, hypotenuse 26 m, angle 33°, x opposite

f — right triangle, angle 63°, side 8 cm, x opposite

2 Find θ:

a — right triangle, hypotenuse 10, adjacent 4, angle θ

b — right triangle, legs 5 and 7, θ at top right

c — right triangle, sides 13 and 19, θ at top

d — right triangle, sides 6 and 3, θ at bottom

e — right triangle, sides 17 and 32, θ at bottom

f — right triangle, sides 14 and 8, θ at top

3 Find x by using Pythagoras' theorem:

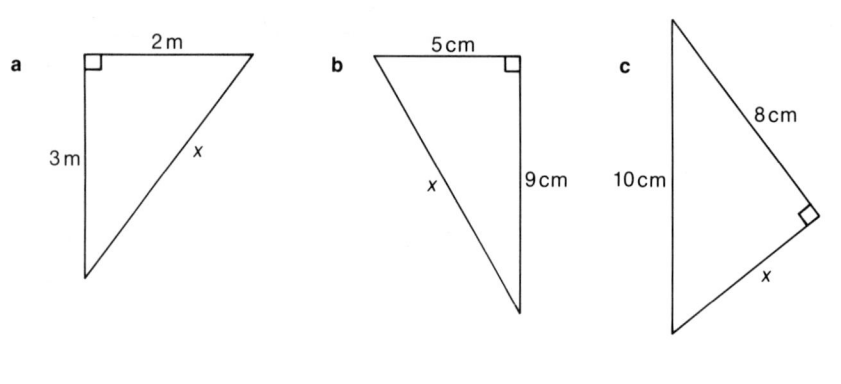

a) legs 2m, 3m, hypotenuse x

b) leg 5cm, hypotenuse 9cm, other leg x

c) legs 8cm and x, hypotenuse 10cm

d) legs x and 19m, hypotenuse 23m

e) legs 83m and x, hypotenuse 172m

f) legs 43cm and x, hypotenuse 61cm

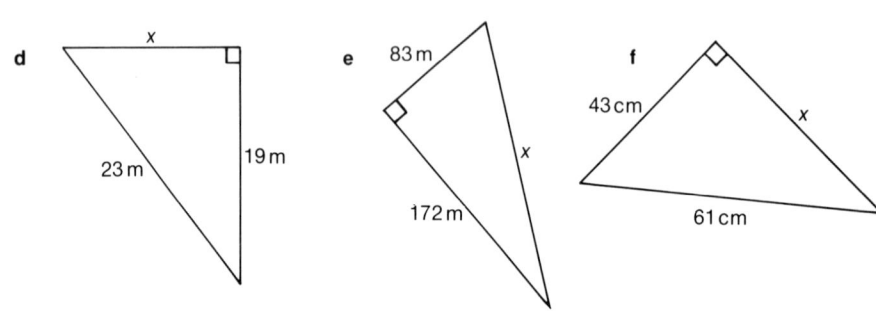

4 Find x:

a) 42°, opposite side 6cm, x

b) 76°, 4m, x

c) 17m, 51°, x

d) 19°, 23cm, x

e) 69°, 3.8m, x

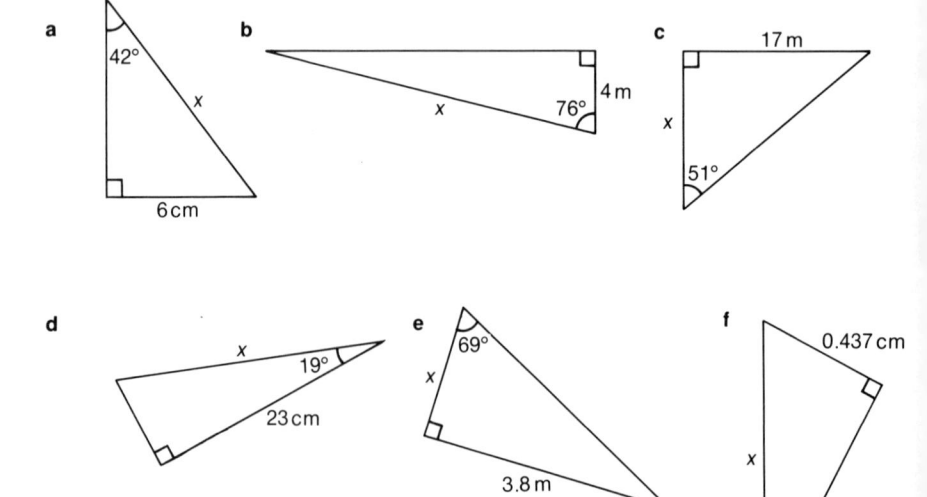

f) 0.437cm, 39°, x

5 Find the quantities indicated by letters and the area of each triangle:

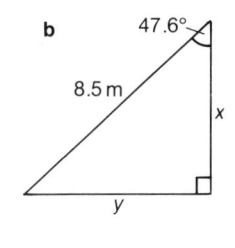

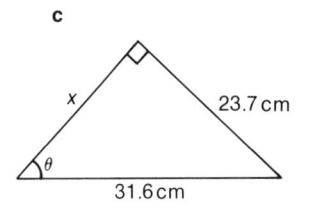

a triangle with 2.8 m, 5.2 m, angle θ, side x

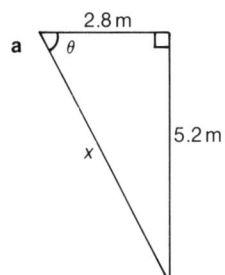

b triangle with 47.6°, 8.5 m, sides x and y

c triangle with 23.7 cm, 31.6 cm, side x, angle θ

d triangle with 79.5 m, 23.4°, sides x and y

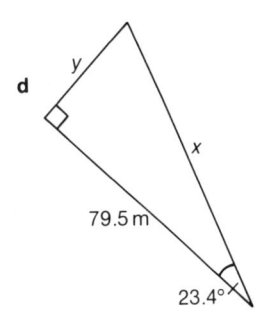

6 Find the quantities indicated by letters, in each case starting by drawing one or more perpendiculars:

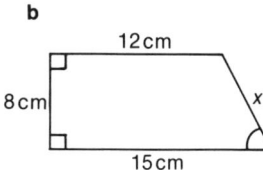

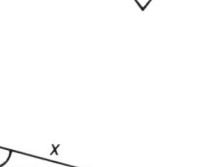

a isosceles triangle, 66°, 4 m, 4 m, base x

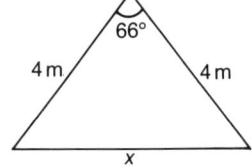

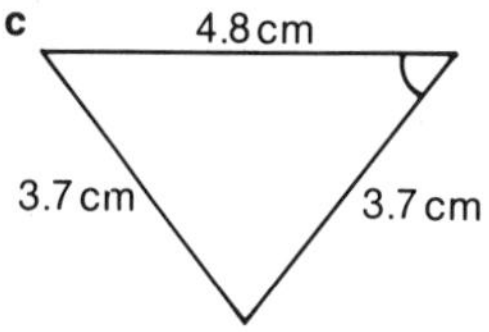

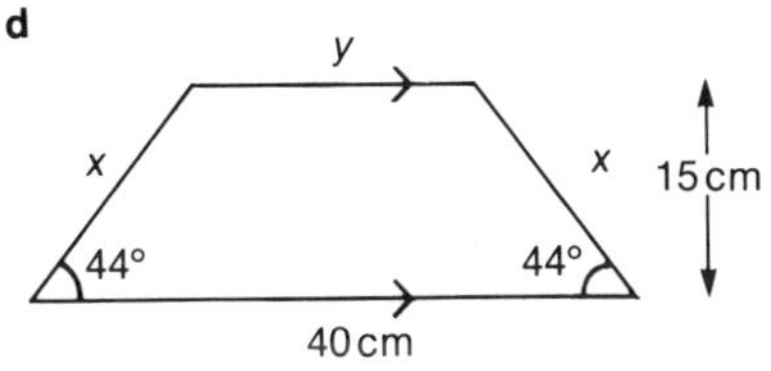

b quadrilateral with 12 cm, 8 cm, 15 cm, side x

c triangle with 4.8 cm, 3.7 cm, 3.7 cm

d trapezium with y, 40 cm, 44°, 44°, x, 15 cm

e triangle with 17 m, 76°, sides x

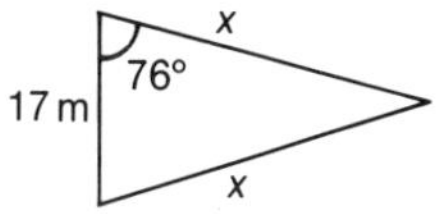

7 Without using a calculator, find
  a $\cos \theta$ and $\tan \theta$, given that $\sin \theta = \tfrac{3}{5}$,
  b $\sin \theta$ and $\cos \theta$, given that $\tan \theta = \tfrac{5}{12}$,
  c $\sin \theta$ and $\tan \theta$, given that $\cos \theta = \tfrac{7}{25}$,
  d $\sin \theta$ and $\cos \theta$, given that $\tan \theta = 1\tfrac{7}{8}$,
  e $\cos \theta$ and $\tan \theta$, given that $\sin \theta = \sqrt{3}/2$,
  f $\sin \theta$ and $\tan \theta$, given that $\cos \theta = 1/\sqrt{10}$.

Problems involving right-angled triangles in two dimensions

Exercise 35A

1. From a point P on the ground which is 27 m from the foot of a vertical post, the angle of elevation of the top of the post is 34°. Work out
   a the height of the post,
   b the angle of elevation from P of the point which is halfway up the post.

2. A car is driven 50 km due east from a point P to a point Q, then 20 km due south to a point R. Work out
   a the final distance PR of the car from its starting point,
   b the final bearing of the car from its starting point.

3. An observer looking straight out to sea from the top of a vertical cliff sees a girl swimming directly towards him. The height of the cliff is 70 m.
   a When the girl is 180 m from the base of the cliff, what is her angle of depression from the observer?
   b How much further has the girl swum when her angle of depression from the observer has become 40°?

4. The diagram on the left shows four towns, A, B, C, D, which are positioned such that A is due west of B and C, and D is due south of B.
   a State the bearing of D from C.
   b Work out the distance of D from C.

   Given, further, that the bearing of A from D is 340°, work out
   c the distance of A from D,
   d the distance of A from C.

5. The figure ABCD on the left is a sketch of a kite a girl is making. Work out
   a the length of the diagonal AC,
   b angle BAD,
   c the length of the diagonal BD,
   d the area of the kite.

6. A train travels 48 km on a bearing of 068°, then 20 km due west. Work out
   a how far north of its starting point the train now is,
   b how far east of its starting point it is,
   c the final bearing of the train from its starting point.

7. The figure on the left is a sketch of a plot of land in the shape of a trapezium. By drawing perpendiculars to produce right-angled triangles, work out
   a the height of the plot, h,
   b the length of the base of the plot, b,
   c the area of the plot.

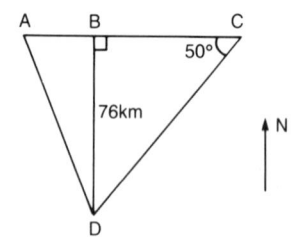

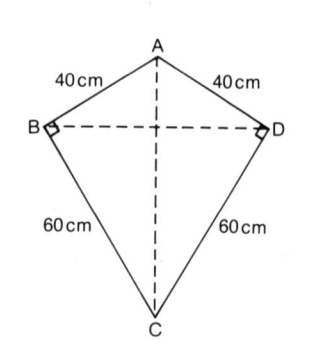

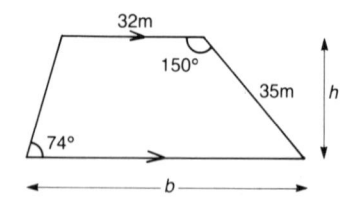

8 In the diagram below CD represents a window in a vertical wall. From a point A on the ground, which is 5 m from the wall, the angles of elevation of C and D are 30° and 40°, respectively. Work out
  a the height of the base of the window, BC,
  b the height of the top of the window, BD,
  c the vertical length of the window, CD.

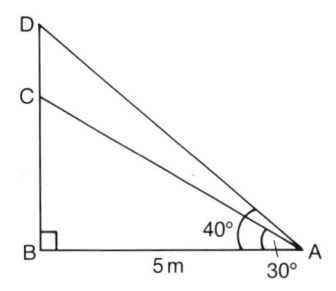

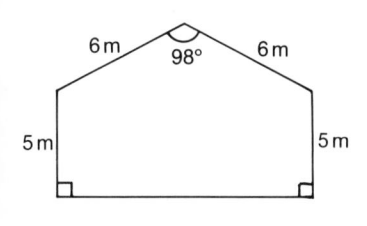

9 The figure on the left shows one wall of a vertical building. Work out
  a the width of the wall,
  b the height of the wall,
  c the area of the wall.

10 A ladder inclined at 65° to the horizontal reaches a point on a vertical wall which is 8 m above the ground. Find
  a the length of the ladder,
  b the distance of its foot from the base of the wall.

The foot of the ladder is now pushed in towards the wall so as to make the top of the ladder move 50 cm higher. Work out
  c how far the foot of the ladder is moved.

11 An aeroplane starts at a point P which is 140 km from a town T on a bearing of 100° from T. It flies in a straight line on a bearing of 220°. Draw a diagram showing the aeroplane's path and mark on your diagram the point Q at which the aeroplane is at its shortest distance from T. Work out
  a the bearing of Q from T,
  b the distance QT.

The aeroplane carries on flying until it reaches a point R which is 250 km from Q. Work out
  c the distance RT,
  d the bearing of R from T.

Exercise 35B

1 A girl walks on a bearing of 069° until she is 215 m north of her starting point. Work out
  a how far east of her starting point she is at the end of her journey,
  b how far she has walked.

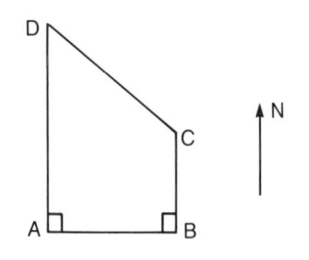

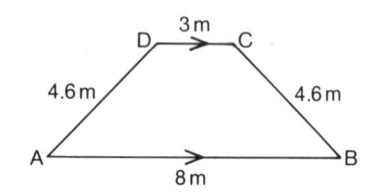

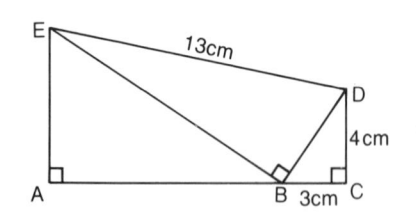

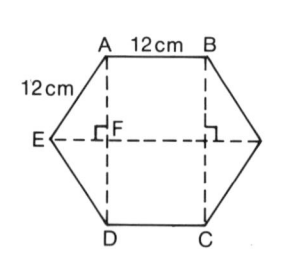

2 A tree standing on level ground is 20 m high.
  a Work out the angle of elevation of the top of the tree from a point on the ground which is 35 m from its foot.
  b From a certain point on the ground the angle of elevation of the top of the tree is 70°. How far is this point from the foot of the tree?

3 The diagram shows the positions of four cities, A, B, C and D. Given that A is 170 km due south of D, and C is 125 km from D on a bearing of 140° from D, work out
  a the distance AB,
  b the distance BC,
  c the bearing of A from C.

4 From the top of a tower which is 42 m high, the angle of depression of the top of a vertical wall is 23°. Given that the wall is 64·5 m from the tower, work out the height of the wall.

5 The figure ABCD on the left, which is an isosceles trapezium, represents the end view of the roof of a house. Work out
  a the vertical depth of the roof (the distance between AB and DC),
  b the inclination of AD and BC to the horizontal,
  c the area of the figure ABCD.

6 A car is driven 40 km on a bearing of 210°, then 70 km due east. Work out its final distance and bearing from its starting point.

7 Without using a calculator, work out, in the figure on the left,
  a the length BD,
  b the length BE.

  Prove also
  c that angle ABE is equal to angle BDC,
  and by using the cosine and sine of this angle work out (without a calculator)
  d the length AB,
  e the length AE.

8 Two points P and Q are on the same horizontal level and 2·6 m apart. A point R, which is 60 cm above the line PQ and in the same vertical plane, is 1·7 m from P. Work out
  a the angle of elevation of R from P,
  b the angle of elevation of R from Q.

9 The area of a regular hexagon of side 12 cm is required. To work this out, the hexagon is divided up into a rectangle and four right-angled triangles, as shown in the diagram on the left.

  State the size of angle AEF and hence work out
  a EF,
  b AF,
  c the area of triangle AEF,
  d the area of rectangle ABCD,
  e the area of the whole hexagon.

10 From the top of a vertical tower AB of height 25 m, the angle of depression of a point P, which is on the ground and due east of the tower, is 37°. Another point Q, which is also on the ground and due

east of the tower, is 20 m further from the tower than P. Work out
a the distance AP of P from the foot of the tower,
b the angle of depression of Q from the top of the tower.

11 A ship starts at a port which is 35 km due east of a lighthouse L, and sails on a bearing of 330° until it is due north of L. It then sails on a bearing of 230° until it is due west of L, when it drops anchor. Work out
a the ship's shortest distance from L,
b its bearing from L at this point,
c how far from L it is when it drops anchor,
d how far it travels altogether.

Simple three-dimensional problems; harder two-dimensional problems on right-angled triangles

Exercise 36A

1 ABC is a horizontal triangle in which AB = AC = 12 m and BC = 8 m. BX and CY are vertical posts, and the angles of elevation of X and Y from A are 22° and 48°, respectively. Find
a the height of the post BX,
b the height of the post CY,
c the angle of elevation of Y from X.

2 In the figure on the left tan A = $\frac{4}{3}$ and tan B = $\frac{1}{2}$. Work out the length AB without using a calculator.

3 A point P is 17 m above horizontal ground, and M, N are points on the ground which are due south of P and due east of P, respectively. Given that the angles of depression of M and N from P are, respectively, 30° and 40°, work out
a the distance MN,
b the bearing of M from N.

4 A ship sails a distance of 250 km on a bearing of 070°, then sails a distance of 180 km on a bearing of 330°. Work out
a how far north of its starting point the ship now is,
b how far east of its starting point it is,
c its final bearing from its starting point.

5 Three points A, B, C, on the same horizontal level, are positioned such that A is due west of B and due south of C. At C there is a vertical pole CX of height 12 m. Given that the distance AX is 14 m, and the angle of elevation of X from B is 54°, find the bearing of B from C.

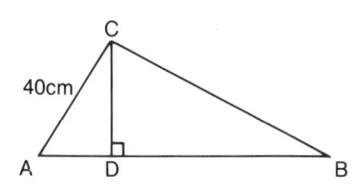

diagram 1

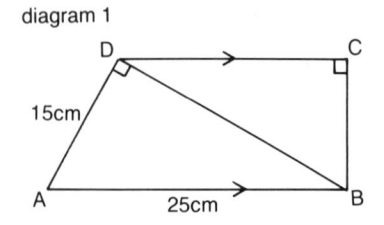

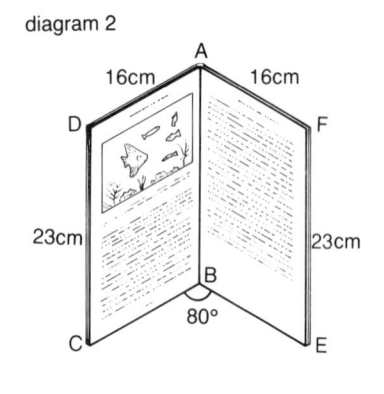

6 The diagram 1 on the left shows a trapezium ABCD in which angles BCD and ADB are right angles. Without using a calculator, work out the area of the trapezium.

7 In the diagram 2 on the left ABCD and ABEF are a pair of rectangular pages of a book. When the pages are open at an angle of 80°, as shown, work out the angle between the diagonals AC and AE.

8 A train starts at a point P at 14·00 h and travels on a bearing of 214° at a constant speed of 104 km h^{-1} for 30 minutes. It then travels due east at a different constant speed, passing the point which is exactly due south of P at 14·48 h. The train carries on travelling due east at the same speed until 15·10 h. Work out
 a the speed of the train when it is travelling due east,
 b its final distance and bearing from P.

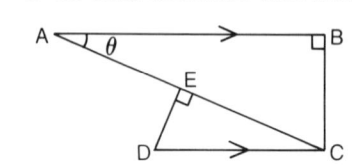

diagram 2

9

In the above figure $\tan \theta = \frac{5}{12}$.
 a Write down the values of $\sin \theta$ and $\cos \theta$.

Given, further, that AE = 29 cm and EC = 36 cm, work out, without using a calculator,
 b the length BC,
 c the length DC.

10 From the top of a cliff 75 m high, a woman sights a boat, due south of her, with an angle of depression of 37°. She walks along the top of the cliff (which is horizontal) in a due easterly direction until the angle of depression of the boat is 26°. Then she walks 150 m in the opposite direction. Work out
 a how far due east the woman walks,
 b the angle of depression of the boat from her final position.

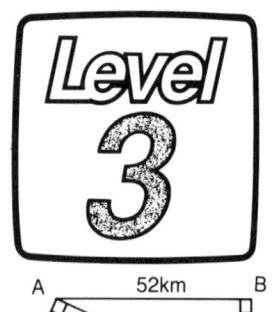

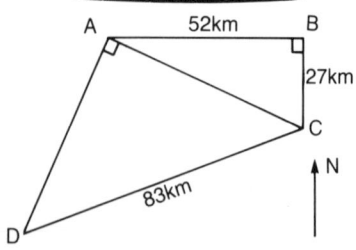

Exercise 36B

1 AX, BY, CZ are three vertical posts situated at the vertices of a horizontal triangle ABC in which AB = 6 m, BC = 9 m and CA = 12 m. Given that AX = 7 m, CZ = 5 m and the angle of elevation of Y from X is 38°, find
 a the angle of elevation of X from Z,
 b the height of the post BY,
 c the angle of elevation of Y from Z.

2 The diagram on the left represents four towns, A, B, C, D, which are positioned such that B is due north of C and due east of A. Find
 a the distance between A and D,
 b the bearing of A from C,
 c the bearing of D from C,
 d the bearing of A from D.

3 The diagram on the left shows two vertical walls, ABCD and ABPQ, which have the same height and meet at right angles. Given that the angle of elevation of A from P is 47°, find 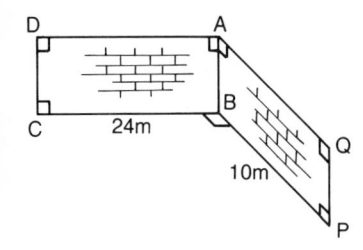
   a the angle of elevation of A from C,
   b the angle of elevation of D from P.

4 ABC is an isosceles triangle in which AB = AC, BC = 96 cm and sin B = 0·28.
   a Express 0·28 as a fraction in its lowest terms and hence find the values of cos B and tan B without using a calculator.
   b Work out the area of triangle ABC without using a calculator.

5 The diagram on the left shows a tetrahedron ABCD in which BCD is a horizontal right-angled isosceles triangle and the edge AD is vertical. Work out 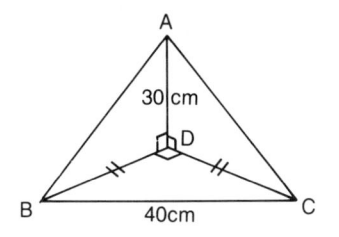
   a the length of the edge AB,
   b the angle of elevation of A from B,
   c the angle of elevation of A from the mid-point of BC.

6 A train travels on a bearing of 052° from a station P to a station Q, stops for 10 minutes, then travels on a bearing of 135° to a station R which is due east of P. The train's average speed throughout the entire journey is 80 km h^{-1} and it takes 45 minutes to travel from P to Q. Work out
   a the distance QR,
   b the total time the train takes to travel from P to R, to the nearest mintue,
   c how far R is east of P,
   d the time the train would have saved, to the nearest minute, by travelling in a straight line from P to R at the same average speed and without stopping.

7 A, B, C are points on horizontal ground such that B is due north of C and due east of A. At A and B are vertical posts AX and BY, of heights 12 m and 10 m, respectively. Given that the angle of elevation of X from Y is 20°, and the angle of depression of C from Y is 35°, work out the distance and bearing of A from C.

8 A rhombus ABCD has sides of 18 cm and angle ABC is 76°. Find
   a the lengths of the diagonals AC and BD,
   b the area of the rhombus.

9 The diagram on the left shows a trapezium ABCD in which cos A = $1/\sqrt{5}$ and cos B = $\frac{15}{17}$. Without using a calculator, find the area of the trapezium.

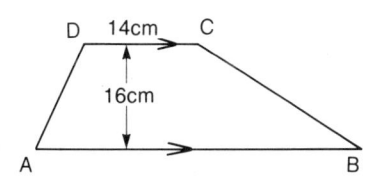

10 From a window of height 28 m a man sees a car on a bearing of 320° with an angle of depression of 23°. The car is travelling due east along a straight road. Work out
   a the angle of depression of the car when it is at its closest point to the window,
   b the bearing of the car from the window when it has passed the closest point and its angle of depression from the window is 18°.

Level 3

Trigonometric graphs

Note: *This topic is not required by all the GCSE examining groups.*

Exercise 37A

1. Letting x have the values 0, 30, 60, 90, etc., make a table for the equation $y = \sin x°$ for $0 \leqslant x \leqslant 360$. Draw the graph of the equation, using a scale of 2 cm to 50 units on the x-axis and a scale of 8 cm to 1 unit on the y-axis. Use the graph to find two approximate solutions of each of the following equations:
   a $\sin x° = 0.8$,
   b $\sin x° = -0.4$.

   Work out also, as accurately as possible,
   c the set of possible values of x, given that $y < -0.5$,
   d the set of possible values of y, given that $45 < x < 90$.

2. **Sketch** together (not necessarily using graph paper) the graphs of $y = \sin x°$ and $y = \cos x°$ for $0 \leqslant x \leqslant 360$.
   a State the transformation which maps the graph of $y = \cos x°$ onto the graph of $y = \sin x°$.
   b State the two values of x for which $\sin x° = \cos x°$.

3. Letting x have the values 100, 110, 120, etc., draw the graph of $y = \tan x°$ for $90 < x < 270$. Take scales of 2 cm to 20 units on the x-axis and 2 cm to 1 unit on the y-axis. Use the graph to estimate solutions of the following equations:
   a $\tan x° = 3$
   b $\tan x° = -4$
   c $\tan 2x° = 2.5$
   d $\tan(x + 20)° = -1$

4. Letting x have the values 0, 20, 40, etc., draw the graph of $y = 1 - \cos x°$ for $0 \leqslant x \leqslant 180$. Take a scale of 2 cm to 20 units on the x-axis and a scale of 8 cm to 1 unit on the y-axis.
   a Describe how the gradient of the graph changes as x increases from 0 to 180 and estimate the maximum value of the gradient.

   Draw on the same axes the graph of $y = \dfrac{x}{100}$. Hence

   b estimate a solution of the equation $1 - \cos x° = \dfrac{x}{100}$.

5. Letting x have the values 0, 20, 40, etc., and using the scales given in question **4**, draw the graph of $y = \sin x° - \cos x°$ for $0 \leqslant x \leqslant 180$. Estimate
   a the maximum value of y and the value of x at which it occurs,
   b the set of values of x for which $y > 1.2$.

6. Letting x have the values 0, 20, 40, etc., and using the scales given in question **4**, draw on the same axes the graphs of $y = 1 + \sin x°$, $y = \tan \tfrac{1}{2}x°$ and $y = 2 - \dfrac{x}{50}$ for $0 \leqslant x \leqslant 140$. Hence estimate

solutions of the following equations:
a $1 + \sin x° = \tan \tfrac{1}{2}x°$
b $\tan \tfrac{1}{2}x° = 2 - \dfrac{x}{50}$
c $\sin x° + \dfrac{x}{50} = 1$

Exercise 37B

Level 3

1. Letting x have the values 0, 30, 60, 90, etc., draw the graph of $y = \cos x°$ for $0 \leqslant x \leqslant 360$. Take scales of 2 cm to 50 units on the x-axis and 8 cm to 1 unit on the y-axis. Use the graph to estimate
   a two solutions of the equation $\cos x° = 0\cdot45$,
   b two solutions of the equation $\cos x° = -0\cdot8$,
   c the set of possible values of x, given that $y < 0\cdot2$,
   d the set of possible values of y, given that $225 < x < 315$.

2. State the equations of the axes of symmetry (if any) and the centre of rotational symmetry (if any) of
   a the section of the graph of $y = \sin x°$ between $x = 0$ and $x = 360$,
   b the section of the graph of $y = \cos x°$ between $x = 0$ and $x = 360$,
   c the section of the graph of $y = \tan x°$ between $x = 90$ and $x = 270$.

3. Letting x have the values 0, 5, 10, etc., draw the graph of $y = \tan 2x°$ for $0 \leqslant x < 45$. Take scales of 2 cm to 5 units on the x-axis and 2 cm to 1 unit on the y-axis. Use the graph to estimate solutions of the equations
   a $\tan 2x° = 1\cdot5$
   b $\tan 2x° = 4$.

   By drawing certain straight lines to intersect the graph of $y = \tan 2x°$, estimate also solutions of the equations
   c $\tan 2x° = \dfrac{x}{10}$
   d $\tan 2x° = 5 - \dfrac{x}{5}$

4. Letting x have the values 0, 10, 20, etc., draw the graph of $y = 1 - 2\sin 2x°$ for $0 \leqslant x \leqslant 90$. Take a scale of 2 cm to 10 units on the x-axis and a scale of 10 cm to 1 unit on the y-axis.
   a Find the minimum value of y and the value of x at which it occurs.
   b Estimate the gradient of the graph at the point where $x = 20$.

5. Letting x have the values 0, 5, 10, etc., draw the graph of $y = 4\sin x° - 3\tan x°$ for $0 \leqslant x \leqslant 40$. Take scales of 2 cm to 5 units on the x-axis and 4 cm to 0·1 units on the y-axis. Estimate
   a the maximum value of y and the value of x at which it occurs,
   b the set of values of x for which $y > 0\cdot2$.

Level 3

Sine rule, cosine rule, the formula $A = \frac{1}{2}ab \sin C$

Note: *These topics are not required by all the GCSE examining groups.*

Exercise 38A

1. In each of the following cases work out the quantities denoted by letters and the area of the triangle:

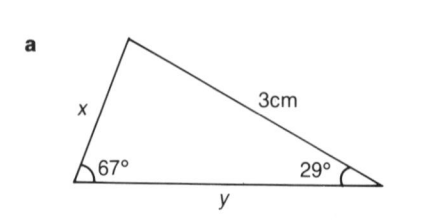

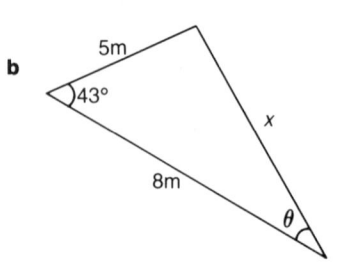

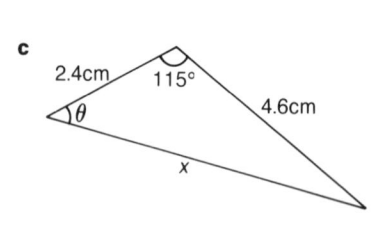

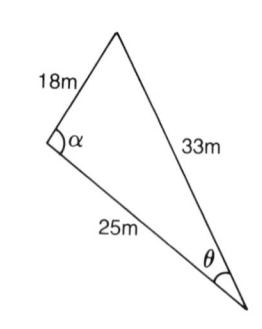

   a Triangle with sides x, 3cm, angles 67°, 29°, base y.

   b Triangle with sides 5m, 8m, x, angle 43°, angle θ.

   c Triangle with sides 2.4cm, 4.6cm, x, angle 115°, angle θ.

   d Triangle with sides 18m, 25m, 33m, angles α, θ.

2. Three villages, A, B, C, are positioned such that B is 40 km due south of A, and C is on bearings of 110° from A and 030° from B. Work out

   a the distance of A from C,

   b the distance of B from C.

3. In the diagram on the left AD represents a vertical wall and B, C are points on the horizontal ground which are 14 m apart. Given that the angles of elevation of D from B and D from C are 42° and 26°, respectively, as shown, work out

   a angle BDC,

   b the distance BD,

   c the height of the wall, AD.

4. A golfer aims to putt a ball into a hole which is 11·7 m from the position of the ball.

   a If she putts the ball a distance of 12·3 m at an angle of 8° from the true direction of the hole, how far from the hole will the ball finish?

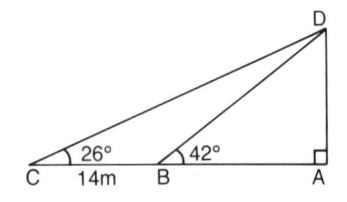

b Given that she putts the ball a distance of 11·2 m, and it finishes 90 cm from the hole, work out the angle between the direction of the putt and the true direction of the hole. (Assume in both cases that the ball travels in a straight line.)

5 The figure ABCD below represents a plot of land which is divided into two parts by a fence BD. Work out
  a the area of triangle ABD,
  b the length of the fence, BD,
  c the area of the whole plot.

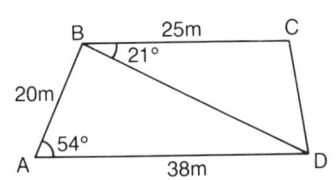

6 The driver of a car is initially 75 km from a town T on a bearing of 035° from T. He drives along a straight motorway on a bearing of 300°, and finishes on a bearing of 330° from T. Work out
  a the distance he drives,
  b his final distance from T.

7 Three points P, Q, R are such that the distance and bearing of Q from P are 53 m and 071°, while the distance and bearing of R from P are 94 m and 122°. Work out
  a the area of the triangle PQR,
  b the distance QR,
  c the bearing of Q from R.

8 In the figure on the left work out
  a the length AC,
  b angle CAD,
  c the area of the whole figure ABCD.

9 A building is 30 m high. Two points P, Q on horizontal ground are, respectively, due east and south-west of the building; the angles of depression of P and Q from the top of the building are, respectively, 40° and 34°. Find
  a the distance PQ,
  b the bearing of Q from P.

10 A train travelling at a constant speed of 78 mph on a bearing of 310° is due south of a church steeple at 11·30 a.m. At 11·40 a.m. the steeple is observed to be on a bearing of 060° from the train. Work out the distance of the train from the steeple at
  a 11·30 a.m.,
  b 11·40 a.m.

Calculate also the time, to the nearest minute, at which the train is
  c due west of the steeple,
  d at its shortest distance from the steeple.

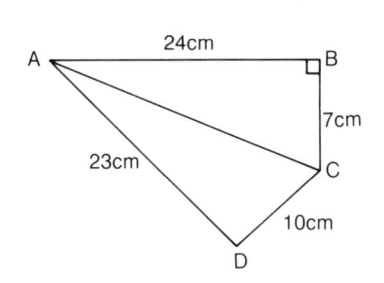

Exercise 38B

1 In each of the following cases work out the quantities denoted by letters and the area of the triangle:

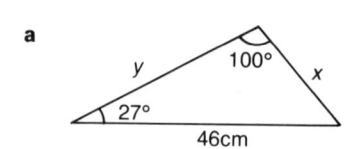

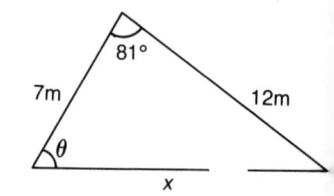

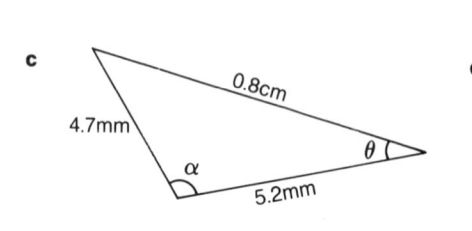

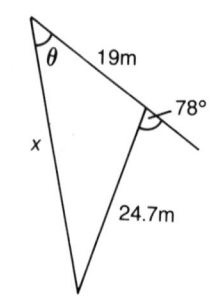

a Triangle with angle 27°, angle 100°, side 46cm between them, sides y and x.

b Triangle with sides 7m and 12m, included angle 81°, opposite side x, angle θ opposite the 12m side.

c Triangle with sides 4.7mm, 0.8cm, 5.2mm, angles α and θ.

d Triangle with sides 19m and 24.7m, angle θ, exterior angle 78°, side x.

2 A car is driven 30 miles due east from a point P to a point Q; then it is driven in a north-westerly direction to a point R. Given that the bearing of R from P is 35°, work out
a the distance RQ,
b the distance PR.

3 In the diagram on the left AT represents a vertical tower, and P, Q are points on the horizontal ground which are, respectively, due west and due east of the tower. Given that the angles of elevation of the top of the tower from P and Q are 49° and 22°, respectively, and the distance between P and Q is 62 m, find
a the distance PT,
b the height of the tower, AT.

4 In the diagram below work out
a the length BD,
b angle CBD,
c the area of the whole figure ABCD.

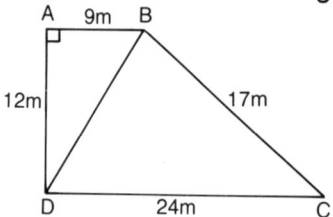

(Diagram: ABCD with A top-left, B top-right of top segment AB = 9m, right angle at A, AD = 12m, BC = 17m, DC = 24m.)

5 Marisa walks 4 miles on a bearing of 124° from her home H to a wine bar W; then she walks on a bearing of 047° to the cinema C which is due east of her home. Work out the distance by which her journey would have been reduced if she had walked in a straight line from H to C.

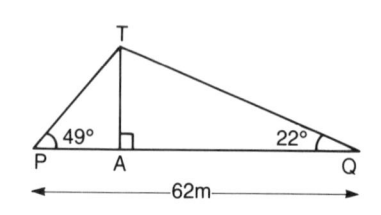

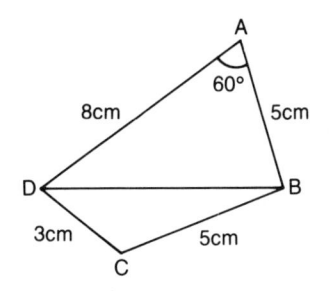

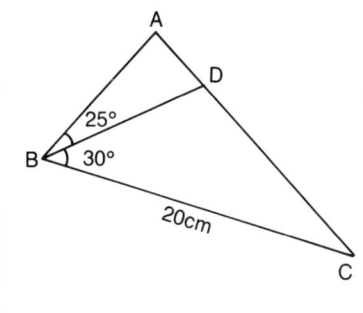

6 **a** In the figure on the left use the fact that $\cos 60° = \frac{1}{2}$ to prove that BD = 7 cm without using a calculator.
  b Prove that angle C is 120°.
  c Calculate the area of the quadrilateral ABCD.

7 The distance and bearing of a point M from a point N are 87 km and 306°, while the distance and bearing of another point L from N are 103 km and 274°. Work out
  a the distance LM,
  b the bearing of L from M,
  c how far L is south of M.

8 A, B, C are three points on horizontal ground such that B is on a bearing of 140° from A, C is on a bearing of 210° from A, and B is 42 m due east of C. At A is a vertical pole AP, and the angle of elevation of P from B is 27°. Work out
  a the height of the pole, AP,
  b the angle of elevation of P from C.

9 In the figure on the left the area of triangle BDC is 60 cm². Work out
  a the length BD,
  b angle ADB,
  c the area of triangle ABD.

10 A ship sails at a constant speed on a bearing of 240°. At 14·00 h it is at a point which is 250 km from a port P on a bearing of 040° from P, and it reaches the point which is exactly due north of P at 17·15 h. Work out
  a the speed of the ship,
  b its shortest distance from P,
  c the time, to the nearest minute, at which it is at its shortest distance from P,
  d the time, to the nearest minute, at which it is exactly north-west of P.

Mensuration

Quick revision exercise 39

1. Find the circumference and area of a circle with
   a. a radius of 5 cm, taking π to be 3,
   b. a diameter of 14 cm, taking π to be 22/7,
   c. a radius of 20 m, taking π to have the value given by a calculator,
   d. a diameter of 1·8 m, taking π to be 3,
   e. a radius of 14 mm, taking π to be 22/7,
   f. a diameter of 2·73 cm, using the value of π given by a calculator.

2. Find the area of each of the trapeziums below, using the formula **'average of parallel sides times distance between them'**.

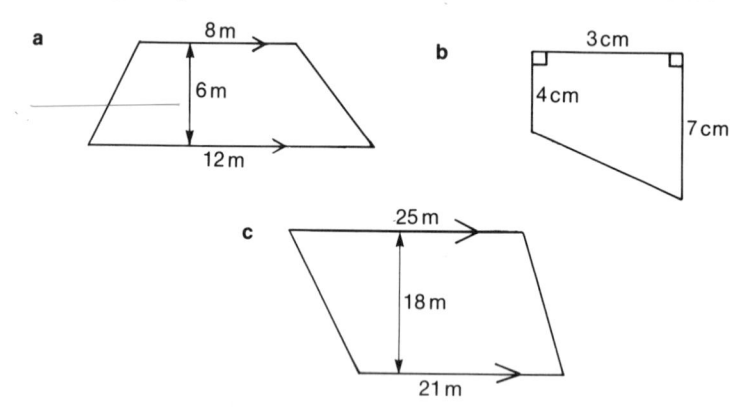

   a. 8 m (top), 6 m (height), 12 m (bottom)

   b. 3 cm (top), 4 cm (left side), 7 cm (right side)

   c. 25 m (top), 18 m (height), 21 m (bottom)

3. Say which two of the following figures could represent the net of a cuboid:

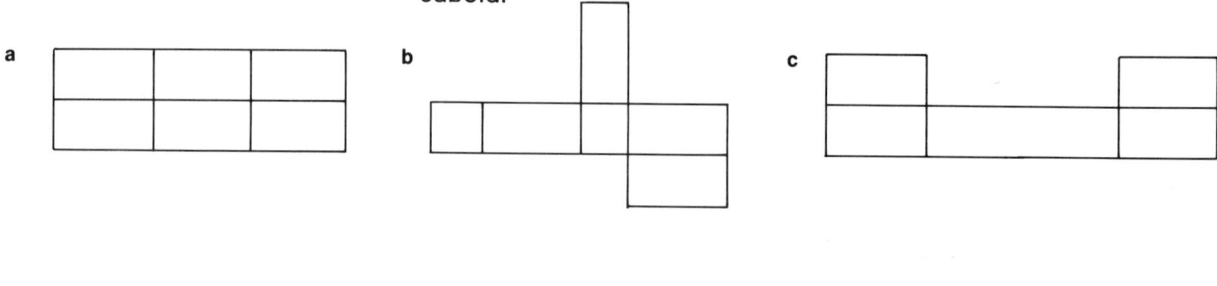

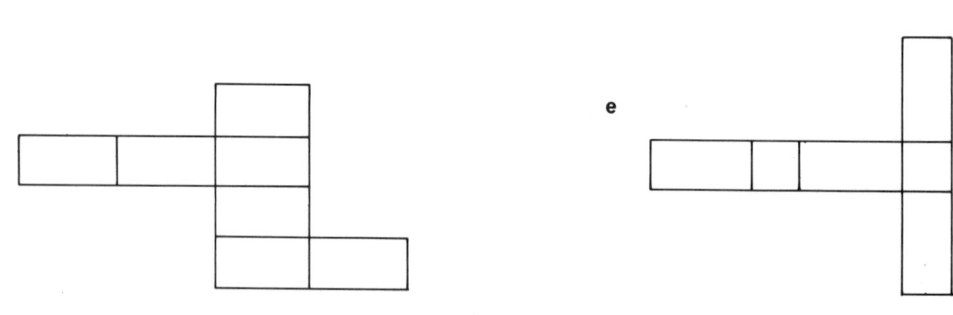

   a, b, c, d, e

4 Each of the diagrams below represents the net of a cuboid. Work out the volume and the surface area of each cuboid.

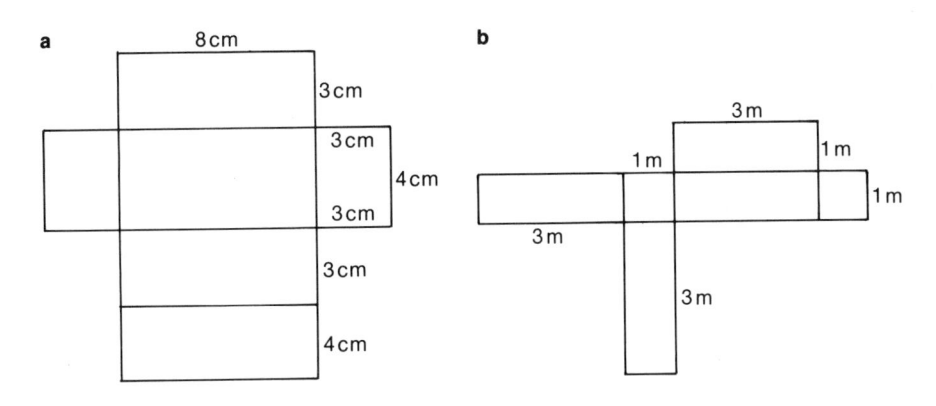

a

8 cm, 3 cm, 3 cm, 4 cm, 3 cm, 3 cm, 4 cm

b

3 m, 1 m, 1 m, 1 m, 3 m, 3 m

5 By dividing the following figures into cuboids, find their volumes:

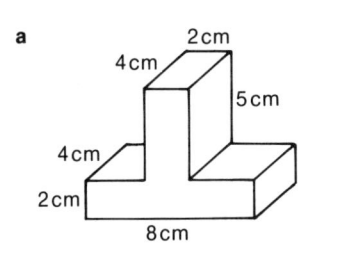

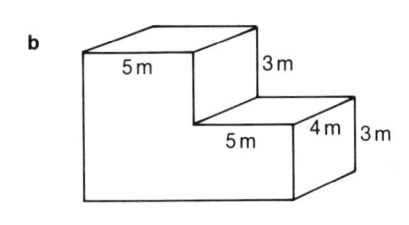

a

2 cm, 4 cm, 5 cm, 4 cm, 2 cm, 8 cm

b

5 m, 3 m, 5 m, 4 m, 3 m

6 Work out the volume and the surface area of each of the following solid prisms:

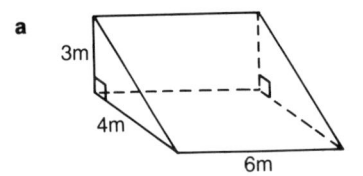

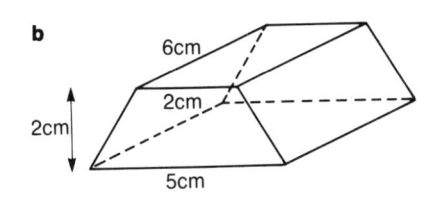

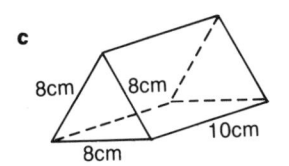

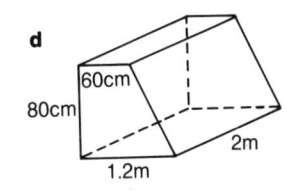

a

3 m, 4 m, 6 m

b

6 cm, 2 cm, 2 cm, 5 cm

c

8 cm, 8 cm, 10 cm, 8 cm

d

60 cm, 80 cm, 1.2 m, 2 m

7 The following figure represents the net of a certain figure. The distances shown are in centimetres.

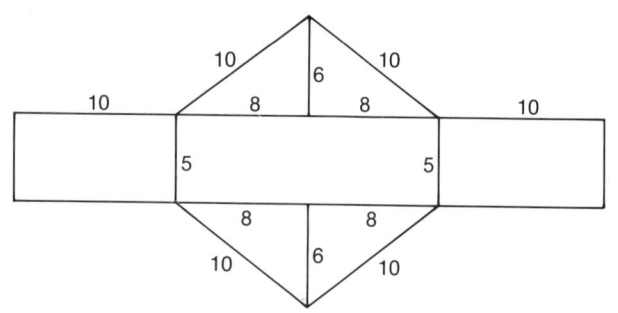

    a What kind of figure can be formed from the net?
    b Work out the volume and the surface area of the figure that can be formed.

8 Using the value of π given by a calculator, work out the volume and the total surface area of a cylinder with
    a a radius of 6 cm and a length of 25 cm,
    b a diameter of 48·3 mm and a length of 9·7 cm.

9 Using the value of π given by a calculator, work out the radius of
    a a circle of area 40 cm²,
    b a cylinder of volume 1200 cm³ and length 11 cm,
    c a cylinder of length 4·2 cm and curved surface area 36 cm².

10 Expressing the answer as a power of 10 where appropriate, state the number of
    a mm² in 1 cm²,   **e** m² in 1 km²,
    b mm³ in 1 cm³,   **f** m³ in 1 km³,
    c cm² in 1 m²,   **g** m² in 1 hectare,
    d cm³ in 1 m³,   **h** cm² in 1 hectare.

Elementary techniques

Note: *In the remaining exercises, use the value of π given by a calculator unless otherwise stated.*

Exercise 40A

1 A cuboidal metal block of length 40 cm, width 35 cm and height 28 cm is melted down and made into cylinders of radius 3 cm and length 12 cm. Work out
    a the volume of one cylinder, to one decimal place,
    b the number of cylinders obtained,
    c the volume of metal left over, to the nearest cm³.

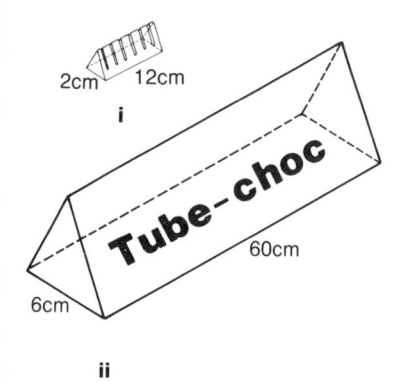

2 A certain type of chocolate bar is made in the form of a prism of length 12 cm in which the cross-section is an equilateral triangle of side 2 cm (diagram **i**). The bars are supplied to shops in cardboard containers of length 60 cm in which the cross-section is an equilateral triangle of side 6 cm (diagram **ii**). Work out
  a the volume of chocolate in each bar,
  b the number of bars that fit into each container.

3 Each wheel of a toy car has a radius of 1·2 cm. Work out
  a the circumference of each wheel,
  b the distance travelled by the car when each wheel rotates 40 times,
  c the number of **complete** revolutions each wheel makes when the car travels 200 cm.

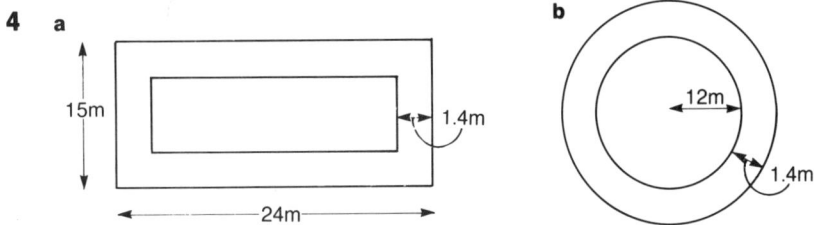

4 a   **b**

Each of the above diagrams represents a lawn which is surrounded by a path of width 1·4 m. The first lawn shown is rectangular and the second is circular. By subtracting the area of the lawn from that of the whole plot, work out the area of the path in each case.

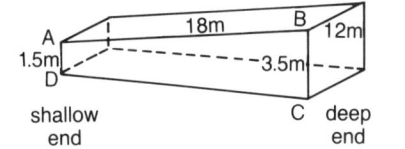

5 The diagram on the left represents a swimming pool, viewed from the side, which has the form of a prism whose cross-section is a trapezium. Work out
  a the area of the cross-section, ABCD,
  b the volume of the pool,
  c the length CD,
  d the area of the pool's surface which is in contact with water when the pool is full.

6 A cylindrical vessel of radius 9 cm and height 16 cm is three-quarters full of water. Work out
  a the volume of water in the vessel, in terms of π.

The water is poured into another cylindrical vessel, of radius 6 cm. Without using a calculator, work out
  b the height reached by the water in the second vessel, assuming that no water is lost.

The water is finally poured into a third cylindrical vessel, and reaches a height of 3 cm. Again assuming that no water is lost, work out
  c the radius of the third vessel.

7 A closed cuboidal wooden box is of length 20 cm, width 14 cm and height 12 cm. It is made of wood 0·3 cm thick whose density is such that 10 cm^3 of the wood has a mass of 7·4 g. Work out
  a the volume of wood in the box,
  b the mass of the box when empty.

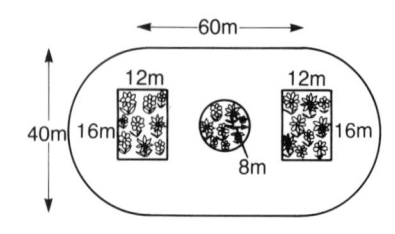

8 The figure on the left represents a plot of land which consists of a rectangle and two semicircular ends. It contains two rectangular flower-beds and a circular flower-bed, as shown. Work out
   a the perimeter of the plot,
   b the area of the plot, including the flower-beds,
   c the area of the plot, excluding the flower-beds.

9 A piece of metal of volume 2·5 cm³ is melted down and made into wire of radius 0·18 mm. Work out
   a the cross-sectional area of the wire, in mm²,
   b the cross-sectional area of the wire, in cm²,
   c the length of wire obtained, in metres.

10

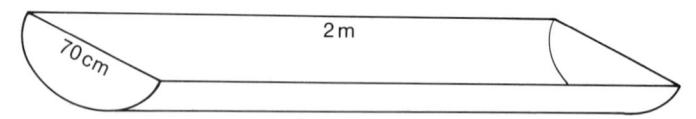

The above diagram shows a water trough whose cross-section is a semicircle. Taking π to be 22/7, work out
   a the volume of the trough, in m³,
   b the total internal surface area of the trough, in m².

Exercise 40B

1

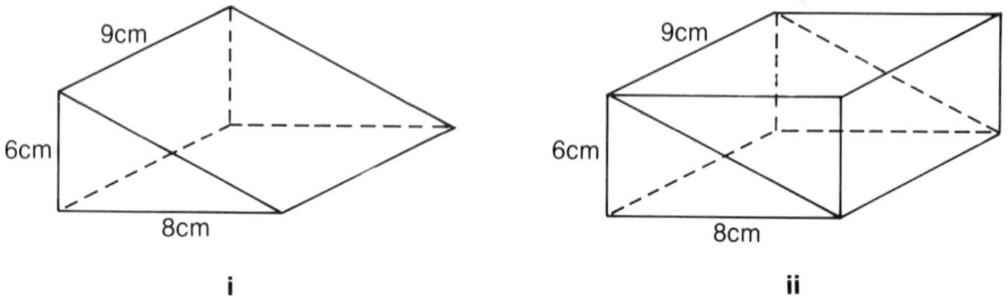

Diagram **i** above shows a wooden wedge which has the form of a triangular prism. The wedges are stacked in pairs, so that each pair forms a cuboid (diagram **ii**). Work out
   a the volume of one wedge,
   b the surface area of one wedge,
   c the number of wedges that will fit into a cuboidal box of length 56 cm, width 45 cm and height 12 cm.

2 Five metal prisms of cross-sectional area 25 cm² and length 6 cm are melted down and re-cast into a cube. Work out
   a the volume of the five prisms,
   b the side-length of the cube.

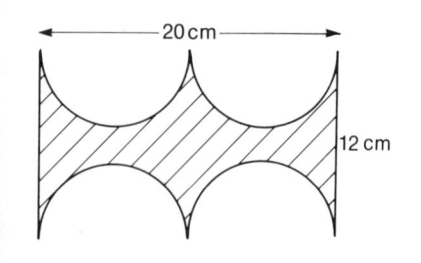

3 The figure on the left can be regarded as a rectangle from which four semicircles have been cut out. Work out
   a the perimeter of the figure,
   b the area of the figure.

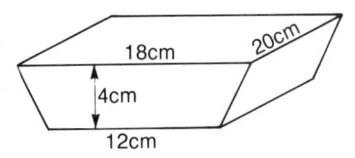

4 A metal pipe with a circular cross-section is 4 m long. Its internal radius is 12 cm and the thickness of the metal is 4 cm. Work out, in m³, the volume of metal in the pipe.

5 The diagram on the left shows an empty cardboard tray whose cross-section is a vertical isosceles trapezium. Work out
 a the capacity of the tray,
 b the area of cardboard needed to make the tray.

6 The wheels of a car make exactly 1600 revolutions when the car travels 2 km. Work out
 a the circumference of each wheel,
 b the radius of each wheel.

7 The cross-section of a vertical vessel is a rectangle of length 25 cm and breadth 20 cm. If 0·025 m³ of water is poured into the vessel, work out
 a the height to which the water will reach.

The water is then poured into a cylindrical vessel, and reaches a height of 70 cm. Assuming that no water is lost, work out
 b the radius of the cross-section of the cylindrical vessel.

8 A closed cuboidal box has external dimensions of 50 cm by 55 cm by 58 cm and is made of metal 0·2 cm thick. Work out
 a the capacity of the box, in m³,
 b the volume of metal in the box, in cm³.

Given that the mass of the empty box is 27·4 kg, work out
 c the density of the metal, in gcm^{-3}.

9 The diagram on the left shows a plot of land which can be considered to consist of a trapezium together with a semicircle. Work out

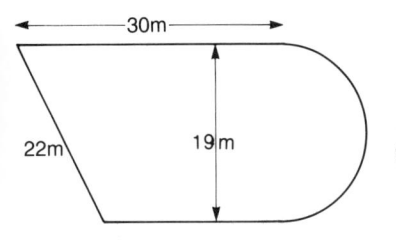

Arcs, sectors, segments; further standard bodies

Quick revision exercise 41

Questions **1** and **2** refer to the diagram overleaf, in which the arc ABC subtends an angle of θ at the centre of a circle of radius r. Note that θ may be acute, obtuse or reflex.

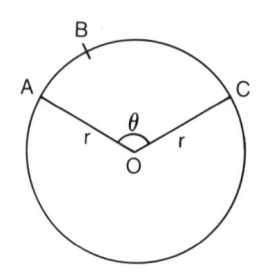

1. Work out the length of arc ABC and the area of sector OABC, given that
   a $r = 4$ cm and $\theta = 60°$,
   b $r = 7$ cm and $\theta = 45°$,
   c $r = 2·6$ cm and $\theta = 156°$,
   d $r = 19$ cm and $\theta = 270°$,
   e $r = 11·2$ cm and $\theta = 318°$.

2. Find the value of θ, given that
   a arc ABC $= 10$ cm and $r = 12$ cm,
   b arc ABC $= 28$ cm and $r = 5$ cm,
   c area of sector OABC $= 15$ cm² and $r = 4$ cm,
   d area of sector OABC $= 4\pi$ cm² and $r = 6$ cm.

3. A chord of a circle of radius 9 cm subtends an angle of 120° at the centre of the circle. Find the area of the minor segment cut off by the chord.

4. A chord of a circle of radius 3·7 cm subtends an angle of 78° at the centre of the circle. Find the area of the major segment cut off by the chord.

5. A chord of length 8 cm subtends an angle of 100° at the centre of a circle. Find the area of the minor segment cut off by the chord.

6. Find the area of the major segment cut off by a chord of length 20 cm in a circle of radius 20 cm.

7. Use the formula $V = \dfrac{4\pi r^3}{3}$ to work out
   a the volume of a sphere of radius 4·5 cm,
   b the radius of a sphere of volume 200 cm³.

8. Use the formula $A = 4\pi r^2$ to work out
   a the surface area of a sphere of radius 12 cm,
   b the radius of a sphere of surface area 54 cm²,
   c the surface area of a sphere of volume 100 cm³.

9. Use the formula $V = \tfrac{1}{3}$ **area of base × height** to work out
   a the volume of a pyramid of height 2 m whose base is a square of side 90 cm,
   b the volume of a cone of radius 8·3 cm and height 20·6 cm,
   c the volume of a tetrahedron of height 11 cm whose base is an equilateral triangle of side 7 cm.

10. The formula $A = \pi r l$ gives the curved surface area of a right cone of radius r and slant length l. Work out

a the **total** surface area of a right cone of radius 6 cm and slant length 10 cm,
b the total surface area of a right cone of volume 12π cm^3 and height 4 cm,
c the volume of a right cone of radius 6 cm and curved surface area 400 cm^2.

Exercise 42A

1 The second-hand of a watch is 1·2 cm long. Work out
  a the distance moved by the tip of the hand in 20 seconds,
  b the area swept out by the hand in this time.

2 Six metal spheres, each of radius 2 cm, are melted down and re-cast into a cylinder of the same radius. Work out
  a the total volume of the spheres, as a multiple of π,
  b the length of the cylinder.

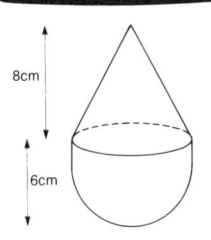

3 The figure on the left shows a solid body which is made of a right cone of height 8 cm and a hemisphere of radius 6 cm. Work out
  a the volume of the body,
  b the surface area of the body.

4 A large wheel, of radius 1·5 m, rolls a distance of 4 m along the ground. Calculate the angle the wheel turns through, to the nearest degree.

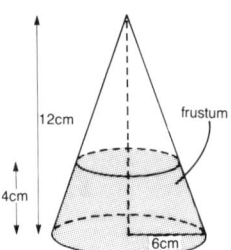

5 A **frustum** of a cone is the figure remaining when a smaller, similar cone is removed by a cut which is parallel to the base of the original cone. In the figure on the left, work out
  a the volume of the original cone,
  b the radius of the cone removed (using similar triangles),
  c the volume of the cone removed,
  d the volume of the frustum.

6 It takes 85 cm^3 of paint to cover the curved surface of a hemispherical dome. Given that a 1 litre pot of paint will cover an area of 12 m^2, work out the radius of the dome.

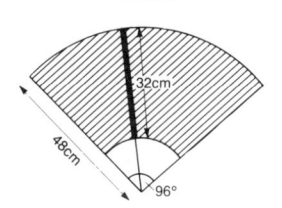

7 The shaded region in the diagram on the left shows the area swept out by the rubber blade of a windscreen wiper which turns through 96°. Work out this area, given that the total length of the rotating arm is 48 cm and the length of the rubber blade is 32 cm.

8 A sector AOB of a circle of centre O is drawn on cardboard. The radius AO is 18 cm and angle AOB is 80°. The sector is cut out and bent into the form of a cone by joining the points A and B. Work out
  a the radius of the base of the cone,
  b the height of the cone.

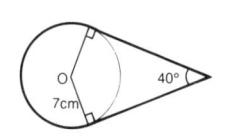

9 The diagram on the left shows a belt passing round a pulley wheel of radius 7 cm. Work out the length of the belt.

10 A cylindrical vessel with a radius of 3·8 cm contains water to a height of 5 cm. Twelve spherical marbles of radius 8 mm are dropped into the vessel and are completely submerged. Work out the new height reached by the water in the vessel.

11 A circular lawn is divided into two sections by a straight narrow path which subtends an angle of 120° at the centre of the circle. Assuming that the area of the path itself is negligible, work out the ratio of the areas of the two sections of lawn.

Exercise 42B

1 A spindle of length 24 cm and maximum diameter 10 cm is made by joining together two right cones, as shown below.

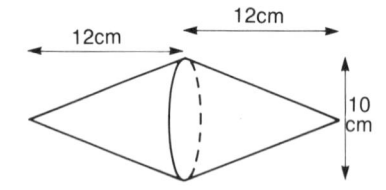

Work out
a the volume of the spindle,
b the surface area of the spindle.

2 The pendulum of a clock is 30 cm long and it turns through an angle of 36° at each swing. Work out the distance moved by the tip of the pendulum in one minute if each swing takes 0·5 seconds.

3 A pie chart of radius 3 cm shows the results of a survey of 600 married couples.
a If 345 of the couples have two children, what will be the area of the sector representing these couples on the pie chart?
b If the couples who have no children are represented on the chart by a sector of area $1·5\pi$ cm², how many of the couples have no children?

4 Metal is supplied to a factory in cuboidal sheets of length 2 m, width 30 cm and thickness 5 cm. The metal is used to make solid pyramids, each of which has a square base of side 8 cm and a height of 12 cm. Work out
a the volume of each pyramid,
b the number of pyramids obtained from each metal sheet,
c the percentage of each sheet which is left over.

5 In the figure on the left, the sides AD and BC are equal in length and AB is an arc of a circle of radius 6 cm which subtends an angle of 40° at its centre, namely the mid-point of CD. Work out
a the perimeter of the figure,
b the area of the figure.

6 A hemispherical bowl has twice the capacity of a cylindrical jar of radius 5 cm and height 9 cm. Work out the internal radius and the internal surface area of the bowl.

7 AOB is a sector of a circle in which the radius AO is 24 cm and angle AOB is 120°. The sector is bent into the form of a cone by joining A and B. Work out
a the radius of the cone,   b the semi-vertical angle of the cone.

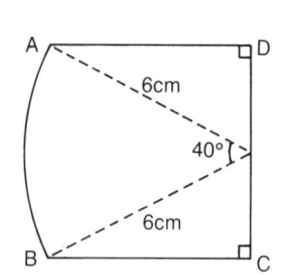

8 A right cone of radius 11 cm and height 20 cm stands with its circular face in contact with the base of a cylindrical vessel of radius 22 cm. Water is poured into the vessel until it reaches a height of 10 cm. Work out
  a the volume of the cone which is submerged,
  b the curved surface area of the cone which is in contact with water.

When the cone is removed from the vessel, work out
  c the new height which will be reached by the water in the vessel.

9 The diagram shows a belt passing round two pulley wheels of radii 14 cm and 7 cm whose centres are 25 cm apart. Work out the length of the belt.

10 A hollow cardboard cone has a height of 15 cm and a radius of 8 cm. A straight cut is made from the apex to a point on the circular base, then the cardboard is unrolled to form a sector of a circle. Work out, to the nearest degree, the angle between the two straight edges of the sector.

11 PQ is a diameter of a circle PQR. Given that RQ = 8 cm and the angle PQR = 60°, work out the area enclosed by the line PQ, the line PR and the minor arc RQ.

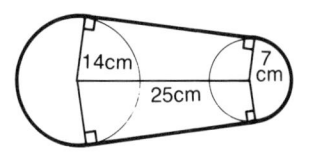

Level 3

Matrices

Note: *The whole of this section is Level 3.*

Basic rules and operations

Exercise 43A

1 State the order of each of the following matrices:

a $\begin{pmatrix} 5 & 1 & 4 \\ x & & y \end{pmatrix}$
b $\begin{pmatrix} w & x \\ y & 3w \end{pmatrix}$
c $\begin{pmatrix} 7 & 2 \\ -9 & 1 \end{pmatrix}$

2 Given that $\mathbf{A} = (6 \quad -1)$ and $\mathbf{B} = (-3 \quad 4)$, work out
a $\mathbf{A} - \mathbf{B}$,
b $2\mathbf{A} + 4\mathbf{B}$,
c $-\mathbf{A} + 2\mathbf{B}$,
d $-2(3\mathbf{A} - \mathbf{B})$.

3 Work out

a $\begin{pmatrix} 3x \\ -y \end{pmatrix} + \begin{pmatrix} -x \\ 2y \end{pmatrix}$
b $2x \begin{pmatrix} y \\ 3xy \end{pmatrix} - y \begin{pmatrix} 2x \\ -x^2 \end{pmatrix}$
c $x \begin{pmatrix} x-2 \\ 3+x \end{pmatrix} - \begin{pmatrix} 3x^2 - 2x \\ x^2 \end{pmatrix}$

4 In each of the following cases find a matrix **X** which satisfies the given equation:

a $3\mathbf{X} = (-6 \quad 4\tfrac{1}{2})$

b $2\mathbf{X} - \begin{pmatrix} 2 \\ -1 \end{pmatrix} = \begin{pmatrix} 7 \\ -3 \end{pmatrix}$

c $\begin{pmatrix} 5 & -2 \\ 7 & -1 \end{pmatrix} - 2\mathbf{X} = \begin{pmatrix} 1 & 3 \\ -1 & -4 \end{pmatrix}$

d $5\mathbf{X} + \begin{pmatrix} 7 \\ 8 \end{pmatrix} = 2\mathbf{X} - \begin{pmatrix} 5 \\ -2 \end{pmatrix}$

5 Find x and y from each of the following matrix equations:

a $\begin{pmatrix} 8 \\ 3y \end{pmatrix} = \begin{pmatrix} 2x \\ -3 \end{pmatrix}$

b $2(y \quad 5) = (3x \quad 5x)$

c $\begin{pmatrix} 2x - y \\ 3 \end{pmatrix} = \begin{pmatrix} -6 \\ x+y \end{pmatrix}$

d $x \begin{pmatrix} -1 \\ 2 \end{pmatrix} - 3 \begin{pmatrix} y \\ 4 \end{pmatrix} = -\begin{pmatrix} 11 \\ y \end{pmatrix}$

6 Work out

a $(3 \quad 2 \quad 5) \begin{pmatrix} 4 \\ 8 \\ 1 \end{pmatrix}$

b $(-4 \quad 7) \begin{pmatrix} -2 \\ -1 \end{pmatrix}$

c $(8x \quad 3y) \begin{pmatrix} 2y \\ -4x \end{pmatrix}$

d $(-x \quad 2 \quad y) \begin{pmatrix} y+2 \\ x-y \\ 1+x \end{pmatrix}$

7 Work out

a $\begin{pmatrix} 5 & 4 \\ -1 & 3 \end{pmatrix} \begin{pmatrix} 2 \\ -1 \end{pmatrix}$

b $(-2 \quad 7 \quad 3) \begin{pmatrix} 4 & 3 \\ 1 & -2 \\ -2 & 8 \end{pmatrix}$

c $\begin{pmatrix} 20 & 15 \\ -5 & -10 \end{pmatrix} \begin{pmatrix} 3 & -5 & -1 \\ -4 & 10 & 2 \end{pmatrix}$ d $\begin{pmatrix} -x \\ 3x \\ 2x \end{pmatrix} (5 \quad -2 \quad 4)$

8 $A = \begin{pmatrix} 2 & 3 \\ -1 & 6 \end{pmatrix}$, $C = \begin{pmatrix} 1 & 7 \\ -2 & 3 \\ 4 & 0 \end{pmatrix}$,

$B = (-5 \quad 0 \quad 2)$, $D = \begin{pmatrix} 3 \\ 2 \end{pmatrix}$.

With the definitions of **A, B, C, D** given above, say in each of the following cases whether or not the given product is possible. If the product is possible, work it out.

a D^2
b CB
c AD
d A^2
e AC
f BC
g DB

9 Find the quantities indicated by letters in each of the following cases:

a $(-x \quad 3 \quad x) \begin{pmatrix} 2 \\ x \\ -4 \end{pmatrix} = (6)$ d $\begin{pmatrix} y & 2x \\ 2y & 3 \end{pmatrix} \begin{pmatrix} 1 \\ 4 \end{pmatrix} = \begin{pmatrix} x^2 \\ 30 \end{pmatrix}$

b $\begin{pmatrix} 3 & y \\ x & 6 \end{pmatrix} \begin{pmatrix} 1 \\ 2 \end{pmatrix} = \begin{pmatrix} x \\ -y \end{pmatrix}$ e $\begin{pmatrix} t & 2 \\ w & 4 \end{pmatrix} \begin{pmatrix} 3 & -1 \\ v & 2 \end{pmatrix} = \begin{pmatrix} 5 & r \\ 2 & 6 \end{pmatrix}$

c $(x \quad y) \begin{pmatrix} 2 & 4 \\ -5 & -3 \end{pmatrix} = (20 \quad 19)$

10 Find the inverse of each of the following matrices when the matrix has an inverse. If the matrix does not have an inverse, give the answer 'singular'.

a $\begin{pmatrix} 5 & 2 \\ 7 & 3 \end{pmatrix}$ f $\begin{pmatrix} 2\frac{1}{2} & -5 \\ 3 & -6 \end{pmatrix}$

b $\begin{pmatrix} 2 & 3 \\ 6 & 9 \end{pmatrix}$ g $\begin{pmatrix} -8 & 9 \\ 4 & -4 \end{pmatrix}$

c $\begin{pmatrix} 4 & -2 \\ -5 & 3 \end{pmatrix}$ h $\begin{pmatrix} 3 & -4 \\ -2 & 2\frac{1}{2} \end{pmatrix}$

d $\begin{pmatrix} 7 & -3 \\ 8 & -3 \end{pmatrix}$ i $\begin{pmatrix} -6 & 5\frac{2}{3} \\ 2 & -2 \end{pmatrix}$

e $\begin{pmatrix} -7 & 3 \\ -2 & 1 \end{pmatrix}$

143

Exercise 43B

1 State the order of
 a a matrix with six rows and three columns,
 b a column matrix containing five elements,
 c a square matrix containing nine elements,
 d a row matrix containing seven elements.

2 Given that $\mathbf{P} = \begin{pmatrix} -5 \\ 2 \end{pmatrix}$ and $\mathbf{Q} = \begin{pmatrix} -1 \\ -4 \end{pmatrix}$, work out

 a $\mathbf{P} + \mathbf{Q}$,   c $-3\mathbf{P} - 2\mathbf{Q}$,
 b $2\mathbf{P} - \mathbf{Q}$,   d $-2(5\mathbf{P} + 3\mathbf{Q})$.

3 Work out
 a $(-2x \quad 7y) - (3x \quad -4y)$
 b $2t\begin{pmatrix} w \\ 3 \end{pmatrix} - w\begin{pmatrix} 3t \\ 2 \end{pmatrix}$ c $3r\begin{pmatrix} r-1 \\ 4 \end{pmatrix} - \begin{pmatrix} r^2 - 3r \\ 7r \end{pmatrix}$

4 In each of the following cases find a matrix **Y** which satisfies the given equation:
 a $2\mathbf{Y} = (5 \quad -8 \quad 2\tfrac{4}{5})$
 b $\begin{pmatrix} 20 \\ -18 \end{pmatrix} = \begin{pmatrix} -10 \\ 8 \end{pmatrix} + 3\mathbf{Y}$
 c $\begin{pmatrix} 4 & -1 \\ -3 & 5 \end{pmatrix} - 5\mathbf{Y} = \begin{pmatrix} 2 & -9 \\ 1 & -7 \end{pmatrix} - \mathbf{Y}$

5 Find x and y from each of the following matrix equations:
 a $\begin{pmatrix} 4-x \\ 3y \end{pmatrix} = \begin{pmatrix} x+6 \\ -12 \end{pmatrix}$ c $\begin{pmatrix} x \\ y \end{pmatrix} = \begin{pmatrix} 2y \\ 4/y \end{pmatrix}$
 b $x(-4 \quad y) = 2(-8 \quad -6)$ d $y\begin{pmatrix} 5 \\ -2 \end{pmatrix} - 2\begin{pmatrix} 2x \\ 4 \end{pmatrix} = \begin{pmatrix} 13 \\ -6x \end{pmatrix}$

6 Work out
 a $(5 \quad -1 \quad -3)\begin{pmatrix} 2 \\ 7 \\ 1 \end{pmatrix}$
 b $(-5p \quad 8r)\begin{pmatrix} 2r \\ -p \end{pmatrix}$ c $(-t \quad 2 \quad 3t)\begin{pmatrix} 4-t \\ -5t^2 \\ 3t+1 \end{pmatrix}$

7 Work out
 a $\begin{pmatrix} 7 & 2 \\ -1 & 0 \\ 3 & 4 \end{pmatrix}\begin{pmatrix} -1 \\ 2 \end{pmatrix}$ c $\begin{pmatrix} 7 & 1 & -2 \\ 3 & 0 & -1 \end{pmatrix}\begin{pmatrix} -1 & 2 \\ 2 & 5 \\ -4 & -3 \end{pmatrix}$
 b $(-10 \quad 15)\begin{pmatrix} 2 & -3 & 5 \\ 1 & 0 & 2 \end{pmatrix}$ d $\begin{pmatrix} 2 \\ -1 \end{pmatrix}(4 \quad -3 \quad 6)$

8 The matrix **A** has order 2 × 1, **B** has order 3 × 2, **C** has order 3 × 1 and **D** has order 1 × 3. Say whether each of the following products is possible and, if it is, state its order:
   a BA
   b D²
   c DA
   d CD
   e AC
   f ADC
   g DBC

9 $A = \begin{pmatrix} 5 & -3 \\ 4 & -1 \end{pmatrix}$, $B = \begin{pmatrix} -2 & 1 \\ 3 & 2 \end{pmatrix}$ and $C = (-1 \ \ 2)$. Work out
   a A²   b B³   c CAB

10 Find the quantities indicated by letters in each of the following cases:

   a $(4 \ \ 2p \ \ -p) \begin{pmatrix} p-1 \\ 3 \\ 2 \end{pmatrix} = (6p)$ c $(p \ \ q) \begin{pmatrix} 4 & 5 \\ -3 & -2 \end{pmatrix} = (-24 \ \ -23)$

   b $\begin{pmatrix} x & y \\ 2y & -1 \end{pmatrix} \begin{pmatrix} 3 \\ -2 \end{pmatrix} = \begin{pmatrix} 14 \\ 4y \end{pmatrix}$ d $\begin{pmatrix} 3 & w \\ -1 & 4 \end{pmatrix} \begin{pmatrix} x & -2 \\ 2 & t \end{pmatrix} = \begin{pmatrix} y & x \\ 6 & 2x \end{pmatrix}$

11 Find the inverse of each of the following matrices if the inverse exists. If it does not exist, give the answer 'singular'.

   a $\begin{pmatrix} 7 & 3 \\ 9 & 4 \end{pmatrix}$ f $\begin{pmatrix} 4 & -5 \\ 8 & -9 \end{pmatrix}$

   b $\begin{pmatrix} 3 & -6 \\ -5 & 11 \end{pmatrix}$ g $\begin{pmatrix} 2\frac{1}{4} & -2 \\ -9 & 8 \end{pmatrix}$

   c $\begin{pmatrix} 2 & 4 \\ 5\frac{1}{2} & 11 \end{pmatrix}$ h $\begin{pmatrix} -1 & 2 \\ 1 & -1 \end{pmatrix}$

   d $\begin{pmatrix} -6 & -2 \\ 2 & 1 \end{pmatrix}$ i $\begin{pmatrix} 2\frac{1}{2} & 1\frac{1}{2} \\ 4\frac{1}{2} & 2\frac{1}{2} \end{pmatrix}$

   e $\begin{pmatrix} 2 & -6 \\ 10 & 20 \end{pmatrix}$

Matrix transformations

Level 3

Note: *When using graph paper in Exercises 44A and 44B, use a scale of 1 cm to 1 unit on both axes.*

Exercise 44A

1 a Copy and complete the following equation, representing a transformation of a triangle ABC to an image triangle A'B'C':

$$\begin{matrix} & \underline{A} & \underline{B} & \underline{C} & & \underline{A'} & \underline{B'} & \underline{C'} \end{matrix}$$
$$\begin{pmatrix} 1 & 0 \\ 0 & -1 \end{pmatrix}\begin{pmatrix} 2 & 6 & 6 \\ 2 & 2 & 4 \end{pmatrix} = \begin{pmatrix} & & \end{pmatrix}$$

    b Draw the triangles ABC and A'B'C' on graph paper, and hence describe the transformation represented by the matrix
$$\mathbf{M} = \begin{pmatrix} 1 & 0 \\ 0 & -1 \end{pmatrix}.$$
    c Work out $\mathbf{M}^2$ and $\mathbf{M}^{-1}$, and interpret the results geometrically.

2 Draw the triangle p with vertices $(-2, 2)$, $(-4, 2)$, $(-2, 6)$ and the triangle q with vertices $(2, 2)$, $(2, 4)$, $(6, 2)$.
    a Describe the transformation which maps p to q.

Apply the transformation represented by $\begin{pmatrix} 0 & 1 \\ 1 & 0 \end{pmatrix}$ to p, labelling the image p', and apply the transformation represented by $\begin{pmatrix} -1 & 0 \\ 0 & -1 \end{pmatrix}$ to q, labelling the image q'. Describe the transformations which map
    b p to p',
    c q to q',
    d p' to q,
    e p to q'.

3 Under the transformation represented by the matrix $\begin{pmatrix} 3 & 1 \\ 4 & 2 \end{pmatrix}$ the images of the points A and B are $(8, 10)$ and $(-1, 2)$, respectively. Either by finding the inverse of the above matrix or by solving pairs of simultaneous equations, find the coordinates of A and B.

4   **a** Apply the transformation represented by $\mathbf{N} = \begin{pmatrix} 0 & -1 \\ 1 & 0 \end{pmatrix}$ to the triangle ABC of question 1, and hence describe the transformation.
    b Work out $\mathbf{N}^2$, $\mathbf{N}^3$ and $\mathbf{N}^{-1}$ and, by considering the geometrical meaning of $\mathbf{N}$, describe the transformations represented by these matrices.

5 It can be shown that, under the transformation represented by the matrix $\begin{pmatrix} a & b \\ c & d \end{pmatrix}$, the image of the point $(1, 0)$ is (a, c) and the image of the point $(0, 1)$ is (b, d). By finding the images of $(1, 0)$ and $(0, 1)$ under the following transformations, obtain the matrices representing these transformations:
    a reflection in the y-axis,
    b enlargement of centre the origin and scale factor 3,
    c reflection in the line $y = x$ followed by reflection in the x-axis.

6   **a** Apply the transformation represented by $\mathbf{J} = \begin{pmatrix} 0 & -1 \\ -1 & 0 \end{pmatrix}$ to the triangle whose vertices are P(0, 4), Q(−2, 4), R(−2, 8). Label the image P′Q′R′ and state the coordinates of P′, Q′, R′.

b Apply the transformation represented by $K = \begin{pmatrix} 0 & -1 \\ 1 & 0 \end{pmatrix}$ to the triangle P′Q′R′. Label the image P″Q″R″ and state the coordinates of P″, Q″, R″.

c State the transformation which maps PQR to P″Q″R″, and obtain the matrix representing this transformation by the method used in question **5**. Verify that this matrix is equal to the matrix product **KJ**.

7 Work out the matrices representing the following combinations of transformations and describe the transformations they represent:
a reflection in the x-axis followed by a half-turn about the origin,
b reflection in the line $y = -x$ followed by reflection in the y-axis.

8 **a** Apply the transformation by $\begin{pmatrix} 1 & -1 \\ 1 & 1 \end{pmatrix}$ to the triangle whose vertices are the origin O, the point A(4, 0) and the point B(4, 1). State the coordinates of the images of A and B.
b Given that the transformation can be regarded as the product of an enlargement and another transformation, describe the other transformation and work out the scale factor of the enlargement.

9 Each of the following matrices represents the product of an enlargement and another transformation. By applying the transformation to any appropriate figure, obtain the other transformation and the scale factor of the enlargement:

a $\begin{pmatrix} 3 & 0 \\ 0 & -3 \end{pmatrix}$ **b** $\begin{pmatrix} 0 & 5 \\ 5 & 0 \end{pmatrix}$ **c** $\begin{pmatrix} 2 & 2 \\ -2 & 2 \end{pmatrix}$

10 **a** M is the matrix $\begin{pmatrix} 0.8 & 0.6 \\ 0.6 & -0.8 \end{pmatrix}$. Show that M^2 is the identity matrix $\begin{pmatrix} 1 & 0 \\ 0 & 1 \end{pmatrix}$ and that $M^{-1} = M$. In view of these properties, what kind of transformation must **M** represent?
b Apply the transformation represented by **M** to the triangle whose vertices are the origin, the point (3, 1) and the point (2, 4). Hence describe the transformation fully.

11 **a** By considering the transformation represented by the matrix $N = \begin{pmatrix} 0 & -1 \\ 1 & 0 \end{pmatrix}$, work out the matrices N^8 and N^{11}.
b By considering the transformation represented by the matrix $P = \begin{pmatrix} -2 & 0 \\ 0 & 2 \end{pmatrix}$, work out the matrices P^4 and P^7.

12 The matrices $\mathbf{A} = \begin{pmatrix} 1 & 0 \\ 0 & -1 \end{pmatrix}$ and $\mathbf{B} = \begin{pmatrix} -0.6 & 0.8 \\ 0.8 & 0.6 \end{pmatrix}$ both represent reflections. Work out **AB** and apply the transformation represented by this matrix to the triangle whose vertices are the points (0, 0), (5, 0) and (0, 10). Measure an appropriate angle with a protractor and hence describe the transformation as accurately as possible. What can you say in general about the product of two reflections in non-parallel lines?

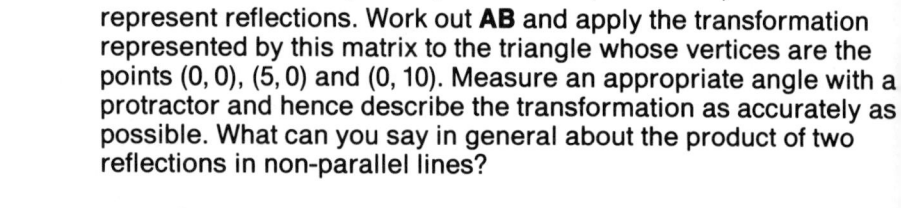

Exercise 44B

Level 3

1 **a** Copy and complete the following equation, representing a transformation of a triangle PQR to an image triangle P'Q'R':

$$\begin{pmatrix} 0 & -1 \\ -1 & 0 \end{pmatrix} \begin{matrix} \text{P} & \text{Q} & \text{R} \\ \begin{pmatrix} 0 & -2 & -2 \\ 2 & 2 & 6 \end{pmatrix} \end{matrix} = \begin{pmatrix} \text{P' Q' R'} \\ \end{pmatrix}$$

b Draw the triangles PQR and P'Q'R' on graph paper, and hence describe the transformation represented by the matrix $\begin{pmatrix} 0 & -1 \\ -1 & 0 \end{pmatrix}$.

c Write down the matrix representing the inverse of the above transformation matrix.

2 Draw the triangle t with vertices (2, 2), (8, 2), (4, 4) and the triangle v with vertices (−2, −2), (−8, −2), (−4, −4). Apply the transformation represented by $\begin{pmatrix} 0 & -1 \\ 1 & 0 \end{pmatrix}$ to t, calling the image t', and apply the transformation represented by $\begin{pmatrix} 0 & 1 \\ 1 & 0 \end{pmatrix}$ to v, calling the image v'. Describe the transformation which maps
a t to v,
b t' to v',
c t to v',
d v to t'.

3 Find the coordinates of the point which

a is mapped to (3, 1) by the transformation $\begin{pmatrix} 4 & 5 \\ 2 & 3 \end{pmatrix}$,

b is mapped to (−11, 6) by the transformation $\begin{pmatrix} -2 & 5 \\ 1 & -3 \end{pmatrix}$,

c is mapped to (1, 2) by the transformation $\begin{pmatrix} -4 & 3 \\ -2 & 2 \end{pmatrix}$.

4 **a** Apply the transformation represented by $\begin{pmatrix} 2 & 0 \\ 0 & 2 \end{pmatrix}$ to the

triangle *m* whose vertices are (1, 1), (3, 1) and (1, 2). Hence describe the transformation.

b Apply the transformation represented by $\begin{pmatrix} -\frac{1}{2} & 0 \\ 0 & -\frac{1}{2} \end{pmatrix}$ to the triangle *n* whose vertices are (8, −2), (0, −2) and (8, −6). Hence describe the transformation.

c Describe the transformation which maps the image of *m* to the image of *n*.

5 By finding the images of the points (1, 0) and (0, 1), work out the matrices which represent the following transformations:
  a reflection in the *x*-axis,
  b an anticlockwise quarter-turn about the origin,
  c reflection in the *y*-axis followed by an enlargement of centre the origin and scale factor 3.

6 By considering any convenient figure, work out the transformation which is equivalent to a clockwise rotation of 90° above the origin followed by reflection in the line $y = x$. Work out the matrix which represents this transformation and, by considering the above pair of transformations, write down the matrix product which gives the same matrix.

7 Work out the matrices which represent the following combinations of transformations and describe the transformations they represent:
  a reflection in the line $y = x$ followed by a half-turn about the origin,
  b reflection in the *y*-axis followed by a clockwise quarter-turn about the origin followed by reflection in the line $y = -x$.

8 a Apply the transformation represented by $\begin{pmatrix} 4 & -3 \\ 3 & 4 \end{pmatrix}$ to the triangle whose vertices are the origin, the point A(2, 0) and the point B(2, 1). State the coordinates of the images of A and B.
  b Given that the transformation is the product of a rotation and an enlargement, work out the angle of rotation to the nearest degree and state the scale factor of the enlargement.

9 a Work out the matrix $\mathbf{P}^2$, given that $\mathbf{P} = \begin{pmatrix} 5/13 & 12/13 \\ 12/13 & -5/13 \end{pmatrix}$. What conclusion can you draw regarding the inverse of $\mathbf{P}$?

  b Apply the transformation represented by $\mathbf{P}$ to the triangle whose vertices are the origin, the point A(3, 2) and the point B(8, 1). Hence describe the transformation completely.

10 By considering the transformations represented by the matrices $\mathbf{J} = \begin{pmatrix} 0 & 1 \\ -1 & 0 \end{pmatrix}$ and $\mathbf{K} = \begin{pmatrix} 0 & 2 \\ 2 & 0 \end{pmatrix}$, work out
  a $\mathbf{J}^{12}$,   **b** $\mathbf{J}^{17}$,   **c** $\mathbf{K}^6$,   **d** $\mathbf{K}^7$.

11 The matrices $\mathbf{R} = \begin{pmatrix} -0.6 & 0.8 \\ 0.8 & 0.6 \end{pmatrix}$ and $\mathbf{S} = \begin{pmatrix} 0.8 & 0.6 \\ 0.6 & -0.8 \end{pmatrix}$ both represent reflections.

  a By considering the images of the point (1, 0) under these transformations, or otherwise, work out the equations of the axes of reflection of **R** and **S**.
  b Work out the angle between the two axes of reflection.
  c Work out the matrix products **RS** and **SR**, and describe the transformations they represent.

12 The matrix $\mathbf{M} = \begin{pmatrix} 0.6 & -0.8 \\ 0.8 & 0.6 \end{pmatrix}$ represents a rotation about the origin. Find the matrix **N** such that both **MN** and **NM** represent a half-turn about the origin.

Vectors

Note: *The whole of this section is Level 3.*

Parallelogram and triangle laws, column vectors

Exercise 45A

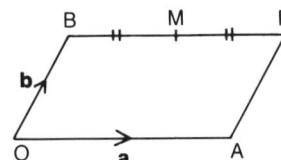

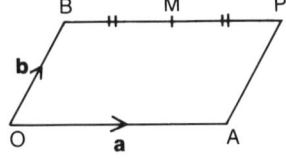

1. The figure on the left shows a parallelogram OAPB in which M is the midpoint of BP. Letting $\vec{OA} = \mathbf{a}$ and $\vec{OB} = \mathbf{b}$, as shown, express the following vectors in terms of $\mathbf{a}$ and $\mathbf{b}$:
   (a) $\vec{PA}$ (b) $\vec{OP}$ (c) $\vec{MP}$ (d) $\vec{OM}$ (e) $\vec{AM}$

2. PQRS is a quadrilateral. Express the following as single vectors:
   (a) $\vec{PQ} + \vec{QR}$
   (b) $\vec{QS} + \vec{SP}$
   (c) $\vec{RQ} + \vec{PS} + \vec{SR}$
   (d) $\vec{PS} - \vec{PR}$ (note that $-\vec{PR} = \vec{RP}$)
   (e) $\vec{RS} - \vec{QS}$
   (f) $\vec{PQ} - \vec{PS} - \vec{RQ}$

3. Given the vectors shown in the diagram on the left, express the following as single vectors:
   (a) $\mathbf{a} + \mathbf{b}$
   (b) $\mathbf{f} - \mathbf{g}$
   (c) $\mathbf{c} + \mathbf{d} + \mathbf{g}$
   (d) $-\mathbf{f} + \mathbf{e} - \mathbf{d}$
   (e) $\mathbf{b} - \mathbf{c} + \mathbf{a} - \mathbf{d}$

4. ABC is an isosceles triangle in which AB = AC = 13 cm and BC = 10 cm. Work out the values of
   (a) $|\vec{AB} + \vec{AC}|$
   (b) $|\vec{AB} - \vec{AC}|$

5. Given that, in the diagram on the left, $|\mathbf{a}| = 6$ cm and $|\mathbf{b}| = |\mathbf{c}| = 8$ cm, work out the values of
   (a) $|\mathbf{a} + \mathbf{b}|$ (c) $|\mathbf{a} + \mathbf{c}|$
   (b) $|\mathbf{a} - 2\mathbf{b}|$ (d) $|\mathbf{b} - \mathbf{c}|$

6. O is the origin, A is the point (2, 5) and B is the point (7, 1). Express the following as column vectors:
   (a) $\vec{OB}$ (b) $\vec{AO}$ (c) $\vec{AB}$ (d) $\vec{BA}$

7. O is the origin and P, Q are points such that $\vec{OP} = \begin{pmatrix} 4 \\ -2 \end{pmatrix}$ and $\vec{OQ} = \begin{pmatrix} 1 \\ 3 \end{pmatrix}$. M is the midpoint of OP and R is the point such that OPRQ is a parallelogram. Express the following as column vectors:
   (a) $\vec{OM}$ (b) $\vec{OR}$ (c) $\vec{RQ}$ (d) $\vec{QM}$

8 Given that $\mathbf{x} = \begin{pmatrix} 6 \\ -5 \end{pmatrix}$ and $\mathbf{y} = \begin{pmatrix} -2 \\ 7 \end{pmatrix}$, express the following as column vectors:
   (a) $-3\mathbf{x}$ (b) $\mathbf{x} + \mathbf{y}$ (c) $2\mathbf{y} - 3\mathbf{x}$

9 Given that $\mathbf{p} = \begin{pmatrix} 3 \\ 4 \end{pmatrix}$ and $\mathbf{q} = \begin{pmatrix} -5 \\ 12 \end{pmatrix}$, find the modulus (or magnitude) of each of the following vectors:
   (a) $\mathbf{p}$ (b) $\mathbf{q}$ (c) $\mathbf{p} - \mathbf{q}$ (d) $2\mathbf{q} - 6\mathbf{p}$

10 The vector $\mathbf{a} = \begin{pmatrix} 3 \\ -1 \end{pmatrix}$. In each of the following cases find the coordinates of a point P which satisfies the given condition:
   (a) O is the origin and $\overrightarrow{OP} = 2\mathbf{a}$,
   (b) O is the origin and $\overrightarrow{OP} = -5\mathbf{a}$,
   (c) A is the point (3, 8) and $\overrightarrow{AP} = \mathbf{a}$,
   (d) O is the origin, S is the point (2, 3) and $\overrightarrow{OS} + \overrightarrow{OP} = \mathbf{a}$.

11 (a) P is the point $(k, 0)$ and R is the point $(0, 4)$. Find k, given that $\overrightarrow{PR}$ is parallel to the vector $\begin{pmatrix} -6 \\ 12 \end{pmatrix}$.

   (b) Given that the vector $\mathbf{x} = \begin{pmatrix} 3 \\ 4 \end{pmatrix}$, find a vector $\mathbf{y}$ which is opposite in direction to $\mathbf{x}$ and of magnitude 20.

12 O is the origin and J, K, L are points such that $\overrightarrow{OJ} = \begin{pmatrix} 5 \\ 1 \end{pmatrix}$, $\overrightarrow{OL} = \begin{pmatrix} -1 \\ 4 \end{pmatrix}$ and $\overrightarrow{LK} = \begin{pmatrix} 10 \\ 2 \end{pmatrix}$.

   (a) Work out the coordinates of K.
   (b) State two relationships between the lines LK, OJ.
   (c) What kind of figure is OJKL?
   (d) Express $\overrightarrow{JK}$ as a column vector and, letting the midpoint of LK be M, show that $\overrightarrow{JK} = \overrightarrow{OM}$. What conclusion can you draw regarding the figure OJKM?

Exercise 45B

Level 3

1 In the figure below, ABCE is a parallelogram and $BC = 2CD$. Letting $\overrightarrow{AB} = \mathbf{p}$ and $\overrightarrow{AE} = \mathbf{q}$, as shown, express the following vectors in terms of $\mathbf{p}$ and $\mathbf{q}$:
   (a) $\overrightarrow{CE}$ (b) $\overrightarrow{CD}$ (c) $\overrightarrow{AC}$ (d) $\overrightarrow{EB}$ (e) $\overrightarrow{DA}$

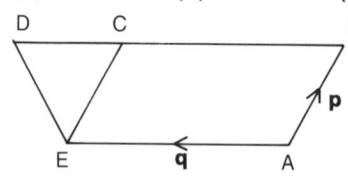

2. ABC is a triangle and P is any point on the side AC. Express the following as single vectors:
   (a) $\vec{BC} + \vec{CP}$
   (b) $\vec{BA} + \vec{PB}$
   (c) $\vec{AB} - \vec{AC}$
   (d) $\vec{CB} - \vec{CP} + \vec{AP}$
   (e) $\vec{PB} - \vec{PA} - \vec{CB}$

3. Given the vectors shown in the diagram on the left, express the following as single vectors:
   (a) **a − e**
   (b) **b + c + d**
   (c) **a + f − h**
   (d) **e + f − c**
   (e) **a − b − g**

4. ABCDEF is a regular hexagon in which $\vec{AB} = $ **x** and $\vec{AF} = $ **y**. By dividing the hexagon into six equilateral triangles, express the following vectors in terms of **x** and **y**:
   (a) $\vec{FC}$
   (b) $\vec{AD}$
   (c) $\vec{EC}$
   (d) $\vec{DB}$

5. Given that, in the diagram on the left, $|\mathbf{a}| = 9$, $|\mathbf{b}| = 16$ and $|\mathbf{c}| = 12$, work out
   (a) $|\mathbf{a} - \mathbf{b}|$
   (b) $|3\mathbf{a} + 2\mathbf{b}|$
   (c) $|\mathbf{a} + \mathbf{c}|$
   (d) $|\mathbf{b} - \mathbf{c}|$

6. O is the origin, A is the point (4, 0), B is (0, 3) and C is (−2, −1). Express the following as column vectors:
   (a) $\vec{AB}$
   (b) $\vec{CO}$
   (c) $\vec{BC}$
   (d) $\vec{CA}$

7. Given that $\mathbf{m} = \begin{pmatrix} -3 \\ 2 \end{pmatrix}$ and $\mathbf{n} = \begin{pmatrix} -1 \\ 4 \end{pmatrix}$, express the following as column vectors:
   (a) $-2\mathbf{n}$
   (b) $\mathbf{m} - \mathbf{n}$
   (c) $2\mathbf{m} + 3\mathbf{n}$

8. ABCD is a quadrilateral in which A is the point (0, 1), $\vec{AB} = \begin{pmatrix} 4 \\ 0 \end{pmatrix}$, $\vec{AD} = \begin{pmatrix} -2 \\ 4 \end{pmatrix}$ and $\vec{DC} = 2\vec{AB}$.
   (a) Work out the coordinates of B, D and C.
   (b) What kind of figure is ABCD?

9. Given that $\mathbf{x} = \begin{pmatrix} 7 \\ 24 \end{pmatrix}$ and $\mathbf{y} = \begin{pmatrix} -8 \\ 16 \end{pmatrix}$, find the modulus of each of the following vectors:
   (a) **x**
   (b) **y**
   (c) **x − y**
   (d) **3y − 2x**

10. O is the origin and A is the point (4, 3). In each of the following cases find the coordinates of a point P which satisfies the given condition;
    (a) $\vec{AP} = \begin{pmatrix} 2 \\ 1 \end{pmatrix}$,
    (b) $\vec{OP} = -2\vec{OA}$,
    (c) $\vec{OP} - \vec{OA} = \begin{pmatrix} -1 \\ 2 \end{pmatrix}$,
    (d) $\vec{PA}$ is parallel to the vector $\begin{pmatrix} 0 \\ 1 \end{pmatrix}$ and $|\vec{PA}| = 5$.

11 (a) O is the origin and R, S are points such that $\vec{OR} = \begin{pmatrix} 5 \\ 2 \end{pmatrix}$ and $\vec{OS} = \begin{pmatrix} 8 \\ k \end{pmatrix}$. Find the two possible values of k, given that $\vec{RS}$ makes an angle of 45° with the x-axis.

(b) Given that $\mathbf{p} = \begin{pmatrix} -12 \\ 5 \end{pmatrix}$, find a vector $\mathbf{q}$ which is opposite in direction to $\mathbf{p}$ and of magnitude 65.

12 In the quadrilateral ABCD, BD is an axis of symmetry and the vector $\vec{BD}$ has the same direction as the vector $\begin{pmatrix} 1 \\ 0 \end{pmatrix}$. Also, A is the point (2, 1), $\vec{AB} = \begin{pmatrix} -3 \\ 3 \end{pmatrix}$ and $|\vec{AD}| = 5$.

(a) Work out the coordinates of B, C, D.
(b) State two relationships between the lines BA, BC.
(c) What kind of figure is ABCD?
(d) Work out the coordinates of the point E such that $\vec{AE} = \vec{BC}$. What kind of figure is ABCE?

Vector geometry

Level 3

Note: In these exercises use only vector methods and not the theorems of ordinary geometry.

Exercise 46A

1 (a) Given that the vectors $\vec{AB}$ and $\vec{PQ}$ are equal, state two relationships between the lines AB and PQ.

(b) ABCD is a quadrilateral in which $\vec{AB} = \vec{DC}$. Use the triangle law to prove that $\vec{AD} = \vec{BC}$. What kind of figure is ABCD?

2 (a) Given that $\vec{AB} = k\vec{BC}$, where k is any number, what conclusion can be drawn regarding the points A, B, C?

(b) A, B, C, P, Q are points such that $\vec{PA} - \vec{PB} = \vec{QB} - \vec{QC}$. Prove that B lies on the line AC and bisects this line.

3 PQRS is a quadrilateral in which $\vec{PR} - \vec{PS} = 3\vec{PQ}$. Prove that SR is parallel to PQ and that SR/PQ = 3. What kind of figure is PQRS?

4 O is the origin and A, B, C are points such that $\vec{OA} = \begin{pmatrix} 2 \\ 1 \end{pmatrix}$, $\vec{OB} = \begin{pmatrix} 4 \\ -2 \end{pmatrix}$ and $\vec{OC} = \begin{pmatrix} 12 \\ -14 \end{pmatrix}$. By considering the vectors $\vec{AB}$ and $\vec{BC}$, prove that A, B, C are collinear and find BC/AB.

5   PQR is a triangle in which M, N are the midpoints of PQ, PR, respectively. Letting $\vec{PM} = \mathbf{a}$ and $\vec{PN} = \mathbf{b}$, express $\vec{MN}$ and $\vec{QR}$ in terms of **a** and **b**. Hence obtain two relationships between the lines MN and QR.

6   A is the point (3, 1), $\vec{AB} = \begin{pmatrix} 1 \\ 2 \end{pmatrix}$, $\vec{AC} = \begin{pmatrix} -2 \\ 2 \end{pmatrix}$, $\vec{AP} = -2\vec{AB}$ and $\vec{AQ} = -2\vec{AC}$. Express $\vec{CB}$ and $\vec{PQ}$ as column vectors and state two relationships between the lines PQ and CB.

7   O, A, B, C are points such that $\vec{OA} = \mathbf{a}$, $\vec{OB} = \mathbf{b}$ and $\vec{OC} = 2\mathbf{a} + \mathbf{b}$. Also P is the point such that $\vec{OP} = \frac{1}{3}\vec{OC}$. By expressing $\vec{AB}$ and $\vec{AP}$ in terms of **a** and **b**, show that P lies on the line AB and work out AP/PB.

8   OPQ is a triangle in which M is the midpoint of OP and N is the point on OQ such that ON = 2NQ. Also R is the point such that $\vec{PN} = 2\vec{NR}$.
   (a) Letting $\vec{OP} = \mathbf{p}$ and $\vec{OQ} = \mathbf{q}$, express $\vec{PQ}$, $\vec{MQ}$, $\vec{PN}$, $\vec{PR}$, $\vec{OR}$ and $\vec{MR}$ in terms of **p** and **q**.
   (b) Name two parallelograms which are formed by the points in the figure.

9   OAB is a triangle in which P is the midpoint of OB and Q is the midpoint of AB. Also G is the point on OQ such that $OG = \frac{2}{3}OQ$. By expressing $\vec{AG}$ and $\vec{AP}$ in terms of $\vec{OA}$ and $\vec{OB}$, or otherwise, show that G lies on AP and work out AG/AP. Hence prove that the three medians of a triangle are concurrent. (A median of a triangle is a line joining a vertex to the midpoint of the opposite side.)

10 In the triangle OAB, M is the midpoint of AB and S is the point on OA such that $OS = \frac{3}{4}OA$. Letting $\vec{OA} = \mathbf{a}$ and $\vec{OB} = \mathbf{b}$, P is the point such that $\vec{BP} = \frac{3}{7}\mathbf{a} - \frac{4}{7}\mathbf{b}$.
   (a) Prove that the points O, P and M are collinear and work out OP/PM.
   (b) Prove that B, P and S are collinear and work out BP/PS.
   (c) Given that OPQB is a parallelogram, work out $\vec{OQ}$ in terms of **a** and **b**.

Exercise 46B

1   The lines AB, PQ meet at M, and M is the midpoint of AB and PQ. Let $\vec{MA} = \mathbf{a}$ and $\vec{MP} = \mathbf{p}$.
   (a) Express $\vec{MB}$ and $\vec{MQ}$ in terms of **a** and **p**.
   (b) Use the triangle law to prove that $\vec{AP} = \vec{QB}$. What kind of quadrilateral is APBQ?

2   O, A, B, C are points such that $\vec{OA} = \mathbf{a}$, $\vec{OB} = \mathbf{b}$ and $\vec{OC} = 3\mathbf{a} - 2\mathbf{b}$. By expressing $\vec{AC}$ and $\vec{CB}$ in terms of **a** and **b**, show that A, B, C are collinear and find AC/CB.

3. O is the origin and A, B, C are points such that $\overrightarrow{OA} = \begin{pmatrix} 2 \\ 1 \end{pmatrix}$, $\overrightarrow{OB} = \begin{pmatrix} 2 \\ 6 \end{pmatrix}$ and $\overrightarrow{OC} = \begin{pmatrix} -4 \\ 3 \end{pmatrix}$.
   (a) Prove that $\overrightarrow{CB} = 3\overrightarrow{OA}$.
   (b) Work out $|\overrightarrow{OC}|$ and $|\overrightarrow{AB}|$.
   (c) What kind of quadrilateral is OABC?

4. PQRS is a quadrilateral in which $\overrightarrow{PR} - \overrightarrow{PS} = \overrightarrow{PQ} + 2\overrightarrow{PS}$. Prove that QR is parallel to PS and work out QR/PS.

5. O, A, B are points such that $\overrightarrow{OA} = 6\mathbf{a}$ and $\overrightarrow{OB} = 3\mathbf{b}$. P is the point such that $\overrightarrow{BP} = 3\mathbf{a}$ and Q is the point on AB such that AQ = 2QB.
   (a) Express $\overrightarrow{OP}$, $\overrightarrow{AB}$, $\overrightarrow{AQ}$ and $\overrightarrow{OQ}$ in terms of $\mathbf{a}$ and $\mathbf{b}$.
   (b) Show that O, Q, P are collinear and state the value of OQ/QP.

6. A is the point (0, 2) and P, Q, R, S are points such that
   $\overrightarrow{AP} = \begin{pmatrix} 1 \\ -2 \end{pmatrix}$, $\overrightarrow{AQ} = \begin{pmatrix} 4 \\ 2 \end{pmatrix}$, $\overrightarrow{AR} = -\overrightarrow{AP}$ and $\overrightarrow{AS} = -\overrightarrow{AQ}$. Prove that PQRS is a rhombus.

7. OAB is a triangle in which Q is the midpoint of OA and P, R divide OA in the ratios 1:2 and 2:1, respectively. Also S divides OB in the ratio 2:1.
   (a) Letting $\overrightarrow{OA} = \mathbf{a}$ and $\overrightarrow{OB} = \mathbf{b}$, express $\overrightarrow{AB}$, $\overrightarrow{RS}$, $\overrightarrow{BQ}$ and $\overrightarrow{SP}$ in terms of $\mathbf{a}$ and $\mathbf{b}$. Hence prove that AB is parallel to RS and BQ is parallel to SP.
   (b) T is the point such that $\overrightarrow{OT} = \frac{1}{3}\mathbf{a} + \frac{1}{3}\mathbf{b}$. Prove that T lies on the lines RS and BQ.

8. ABCD is a quadrilateral in which J, K, L, M are the midpoints of AB, BC, CD and DA, respectively. By expressing $\overrightarrow{JK}$ and $\overrightarrow{ML}$ in terms of $\overrightarrow{AC}$, prove that $\overrightarrow{JK} = \overrightarrow{ML}$. What kind of figure is JKLM?

9. OACB is a parallelogram in which M is the midpoint of OB and N is the midpoint of BC. $\overrightarrow{OA} = \mathbf{a}$, $\overrightarrow{OB} = \mathbf{b}$ and P is the point such that $\overrightarrow{AP} = \frac{2}{5}\mathbf{b} - \frac{4}{5}\mathbf{a}$.
   (a) Prove that A, P, M are collinear and work out AP/PM.
   (b) Prove that O, P, N are collinear and work out OP/PN.
   (c) Given that Q is the point such that OAQP is a parallelogram, express $\overrightarrow{NQ}$ in terms of $\mathbf{a}$ and $\mathbf{b}$.

10. O, A, B, P are points such that $\overrightarrow{OA} = \mathbf{a}$, $\overrightarrow{OB} = \mathbf{b}$ and $\overrightarrow{OP} = \frac{1}{4}\mathbf{a} + \frac{3}{4}\mathbf{b}$.
    (a) Prove that A, P, B are collinear and work out AP/PB.

    Q is the point such that $\overrightarrow{OQ} = \frac{5}{4}\mathbf{a} - \frac{1}{4}\mathbf{b}$.
    (b) Prove that Q, A, P are collinear and work out QA/AP.

    R is the point such that $\overrightarrow{RA} = \mathbf{b}$.
    (c) Prove that OPQR is a parallelogram.

GCSE Specimen Papers

All the questions in the papers which follow are taken from the specimen papers issued by the GCSE examining groups. The system used by most of the groups is that Level 2 candidates attempt Papers 2 (see Book A) and 3, while Level 3 candidates attempt Papers 3 and 4. The papers below are assembled in accordance with this system.
   The examining groups are indicated by the following abbreviations:
   LEAG = London and East Anglian Group
   SEG = Southern Examining Group
   MEG = Midland Examining Group
   NEA = Northern Examining Association

Paper 3 (Approximately 2 hours)

1 **a** The attendance at United's last match was 15 374. Write the attendance figure correct to three significant figures.
   b The attendance at City's last match was given as 24 000, correct to the nearest 100. Write down the lowest and highest possible attendances. *(MEG)*

2 The diagram on the left shows a rectangular allotment garden, 30 m by 10 m. It contains a fruit section in the shape of a circle of diameter 8 m. In the rest of the garden vegetables are grown.
   a Taking π to be 3, find the area of the circular fruit section.
   b Find the area of the shaded vegetable section. *(MEG)*

3 The distance of the earth from the sun is 93 million miles. Express this distance in standard form. *(NEA)*

4 The diagram on the left shows a hexagon with just two lines of symmetry. Find the value of x when y is 25°. *(SEG)*

5 The graph of the line with equation $5x + 12y = 60$ cuts the x-axis at A and the y-axis at B.
   a Find the coordinates of A.
   b Find the coordinates of B.
   c Calculate the length of AB. *(MEG)*

6

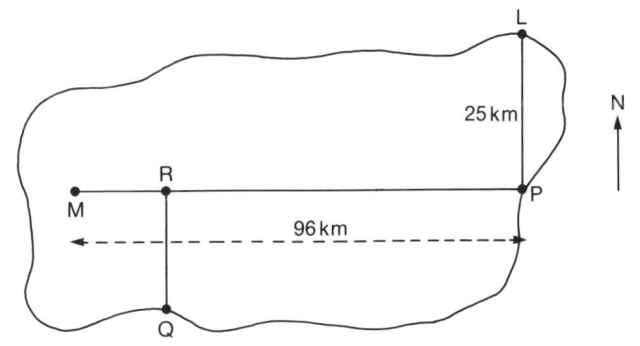

The above diagram is a sketch map of an island. The lighthouse L is 25 km due north of Portpearl (P) and the Mount (M) is 96 km due west of Portpearl.

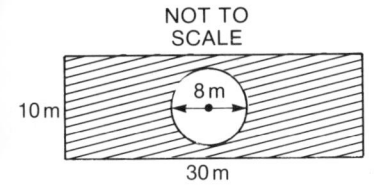

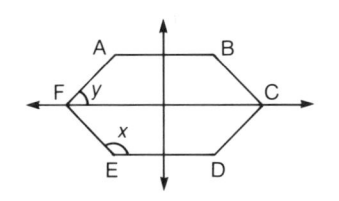

a Calculate, to the nearest kilometre, the distance of the lighthouse from the Mount.
   b Calculate, to the nearest degree, the size of angle LMP and hence find the bearing of L from M.

   The Quay (Q) is 20 km from the Mount on a bearing of 125°. The Rooftop Hotel (R) is due north of the Quay and due east of the Mount.
   c Draw a rough sketch of triangle MRQ and mark on it the length of MQ and the size of each of its angles.
   d Calculate, in kilometres to one decimal place, the distance of the Rooftop Hotel from (i) the Mount, (ii) Portpearl. *(LEAG)*

7 v, u, a and t are related by the formula $v = u + at$.
   a Find v when $u = 60$, $a = -10$ and $t = 4$.
   b Find u when $v = 55$, $a = 4$ and $t = 12$.
   c Express a in terms of v, u and t. *(MEG)*

8 Ravinder's father said he would reward Ravinder if his mean (average) mark for his six examinations was 65 or more. After five examinations Ravinder's average mark was exactly 60. For his seventh examination Ravinder got 84. Find his final mean (average) mark. *(MEG)*

9 Alan, Brian and Charles stake £5 on the football pools each week. Alan pays £1, Brian £1·50 and Charles £2·50. They agree to share any winnings in proportion to their payments. One week they win £375. Find Brian's share of this. *(NEA)*

10 Two bags contain coloured beads.

   Bag A contains 3 blue beads and 1 red bead.
   Bag B contains 3 blue beads and 3 red beads.

   Two draws are made, at random in each case.

   Draw 1—a bead is taken from Bag A and put in Bag B.
   Draw 2—a bead is taken from Bag B.

   Copy the tree diagram on the left and write the appropriate probabilities on the branches. *(NEA)*

11 **a** Express $\dfrac{3^2 \times 3^4}{3^8}$ as a single power of 3.
   b State your answer as a fraction. *(NEA)*

12 Using a scale of 1 cm to 1 unit on each axis, and letting both x and y cover the range -6 to $+6$, draw on graph paper the triangle T whose vertices have coordinates of (1, 1), (5, 1) and (5, 3).
   a A is the image of triangle T after it has been rotated through a half-turn about the origin (0, 0). Draw A and state the coordinates of its vertices.
   b B is the image of triangle T after it has been rotated through a half-turn about the point (3, 0). Draw B and state the coordinates of its vertices.

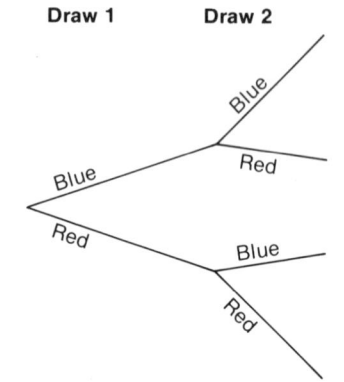

c C is the image of triangle T after it has been reflected in the y-axis. Draw C and state the coordinates of its vertices.
d Describe fully the transformation which maps A onto B.
e Describe fully the transformation which maps A onto C.
(LEAG)

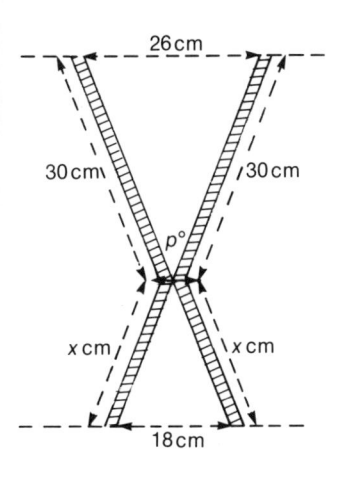

13 The diagram on the left shows the end view of a household newspaper rack.
a Use the information given in the diagram to calculate the size of the angle $p°$, giving the answer correct to the nearest degree.
b Calculate the value of x, giving your answer correct to one decimal place. (NEA)

14 a Given that $y = (x - 1)^2$, copy and complete the following table.

x	−1	−0.5	0	0.5	1	1.5	2	2.5	3
y		2.25	1	0.25		0.25	1		4

b Using a scale of 4 cm to represent 1 unit on each axis, draw the graph of $y = (x - 1)^2$ for values of x from −1 to 3 inclusive.
c By drawing a tangent, estimate the gradient of the graph at the point (2, 1).
d Use your graph to find the values of x for which $(x - 1)^2 = 3$.
(MEG)

15 In her will, Granny leaves all her money to be shared by her three grandchildren. Anne is to have £400 more than Beatrice. Clarissa is to have three times as much as Beatrice.
a If Beatrice receives £x, then Anne receives £(x + 400). Write an expression for the amount Clarissa receives in terms of x.
b Suppose Clarissa receives £300. How much does Anne receive?
c When Granny died, Anne and Clarissa received the same amount of money. How much did Granny leave? (SEG)

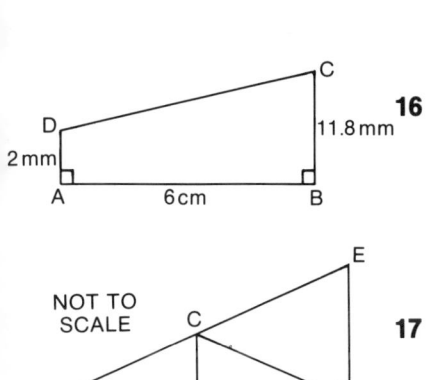

16 The diagram on the left shows the cross-section ABCD of a plastic door wedge.
a Write down, in cm, the length of BC.
b Calculate, in cm², the area of the cross-section ABCD.
c Given that the wedge is of width 3 cm, calculate the volume, in cm³, of plastic required to make (i) 1 wedge, (ii) 1 000 000 wedges. (LEAG)

17 In the diagram on the left, triangle ADE is the image of triangle ABC after an enlargement of scale factor +2, using A as the centre of enlargement. Angles ABC and ADE are right angles.
a Write down the length of AE if AC = 7 cm.
b Write down the size of angle CED if angle ACB = 70°.
c Name an isosceles triangle in the diagram.
d Name two triangles in the diagram which are congruent to each other. (MEG)

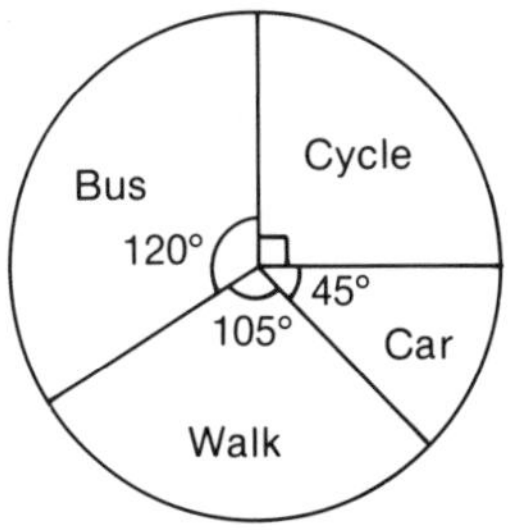

18 The pie chart shows how the 24 pupils in a class travelled to school.
a How many of these pupils came to school by bus?
b What fraction of the class travelled by car? Write your answer as simply as possible. (MEG)

159

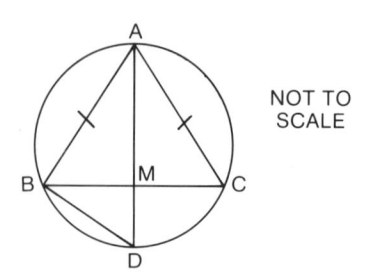

19 In the diagram on the left AB and AC are chords of a circle and AB = AC. The diameter AD meets the chord BC at M, and angle ACM = 62°.
  a (i) Write down the size of angle ABD.
    (ii) Calculate the size of angle DBM.
  b Given that BM = MC = 5 cm, calculate correct to one decimal place
    (i) the length of AM,
    (ii) the length of AB. (MEG)

Paper 4 (Approximately 2½ hours)

1 Factorise completely $3x^2 - 48$. (NEA)

2 a The size of each exterior angle of a regular polygon is $x°$ and the size of each interior angle is $4x°$. Find the value of x and the number of sides of the polygon.
  b AB is a chord of a circle and AC is a diameter. The length of AB is 14 cm and the radius of the circle is 25 cm. Calculate the length of the chord BC. (MEG)

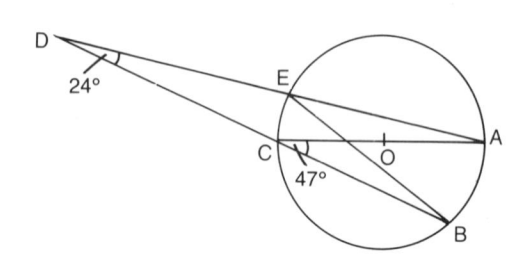

3 In the above diagram, O is the centre of the circle, angle CDE = 24° and angle BCA = 47°. Find
  a angle EAC,
  b angle CBE. (LEAG)

4 a Given that $f(x) = 8^x$, calculate
    (i) $f(\frac{2}{3})$,
    (ii) $f(-\frac{1}{3})$.
  b Find the smallest integer which satisfies the inequality
    $$5x - 7 > 2x + 13$$ (NEA)

5 It is given that $\mathbf{M} = \begin{pmatrix} 3 & 1 \\ 1 & 2 \end{pmatrix}$ and $\mathbf{N} = \begin{pmatrix} 1 & 4 \\ -3 & 2 \end{pmatrix}$.
  a Express $\mathbf{M} + 3\mathbf{N}$ as a single matrix.
  b Express $\mathbf{M}^2$ as a single matrix. (MEG)

6 Frojus are made of frozen fruit juice. They are sold in the shape of a triangular prism which is 11 cm long and whose regular cross-section is an equilateral triangle of side 2·5 cm. Given that the fruit juice used increases in volume by 5% when frozen, calculate the volume of fruit juice required to make one 'Froju'.

(NEA)

7 Jasbir is doing a simple experiment to test the relationship between two quantities m and l. His theory is that m varies as the square of l. He has already found that $m = 18$ when $l = 6$. Assuming that his theory is correct, what value of m should he obtain when $l = 4$? *(LEAG)*

8 As shown on the left the top part of a cone is removed to leave the lower part B. The vertical heights of A and B are equal. If the volume of A is $3·14 \, cm^3$, what is the volume of the whole cone? *(SEG)*

9 A function f(x) is defined as

$$f(x) = x^2 + 5x - 24$$

a Evaluate
  (i) f(−2)
  (ii) f(−3).
b Find the values of x for which
  (i) f(x) = 0,
  (ii) f(x) = −24. *(SEG)*

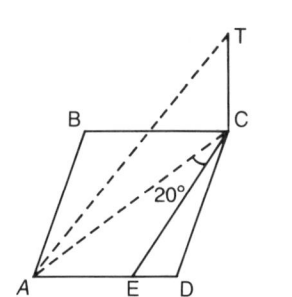

10 The figure on the left shows a vertical flagpole CT, of height 11·2 m, situated at the corner C of a horizontal square plot ABCD. The angle of elevation of the top of the flagpole T from A is 19°.
a Calculate, in metres to one decimal place, the length of AC.
b Show that the length of the side of the square is approximately 23 m.

A point E is marked on AD so that the angle ACE is 20°.
c Find
  (i) the length of EC to two decimal places,
  (ii) the angle of elevation of T from E to the nearest degree.

(LEAG)

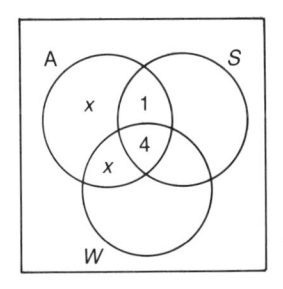

11 Nineteen girls are employed in an office. The Venn diagram shows some details about the numbers who can do audio-typing (A), shorthand-typing (S) and use the word-processor (W). They all have at least one of these skills.
a 11 girls can do audio-typing. Find x.
b If six girls cannot do either method of typing, how many can do shorthand-typing?
c Nobody does only shorthand-typing. Find
  (i) how many can use the word-processor,
  (ii) how many can both use the word-processor and do shorthand-typing.
d Copy the Venn diagram and shade the region $W \cap A' \cap S'$. Give a brief description of this set. *(SEG)*

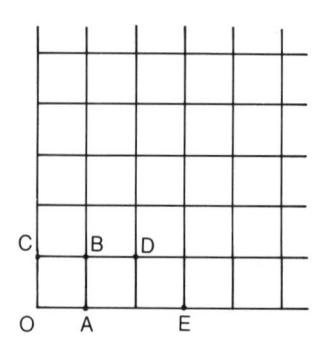

12 In a board game a counter is moved on a rectangular grid according to the score on a die, as in the table below.

Score	Move
1, 3, or 5	One place to right
2 or 4	One place upwards
6	One place to right then one place upwards

The counter starts at O, the bottom left-hand corner of the board. The diagram shows part of the board.
  a Write down the probability that after one throw the counter is at
    (i) A
    (ii) B
    (iii) C
  b Find the probability that after two throws the counter is at D.
  c Find the probability that after three throws the counter is at E.
  (NEA)

13 Given that $T = 2\pi \sqrt{\dfrac{l}{g}}$,

  a estimate the value of T, correct to one significant figure, when $l = 243$ and $g = 981$,
  b express g in terms of T, π and l. *(MEG)*

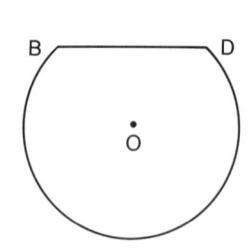

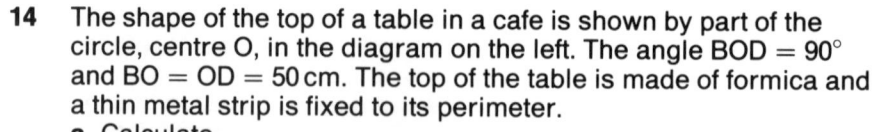

14 The shape of the top of a table in a cafe is shown by part of the circle, centre O, in the diagram on the left. The angle BOD = 90° and BO = OD = 50 cm. The top of the table is made of formica and a thin metal strip is fixed to its perimeter.
  a Calculate
    (i) the length of the metal strip,
    (ii) the area of the formica surface.
  b If the table top is to be cut from a square of formica of area 1 m², what percentage of formica will be wasted? *(SEG)*

15 a Copy and complete the table below for $y = \dfrac{x^2}{4} + \dfrac{4}{x} - 2$.

x	1	1·5	2	2·5	3	3·5	4
$x^2/4$		0·56				3·06	
$4/x$		2·67				1·14	
-2		-2				-2	
y		1·23				2·20	

  b Using a scale of 4 cm to 1 unit on the *y*-axis and 2 cm to 1 unit on the *x*-axis, draw the graph of
  $$y = \frac{x^2}{4} + \frac{4}{x} - 2 \quad \text{for } 1 \leqslant x \leqslant 4$$

  c Using the same axes and scales, draw the graph of $y = \dfrac{x}{4} + 1$.

d Write down the values of x where the two graphs intersect.
e Show that these graphs enable you to find approximate solutions to the equation
$$x^3 - x^2 - 12x + 16 = 0$$
(LEAG)

16 Using a scale of 1 cm to 1 unit on each axis, draw on graph paper the triangle with vertices A(2, 2), B(2, 4) and C(5, 4).
  a Write as a column vector
   (i) the translation from the point B to the point C,
   (ii) the translation from the point B to the point A.
  b Draw on the graph paper the images of the triangle ABC after the transformations determined by
   (i) $P = \begin{pmatrix} -1 & 0 \\ 0 & 1 \end{pmatrix}$ (label the image p)
   (ii) $Q = \begin{pmatrix} 0 & -1 \\ -1 & 0 \end{pmatrix}$ (label the image q)
  c Describe geometrically the single transformation determined by
   (i) **P**,
   (ii) **Q**,
   (iii) the triangle p mapped onto triangle q.
  d If the triangle ABC is transformed by a translation $\begin{pmatrix} 3 \\ -2 \end{pmatrix}$, followed by Q to give a final image of q', describe geometrically the single transformation which will map the triangle q onto the triangle q'. *(SEG)*

17 In the triangle on the left, the point X lies on the side OA of the triangle OAB and $OX = \frac{1}{3}OA$. The vectors **a** and **b** are such that $\overrightarrow{OA} = \mathbf{a}$ and $\overrightarrow{OB} = \mathbf{b}$. The point P is such that $\overrightarrow{OP} = \frac{1}{5}\mathbf{a} + \frac{2}{5}\mathbf{b}$.
  a Express, in terms of **a** and **b**, the vectors
   (i) $\overrightarrow{BX}$
   (ii) $\overrightarrow{BP}$
  b By considering the results of part **a**, or otherwise, show that the line BX passes through P and write down the numerical value of $\frac{BP}{BX}$.
  c Given that the area of triangle OAB is 30 cm², calculate
   (i) the area of triangle ABX,
   (ii) the area of triangle ABP,
   (iii) the area of triangle OPA. *(MEG)*

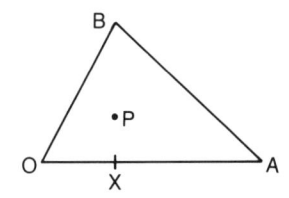

Answers to Exercises

Numerical Topics

Exercise 1A

1 a Odd numbers: 9, 11; **b** Multiples of 4: 20, 24; **c** Square numbers: 25, 36; **d** Powers of 3: 243, 729
2 15, 21, 28 **3 a** 26, 32, 38; **b** 18, 11, 4; **c** −2, 1, 4; **d** 21, $24\frac{1}{2}$, 28 **4 b** 25, 36; **c** Matches 4, 12, 2
40: Extra matches 8, 12, 16; **d** 60, 84 **5** Prime numbers: 13, 17 19, 23 **6 a** 1250, 6250; **b** 25, $-12\frac{1}{2}$;
c 1, 2; **d** 81, $121\frac{1}{2}$ **7 a** 19; **b** 2; **c** 5; **d** 5; **8 a** Rational; **b** Irrational; **c** Irrational; **d** Rational;
e Rational **9 a** 11, 17, 28; **b** 3, 8, 13, 21; **c** 3, 4; **d** 6, 10, 16 **10 a** 3; **b** 6; **c** 10;
d 1, 3, 6, 10, 15, 21; **e** Triangular numbers **11 a** 17, 23; **b** 26, 37; **c** 24, 25; **d** 35, 51; **e** 34, 25;
f 14, 12 **12** 13, 84, 10, 19

Exercise 1B

1 a Even numbers; 10, 12; **b** Multiples of 5; 25, 30; **c** Powers of 2; 32, 64; **d** Perfect cubes; 125, 216
2 1, 9, 25, 49, 81; 8, 16, 24, 32; multiples of 8 **3 b** 7, 9, 11; **c** 22, 28, 34 **4 a** 11; **b** 3; **c** 12 **5 a** 33
40; **b** 24, 13; **c** −1, −4; **d** $-\frac{1}{2}$, 2 **6 a** 112, 224; **b** $\frac{16}{81}, \frac{32}{243}$; **c** $-10\frac{1}{2}, 5\frac{1}{4}$; **d** 108, 648; **e** 81, $60\frac{3}{4}$
7 a Rational; **b** Rational; **c** Irrational; **d** Irrational; **e** Rational; **f** Rational
8 a 1, 4, 6, 4, 1; 1, 5, 10, 10, 5, 1; 1, 6, 15, 20, 15, 6, 1; **b** Powers of 2; **c** 256 **9 b** 1, 4, 9, 16; square
numbers; **c** 36; **d** 4, 10, 18, 28; **e** 40, 54, 70 **10 a** 18, 29; **b** 32, 256; **c** 2, 0 **11 a** 19, 25; **b** 50,
72; **c** 0, −10; **d** 36, 68 **12** 11, 22, 110 **13 a** 2, 6, 12, 20; **b** 30, 42; **c** Each number is twice the
corresponding triangular number

Exercise 2

1 a $\frac{1}{10}$; **b** $\frac{43}{100}$; **c** $\frac{1}{4}$; **d** $\frac{3}{50}$; **e** $\frac{1}{3}$; **f** $\frac{1}{20}$; **g** $\frac{19}{20}$; **h** $\frac{7}{25}$; **i** $\frac{2}{5}$; **j** $\frac{13}{20}$; **k** $\frac{1}{40}$; **l** $\frac{21}{25}$; **m** $\frac{1}{8}$; **n** $\frac{29}{50}$; **o** $\frac{1}{12}$; **p** $\frac{3}{8}$;
q $\frac{9}{40}$ **2 a** 70%; **b** 30%; **c** 80%; **d** 74%; **e** 26%; **f** 57·1%; **g** 8%; **h** $66\frac{2}{3}$%; **i** 44%; **j** 25·3%;
k 30·8%; **l** $14\frac{1}{2}$%; **m** $87\frac{1}{2}$%; **n** 0·29%; **o** 93·0% **3 a** 11; **b** 35p; **c** £1·47; **d** 3570; **e** 9p;
f 190 000; **g** £1·26; **h** £232·87; **i** 20; **j** 6·4 **4 a** 403; **b** £6·46; **c** 14; **d** £943·02; **e** £2070; **f** 494;
g £27·14; **h** £3·77; **i** £8601 **5 a** 30%; **b** 14%; **c** 20%; **d** 8·3%; **e** 16·2%; **f** 46·9% **6 a** £48;
b £2·50; **c** £560; **d** £12 200; **e** 80p; **f** £5·25

Exercise 3A

1 a 9; **b** 8 **2 a** £4500; **b** £3600; **c** 40% **3 a** 40%; **b** 27 **4 a** £40; **b** £46 **5 a** £756;
b £219·24; **c** £536·76 **6 a** 69·8%; **b** 18 090 **7 a** £110·40; **b** £35·64; **c** £146·04 **8 a** 21%;
b 1·6% **9 a** 19; **b** 48p **10 a** £5·10; **b** £23·80; **c** £308·90; **d** £44·40; **e** £3·60 **11 a** £26·03;
b £440; **c** £7·60 **12 a** £2840; **b** £14 200 **13 a** 40 min; **b** 75p

Exercise 3B

1 a 20%; **b** 6 min **2 a** 24; **b** 125 **3 a** £26·41; **b** £45·15 **4 a** 369; **b** 311; **c** 370 **5 a** 40%;
b £35 000; **c** £15 000; **d** 75% **6** £8747·20 **7 a** £4·50; **b** £8·55; **c** 52·6% **8 a** 25%; **b** 15%;
c 50%; **d** 45% **9 a** £1250; **b** £230; **c** 2·9% **10 a** £8·75, £25, £3·75, £28·75; **b** 30%; **c** £31·11;
d 8% **11 a** £4032; **b** £12 000 **12 a** £48 200; **b** £9·50 **13 a** £960; **b** £48 000

Exercise 4A

1 a 5·34; **b** 0·82; **c** 12·08; **d** 1·30 **2 a** 9·2; **b** 17·3; **c** 0·8; **d** 8·7 **3 a** 850; **b** 0·032; **c** 1100;
d 0·60; **e** 150 000 **4 a** 6·23; **b** 12 500; **c** 0·005 01; **d** 20·1; **e** 6300 **5 a** 500; **b** 0·0006;

c 30 000 000   **6**   **a** 215 000;   **b** 210 000;   **c** 215 000   **7**   **a** 333 m²;   **b** 332·53 m²;   **c** 333 m²   **8**   **a** 525;
b 534   **9**   **a** £150, £61, £120;   **b** £330;   **c** £320;   **d** £320   **10**   **a** 3·873 m;   **b** 3·9 m   **11**   **a** 122·0 miles;
b 122 miles;   **c** 100 miles   **12**   82·86 g   **13**   **a** 0·051 mm;   **b** 0·0509 mm

Exercise 4B

1   **a** 0·6;   **b** 12·3;   **c** 5·6;   **d** 28·5   **2**   **a** 4·85;   **b** 0·90;   **c** 17·36;   **d** 2·33   **3**   **a** 29;   **b** 160;   **c** 12 000;
d 0·0053;   **e** 650 000   **4**   **a** 12·46;   **b** 0·4021;   **c** 160·1;   **d** 0·040 72;   **e** 54 240 000   **5**   **a** 12 700 km;
b 13 000 km;   **c** 13 000 km   **6**   **a** 11 350;   **b** 11 449   **7**   **a** 0·0264 g;   **b** 0·026 g;   **c** 0·026 g   **8**   **a** 0·654 m;
b 0·7 m;   **c** 0·7 m   **9**   **a** 5;   **b** 3;   **c** 2   **10**   **a** 3·142;   **b** 3·1416;   **c** 3·141 59   **11**   328·57 ml
12   **a** 4·30 cm;   **b** 4·3014 cm

Exercise 5A

1   80   **2**   12   **3**   0·5   **4**   4   **5**   0·5   **6**   4   **7**   7   **8**   9   **9**   11 cm   **10**   **a** 44 g;   **b** 23   **11**   250 g
12   **a** 0·05 mm;   **b** 4 mm   **13**   **a** 560 km;   **b** 150 miles   **14** $2\frac{1}{2}$ m

Exercise 5B

1   20   **2**   0·2   **3**   0·0004   **4**   1·5   **5**   11   **6**   0·1   **7**   0·2   **8**   0·06   **9**   **a** 380 cm;   **b** 1·4 g;
c 1000 cl   **10**   17 t   **11**   **a** 6 feet 6 inches;   **b** 13 feet;   **c** 26 feet   **12**   **a** 1300 g;   **b** 12   **13**   **a** 164 l;
b 36 gallons   **14**   **a** 630 m;   **b** 8

Exercise 6A

1   **a** 3:4;   **b** 2:3:5;   **c** 3:7;   **d** 5:3:9;   **e** 2:1;   **f** 2:3:4;   **g** 7:9;   **h** 9:2:6;   **i** 3:7;   **j** 2:5   **k** 5:4;   **l** 7:10;   **m** 4:3
2   **a** 39 min;   **b** 52 min;   **c** 10 h;   **d** 30 h   **3**   **a** 4·8 km;   **b** 1·28 km;   **c** 17·5 cm   **4**   **a** 4·95 m;   **b** 120 cm
5   **a** 3, 9;   **b** 15, 10;   **c** 12, 9;   **d** 4, 8, 20;   **e** 14, 7, 21;   **f** 40, 24, 16;   **g** £2·40, £2·80;   **h** £4·10, £14·35
6   £8000, £10 000, £12 000   **7**   **a** 75 kg;   **b** 24 kg   **8**   **a** 15, 10, 20;   **b** 12, 11, 22   **9**   **a** 20, 80, 120;   **b** 5·5,
11, 22, 27·5;   **c** 2, 6, 18, 40;   **d** 4·5, 18, 27, 54   **10**   **a** 2·25 amps;   **b** 120 volts   **11**   **a** 2·6 cm, 3·6 cm;
b 3·3 cm;   **c** 625 g   **12**   **a** 10, 7·5;   **b** 12, 6, 4;   **c** 36, 9, 4;   **d** 2·75, 2·2, 1·1   **13**   **a** 36 min;   **b** 3 h 36 min;
c 1 h 48 min   **14**   **a** $5\frac{1}{2}$ h;   **b** 129 km h⁻¹   **15**   **a** 47%;   **b** 27

Exercise 6B

1   **a** 5:4;   **b** 2:3:5;   **c** 5:7;   **d** 5:3:14;   **e** 7:3:5;   **f** 4:11;   **g** 2:3:4;   **h** 5:3;   **i** 5:8;   **j** 9:16;   **k** 4:3   **2**   **a** $17\frac{1}{2}$
buckets;   **b** 96·25 litres   **3**   **a** 310 miles;   **b** 6·4 inches;   **c** 360 miles   **4**   **a** 2:15;   **b** 63·75 cm;
c 24 cm 8 mm   **5**   **a** 10, 4;   **b** 36, 9;   **c** 9, 27, 36;   **d** 20, 15;   **e** 45 cm, 30 cm, 75 cm;   **f** £1·04, £4·68;   **g** 1,
0·5, 3;   **h** £3·44, £5·16   **6**   70 km   **7** $16\frac{1}{2}$ miles   **8**   112   **9**   **a** 22 750;   **b** 300, 100, 200, 50   **10**   **a** 30, 75,
150;   **b** 2, 4, 20;   **c** 3, 7, 15;   **d** 17·5, 23·75, 41·25   **11**   **a** 540;   **b** 35   **12**   **a** 6, 3;   **b** 60, 40, 30;   **c** 30, 10,
6;   **d** 28, 40, 60   **13**   **a** 95;   **b** 855   **14**   **a** Neither;   **b** Inverse;   **c** Direct;   **d** Inverse;   **e** Neither;
f Direct   **15**   **a** 0·57 amps, 0·67 amps;   **b** 0·45 amps;   **c** 59 ohms

Exercise 7A

1   **a** £1275;   **b** £3900;   **c** 14 weeks;   **d** 29 weeks   **2**   **a** 1·35 km;   **b** 7·2 km;   **c** 6 min 20 s;
d 33 min 20 s   **3**   **a** 37;   **b** 211   **4**   **a** 36 m s⁻¹;   **b** 46 min   **5**   **a** 27 700;   **b** 132 days   **6**   **a** 65 words per
minute;   **b** 975;   **c** 24 min   **7**   **a** 25 853;   **b** £3·96   **8**   **a** 30 mph;   **b** $3\frac{1}{2}$ h;   **c** 22 mph   **9**   **a** 60;   **b** 5100;
c 18   **10**   62 miles   **11**   **a** 270;   **b** 15 h;   **c** 18 articles per hour   **12**   **a** 3 h;   **b** $25\frac{1}{2}$ km;   **c** 12 km h⁻¹

Exercise 7B

1   **a** 40;   **b** 9 min;   **c** 4 min   **2**   **a** 90 km h⁻¹;   **b** 25 m s⁻¹;   **c** 160 m;   **d** 307·5 km   **3**   **a** 9·4;   **b** 13
4   **a** 18 720 m;   **b** 18·72 km h⁻¹;   **c** 17·16 km   **5**   **a** 2·4 dollars per pound;   **b** 1032 dollars;   **c** £208·33

6 a 360 m; b 9 m s^{-1}; c 14 m s^{-1} **7** a £42; b Winter, upper gallery; c Lower gallery
8 7·6 litres per second **9** 2:1 **10** a 1400; b 3 weeks and 3 days; c £89·60; d 20 h

Exercise 8A

1 a 37 kg; b 18 lb; c 29 kg; d 48 lb **2** a 72 days; b 27 **3** a 20 min, 15 min; b 25 miles;
c 75 mph; d 16·20; e 50 mph; f 2 h 45 min **4** a 38 francs; b £2·10
5 a 44 miles per gallon, 45 mph; b 22 mph, 66 mph **6** a Line A: car, 60 km h^{-1};
line B: cyclist, 30 km h^{-1}; line C: runner, 18 km h^{-1}; b 27 min; c 7 km; d 32 min, 16 km **7** a £53;
b 90 miles; c £30; d 20p; e 100 miles **8** a 320 g; b 580; c 30 g **9** a Denise, 30 min;
b 3·21 p.m.; c 45 min; d 5 km; e 50 km h^{-1}; f 5 km h^{-1}

Exercise 8B

1 a 7 h; b 22°C; c −3°C; d 12·40 a.m., 7·20 a.m.; e 48 min; f 8°C **2** a 3·2 km; b 8 min;
c 4·43 p.m.; d 15 min; e 8 km h^{-1}; f 9·6 km h^{-1} **3** a 180; b £160; c 60 **4** a 53 kroner;
b 33 marks **5** a 1180, 260 min; b 120 min, 510 min; c 350; d 160 min **6** a 16·40; b 60 km h^{-1};
c 1 h; d 14·48, 15·28 **7** a £6·40; b 24; c £1·60; d 30p; e 7; f £3·60 **8** a 20 s; b 27 s;
c 12 m s^{-1}; d 40 m s^{-1}; e 340 m; f 240 m **9** a (vi); b (iv); c (iii); d (v); e (i); f (ii)

Exercise 9A

1 a 9; b $\frac{1}{9}$; c 8; d $\frac{1}{8}$; e 625; f $\frac{1}{625}$; g $\frac{1}{49}$; h $\frac{1}{32}$; i $\frac{1}{216}$ **2** a 16; b 81; c $1\frac{1}{2}$; d $\frac{4}{5}$; e $2\frac{1}{4}$
3 a 4; b 25; c 400; d $1\frac{1}{9}$; e 625 **4** a 42·3; b 70·8; c 62 000; d 4·6; e 0·0297; f 5; g 0·07;
h 0·0049; i 0·064 23; j 0·000 037 **5** a Move the decimal point n places to the right; b Move the
decimal point n places to the left **6** a 8·57 × 10^2; b 2·4 × 10^{-1}; c 5·41 × 10^{-4}; d 2·36 × 10^5;
e 7·2 × 10^7; f 9 × 10^{-6} **7** a 3 × 10^{-3}; b 1·04 × 10^6; c 4·9 × 10^{-3}; d 2·3 × 10^{-2}; e 2 × 10^3;
f 5 × 10^{-5}; g 2·5 × 10^2 **8** a 2^8; b 2^{12}; c 2^{x+y}; d 2^7; e 2^{-5}; f 2^{x-y}; g 2^8; h 2^{-6} **9** a 5^3; b 5^{-2}
c 5^{-5}; d 5^{-6x} **10** a 3^6; b 3^{20}; c 3^{xy}; d 3^8; e 3^{15}; f 3^{18}; g 3^6; h 3^{-11}

Exercise 9B

1 a 49; b $\frac{1}{49}$; c $\frac{1}{64}$; d $\frac{1}{1000}$; e $\frac{1}{81}$ **2** a 9; b 16; c $2\frac{1}{2}$; d $\frac{9}{11}$; e $1\frac{7}{9}$ **3** a 10; b 16; c $1\frac{2}{3}$; d 2500
e 8000 **4** a 27; b 6·9; c 58 000; d 0·3; e 8·2; f 0·000 72 **5** a 9·65 × 10^3; b 5·3 × 10^{-2};
c 2·5 × 10^5; d 2 × 10^{-5}; e 4·684 × 10^6 **6** a 6 × 10^{-5}; b 8 × 10^2; c 2·8 × 10^7; d 3 × 10^{-3};
e 4 × 10^{-6}; f 6 × 10^3 **7** a 3^{13}; b 3^2; c 3^{7x}; d 3^{5a}; e 3^4; f 3^{-9} **8** a 7^4; b 7^{-2}; c 7^{-11}; d 7^{2x}
9 a 2^8; b 2^{5x}; c 2^9; d 2^{14}; e 2^{15}; f 2^{24}; g 2^{14}; h 2^{-15}

Exercise 10A

1 1 **2** 3 **3** $\frac{1}{2}$ **4** 2 **5** 5 **6** 9 **7** 8 **8** $\frac{1}{6}$ **9** $\frac{1}{27}$ **10** $\frac{1}{49}$ **11** 27 **12** $\frac{2}{3}$ **13** 1 **14** 4
15 32 **16** $\frac{3}{10}$ **17** $\frac{1}{4}$ **18** $2\frac{1}{3}$ **19** $\frac{1}{125}$ **20** $\frac{16}{81}$ **21** −8 **22** $1\frac{1}{2}$ **23** a 1; b $\frac{1}{9}$; c $\frac{1}{3}$; d 243
24 a $\frac{1}{2}$; b 3; c $1\frac{2}{3}$ **25** a $-\frac{1}{2}$; b 49; c $\frac{5}{6}$ **26** 81 **27** 2 **28** 25 **29** 8 **30** a 16 million;
b 25 million; c 1 July 1980

Exercise 10B

1 7 **2** 11 **3** 1 **4** 3 **5** 4 **6** 4 **7** 125 **8** $\frac{1}{10}$ **9** 12 **10** 1 **11** $\frac{1}{16}$ **12** $15\frac{5}{8}$ **13** 32
14 $2\frac{14}{25}$ **15** 256 **16** $\frac{5}{11}$ **17** $3\frac{1}{3}$ **18** 216 **19** 4 **20** $4\frac{1}{2}$ **21** a 1; b 4; c $\frac{1}{2}$; d 8 **22** a 1;
b $\frac{1}{27}$; c 125 **23** a $2\frac{1}{2}$; b 1000; c $-\frac{1}{3}$ **24** 64 **25** $\frac{1}{3}$ **26** 81 **27** 2 **28** a 40 m s^{-1}; b 20 m s^{-1},
10 m s^{-1}, 5 m s^{-1}; c 5 m s^{-1}; d $t = 0.5$ s

Set Theory

Exercise 11A

1 a Natural numbers below 10; **b** Numbers which are both odd and multiples of 3; **c** Numbers which are either odd or multiples of 3; **d** Even numbers and zero; **e** Numbers which are neither odd nor multiples of 3 **2 a** Jo, Hanif; **b** Jason, Carol, Alvin; **c** Jason, Carol, Alvin, Jo, Hanif, Megan, Alan; **d** Jason, Carol, Alvin, Ramiz, Jaya; **e** Ramiz, Jaya; **f** Megan, Alan; **g** Jason, Carol, Alvin, Jo, Hanif, Ramiz, Jaya **3 a** 8; **b** 6; **c** 1; **d** 5; **e** 3 **4 a** Students who like neither strawberries nor blackberries, $(S \cup B)'$ or $S' \cap B'$; **b** Students who do not like strawberries, S'; **c** Students who like strawberries but do not like blackberries, $S \cap B'$ **5 a** False; **b** True; **c** False; **d** True; **e** True; **f** False; **g** True; **h** True; **i** False; **j** True **6 a** {3, 5, 8, 10, 12}; **b** {7, 11}; **c** {3, 4, 5, 6, 7, 9, 11}; **d** {3, 5}; **e** {4, 6, 7, 8, 9, 10, 11, 12}
7 [diagram] **a** True; **b** True; **c** False; **d** True; **e** False; **f** True; **g** True; **h** False
8 [diagram] **a** The set is empty; **b** The set contains all the members of staff; **c** The set contains all the members of staff; **d** The set is empty **9 a** All the people with ginger hair are over 6 feet; **b** There are no blue-eyed people with ginger hair; **c** There are eight people who are either blue-eyed or over 6 feet; **d** There are three people who have ginger hair and do not have blue eyes; **e** None of the ginger-haired people who are over 6 feet have blue eyes **10 a** b, c, d, e; **b** a, e, f; **c** d; **d** a; **e** b; **f** f; **g** a; **h** a, b, c, d, f **11 a** False; **b** True; **c** False; **d** False; **e** True; **f** True

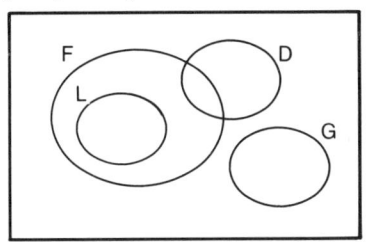

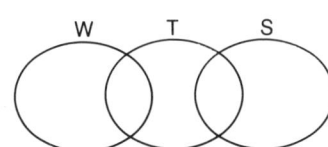

Exercise 11B

1 a {c, f, j}; **b** {a, b, c, d, f, g, h, j} **2 a** Even multiples of 5; **b** Numbers which are either even or multiples of 5; **c** Odd numbers and zero; **d** Odd multiples of 5 **3 a** A, E; **b** A, C, D, E, F; **c** B, D, G; **d** B, G; **e** C, F; **f** B, C, D, F, G **4 a** 11; **b** 4; **c** 5; **d** 2; **e** 8; **f** 4; **g** 7 **5 a** People who do not like hockey, H'; **b** People who like snooker but not hockey, $(S \cap H')$; **c** People who do not like both snooker and hockey, $(S \cap H)'$ **6 a** No students both listened to the radio and played records; **b** 15 students either watched television or played records; **c** All the students who listened to the radio watched television; **d** Three students neither watched television nor played records; **e** Seven students watched television but neither listened to the radio nor played records **7 a** {3, 5}; **b** {2, 3, 4, 5, 6, 7, 10}; **c** {3, 5, 6}; **d** {2, 3, 5, 6, 7} **8 a** False; **b** True; **c** True; **d** True; **e** False; **f** True; **g** True
9 a [diagram] **b** [diagram] **c** [diagram]

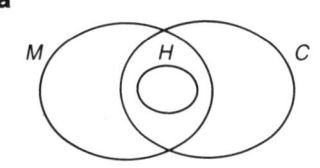

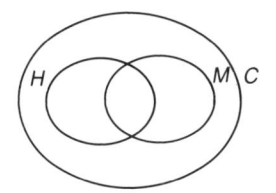

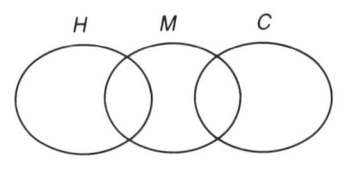

10 a x; **b** u, v, w, x, y, z; **c** x, y; **d** t, y; **e** s, z; **f** u, x, y

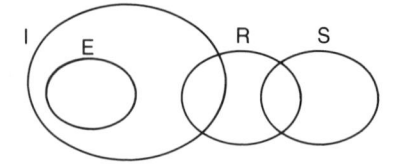

11
a True; **b** False; **c** False; **d** False; **e** True; **f** True; **g** True

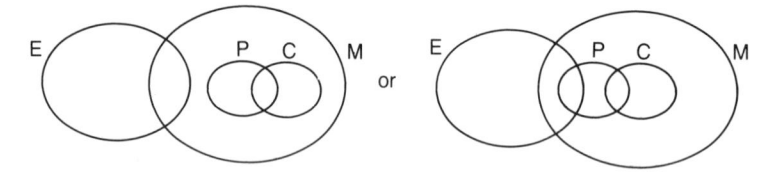

Exercise 12A

1 a 12; **b** 13; **c** 7; **d** 6; **e** 18; **f** 11; **g** 11; **h** 17   **2 a** 23; **b** 15; **c** 70; **d** 34; **e** 18, 22   **3** 2
4 16, 13   **5 a** 14; **b** 24; **c** 50   **6** 19, 14   **7 a** 26; **b** 12; **c** 4; **d** 3; **e** 9; **f** 27; **g** 46
8 'La Meridiana'   'The Punjabi Palace'   **a** 5; **b** 19; **c** 14   **9 a** 12; **b** 8   **10 a** 6; **b** 9; **c** 4; **d** 17; **e** 11

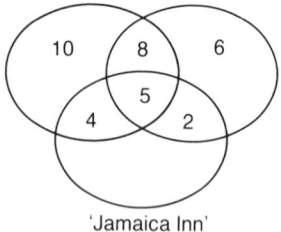

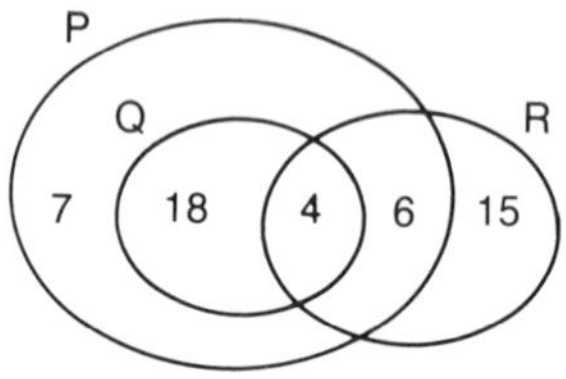

12 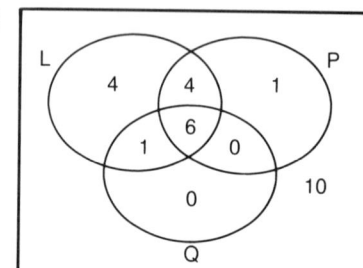 a 7; **b** 4; **c** 22

Exercise 12B

1 a 36; **b** 278; **c** 135; **d** 377; **e** 74; **f** 316   **2 a** 15; **b** 44, 8; **c** 42; **d** 38, 18, 38; **e** 6   **3** 8
4 20, 13   **5 a** 53%; **b** 45%   **6** 11   **7 a** 27; **b** 13; **c** 4; **d** 11; **e** 7; **f** 19; **g** 14
8

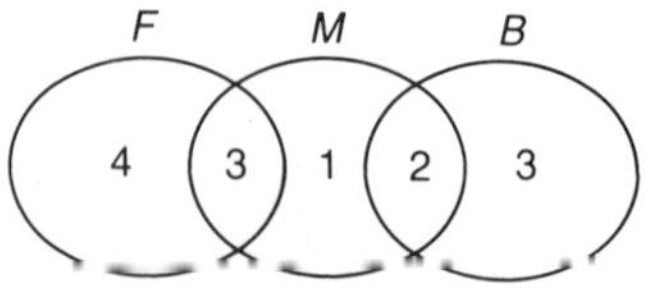

9 a 10%; **b** 80%; **c** 40%; **d** 85%

10

A diagram with sets A, B, C: 10, 4, 8 (in C), 13; 25 outside.

11

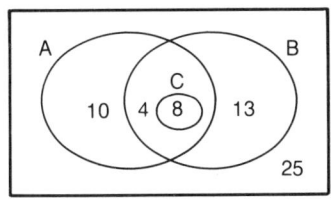

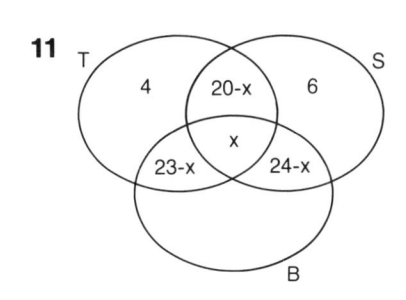

Venn diagram with sets T, S, B: 4, 20−x, 6, x, 23−x, 24−x.

a 15; **b** 35; **c** 7
12 a 25%; **b** 30%; **c** 8%

Statistics

Exercise 13A

1 126°, 108°, 72°, 54° **2** 2, 1, 1⅓ **3 a** Median; **b** Mean; **c** Mode **4 a** Frequencies are 8, 4, 2, 1; **c** 90°, 144°, 72°, 36°, 18°; **d** 365; **e** 292 **5 a** −1, ½, 1½, 11; **b** 41, 35, 37, 50 **6 a** 24; **b** 56; **c** 10; **d** 105°; **e** 12 **7 a** 0; **b** 1; **c** 25; **d** 24; **e** 0·96 **8 a** 0, 1, 1·2; **b** 1, −1, −1·2; **c** 2, 2·5, 2·7 **9 a** 3 kg; **b** 26–28 kg; **d** 27·1 kg **10 a** 94; **b** 33 **11 a** Frequencies are 2, 5, 9, 8, 6; **b** 4, 73–76; **d** 76·0, 76·1 **12 a** Frequencies are 5, 8, 6, 4, 2; **c** 17·6 cm; **d** 4800 **13 a** 3, 9, 17, 27, 36, 40; **b** 28, 35, 40, 37, 29, 18 **14 a** £105, £91, £123; **b** £16; **c** 22 **15 a** 12·5 min, 10·1 min, 16·5 min; **b** 3·2 min; **c** 370 **16 b** 13·2°C

Exercise 13B

1 147°, 105°, 84°, 24° **2** 11, 10, 10·3 **3 a** 10, 8, 7, 3, 2; **c** 120°, 96°, 84° 36°, 24°; **d** 288; **e** 25 **4 a** Mode; **b** Mean; **c** Mode; **d** Mean **5 a** 7, 5, 6, 20; **b** 6, 2, 1·1, 16 **6 a** 10; **b** 8; **c** 22; **d** 54°; **e** 14 **7 a** 3; **b** 4; **c** 3·78; **d** 3, 3, 3·65 **8 a** −4, −3, −2·4; **b** 15, 17·5, 19·5; **c** 15 **9 a** 6 lb; **b** 122–126 lb; **d** 123·3 lb **10 a** 33·4; **b** Mode = 3, median = 4 **11 a** 3, 4, 5, 2, 1, 2; **b** £6; **c** The classes are too wide and thus contain too few items; also the set of 17 values is somewhat too small and too dispersed to justify division into classes **12 b** 4600; **c** 310 **13 a** 3; **b** 4; **c** 10; **d** 6 **14 a** 49, 41, 58; **b** 8·5; **c** 148 **15 a** 67 miles, 42 miles, 90 miles; **b** 24 miles; **c** 44 **16 b** 10·3 s

Probability

Exercise 14A

1 a $\frac{1}{2}$; **b** $\frac{1}{3}$; **c** $\frac{1}{4}$; **d** $\frac{4}{9}$ **2 a** $\frac{4}{25}$; **b** $\frac{9}{25}$; **c** $\frac{3}{8}$; **d** $\frac{9}{40}$ **3 a** $\frac{1}{4}$; **b** $\frac{1}{2}$ **4 a** 0·7; **b** 0·027; **c** 0·147 **5 a** $\frac{1}{5}$; **b** $\frac{2}{5}$; **c** $\frac{4}{15}$ **6 a** $\frac{3}{4}$; **b** $\frac{9}{28}$; **c** $\frac{1}{7}$ **7 a** 35; **b** 50 **8 a** $\frac{3}{20}$; **b** $\frac{1}{4}$; **c** $\frac{27}{40}$; **d** $\frac{1}{5}$ **9 a** $\frac{3}{5}$; **b** $\frac{1}{5}$; **c** 300 000 **10 a** $\frac{1}{7}$; **b** $\frac{5}{7}$; **c** $\frac{6}{7}$ **11 a** $\frac{4}{9}$; **b** $\frac{1}{9}$; **c** $\frac{1}{18}$; **d** $\frac{1}{6}$ **12 a** $\frac{2}{5}$; **b** $\frac{1}{5}$; **c** $\frac{2}{7}$ **13 a** $\frac{6}{7}$; **b** $\frac{30}{49}$ **14 a** 8; **b** $\frac{3}{8}$; **c** $\frac{1}{4}$ **15** $\frac{1}{16}$, $\frac{15}{16}$ **16 a** $\frac{8}{27}$; **b** $\frac{19}{27}$ **17 a** x^2; **b** $(1-x)^2$; **c** $1-x^2$ **18 a** $\frac{1}{3}$; **b** $\frac{1}{3}$; **c** $\frac{1}{9}$; **d** The game is fair because the two players have the same probability of winning

Exercise 14B

1 a $\frac{1}{2}$; **b** $\frac{1}{4}$; **c** $\frac{1}{12}$ **2 a** $\frac{1}{7}$; **b** $\frac{5}{7}$ **3 a** $\frac{3}{8}$; **b** $\frac{13}{45}$; **c** $\frac{13}{120}$ **4 a** 0·4; **b** 0·216; **c** 0·144 **5 a** $\frac{9}{100}$; **b** $\frac{6}{25}$; **c** $\frac{16}{25}$ **6 a** 36; **b** $\frac{1}{6}$; **c** $\frac{2}{9}$; **d** $\frac{3}{4}$ **7 a** 500 000; **b** 20 000; **c** 320 000 **8 a** $\frac{1}{11}$; **b** $\frac{2}{11}$; **c** $\frac{3}{11}$; **d** $\frac{8}{11}$ **9 a** 27; **b** 24 **10 a** $\frac{8}{27}$; **b** $\frac{19}{27}$ **11 a** $\frac{7}{8}$; **b** $\frac{11}{36}$ **12 a** 0·49; **b** 0·09; **c** 0·42 **13 a** $\frac{1}{6}$; **b** $\frac{1}{12}$ **14 a** $\frac{1}{2}$; **b** $\frac{1}{6}$; **c** $\frac{1}{4}$; **d** $\frac{1}{6}$ **15 a** $x^2(1-x)$; **b** $(1-x)^3$; **c** $1-x^3$ **16** The game is fair because each player's probability of winning is $\frac{1}{4}$

Exercise 15A

1 a $\frac{1}{11}$; b $\frac{3}{44}$; c $\frac{8}{33}$; d $\frac{17}{22}$ 2 a $\frac{18}{35}$; b $\frac{3}{7}$ 3 a $\frac{1}{20}$; b $\frac{3}{10}$; c $\frac{1}{10}$ 4 $\frac{17}{20}$ 5 a $\frac{3}{5}$; b $\frac{14}{25}$; c $\frac{19}{25}$; d $\frac{7}{75}$; e $\frac{1}{20}$ 6 a $\frac{3}{10}$; b $\frac{13}{30}$ 7 a 0·59; b 0·41; c 0·49; d 0·55; e 6 8 a 0·64; b 0·48 9 a $\frac{1}{6}$; b $\frac{1}{1}$ c $\frac{1}{6}$; d $\frac{11}{18}$ 10 $\frac{2}{5}$ 11 a $\frac{21}{32}$; b $\frac{17}{32}$; c $\frac{3}{8}$ 12 a $\frac{13}{36}$; b yes; on average a player wins about £1·81 per game, which is more than the fee for playing the game

Exercise 15B

1 a $\frac{2}{7}$; b $\frac{20}{77}$; c $\frac{5}{7}$; d $\frac{40}{77}$ 2 $\frac{1}{2}$ 3 a $\frac{8}{15}$; b $\frac{1}{3}$ 4 the procedure is unfair since Joe has a winning probability of $\frac{1}{2}$ while his brothers have winning probabilities of $\frac{1}{4}$ 5 $\frac{1}{21}$ 6 a $\frac{11}{32}$; b $\frac{1}{8}$; c $\frac{5}{8}$ 7 a $\frac{12}{14}$ b $\frac{23}{144}$; c $\frac{11}{72}$; d 0·21 8 Sylvester's suggested procedure is unfair; Melissa's is fair since each person has a winning probability of $\frac{1}{3}$ 9 a 0·92; b 0·76; c 0·57; d 0·38 e 0·22; f 5 10 $\frac{2}{3}$ 11 a $\frac{3}{20}$; b $\frac{1}{5}$ 12 a $\frac{4}{25}$; b $\frac{12}{25}$; c $\frac{108}{625}$

Algebra

Exercise 16A

1 a 30; b 50; c 5; d 6; e 45; f −12; g −$\frac{1}{2}$; h −$\frac{1}{3}$ 2 a 4; b −27; c 36; d 9; e −25; f −8; g −2; h −$\frac{2}{3}$ 3 a $3x - 2$; b $s - 7y + 3$; c $3abc - 4ab + 4bc$; d $2x - 5x^3$; e $p^3 - p^2$ 4 a $5x - 20y$; b $-a + 2b - c$; c $-24 + 12y + 28w$; d $3t^2 + 2st - t^3$; e $6xy + 15y^2 - 18xy^2$; f $-6p + 10p^2 - 14p^3$; g $-16w^2x + 24wx^3 - 40w^3x^4$; h $-14r^4s + 35r^2s + 21r^2s^4 - 28r^5s^5$ 5 a $3x^2$; b $-5x - 2y$; c $7x - 6$; d $2w^2 - 4w$ 6 a $12(y - 3)$; b $7(1 - 2r - 3s)$; c $8y(2 - 3x)$; d $5x(4x - 3y + 5)$; e $xz(1 - y)$; f $11cd(2ab + b - 3a + 4)$; g $2x^3(1 - 2xy + 3x^2y^2)$; h $3pq^4r^2(2pq - 3r + 4p^4q^2)$ 7 a $x^2 + 7x + 10$; b $t^2 + 2t - 3$; c $m^2 - 16m + 63$; d $10y^2 - 11yr - 6r^2$ e $24x^2 - 41xy + 11y^2$; f $8 + 30w - 27w^2$; g $72 - 58s + 10s^2$; h $23abc - 7a^2b^2 - 6c^2$; i $x^2 + 12x + 36$ j $1 - 6y + 9y^2$; k $16p^2 - 40pr + 25r^2$; l $49r^2s^2 - 28rst + 4t^2$

Exercise 16B

1 a 5; b 500; c 2500; d −20; e −4; f 40; g $\frac{3}{5}$; h $4\frac{1}{2}$ 2 a 6; b −8; c −150; d 0; e 5; f −$1\frac{2}{3}$; g −6; h 5 3 a $3r - 4$; b $3m - 14p$; c $6xy - 2x$; d $t - 7t^3$; e $2a^2b - 3a + b$ 4 a $12w - 42x$; b $-3 + x - 5y$; c $-10y + 20z + 45$; d $5p^2 + 3p^3 - 4p^3q - 2p^4$; e $-10x^2y + 24xy^3 - 6x^3y^2$; f $18a^2bc^4 - 27a^3c^3 + 9a^5b^2c^5$ 5 a $-x - 2x^2$; b $5x - 7$; c $13rt^2 - 2rt$; d $5x + 7y - 9xy$ 6 a $x(4 - y + 3yz)$; b $9(3p - 5q)$; c $2y(2x - 3w - 1)$; d $7r(5t - 8r)$; e $75m(2 + m - 3m^2)$; f $5ac(2bd + bcd^2 - 3cd + 4ab)$; g $3pt(4yt - 5px + 9x^2y)$; h $15wx^2y^3(4wx^3y - 3 + 2w^3xy^3)$ 7 a $y^2 + 7y + 12$; b $r^2 - 3r - 10$; c $x^2 - 11x + 24$; d $8f^2 - 24fg - 14g^2$; e $81w^2 - 25z^2$; f $50 - 20x + 2x^2$; g $8 + 10y - 375y^2$; h $35acd - 6a^2c^2 - 49d^2$; i $p^2 + 20p + 100$; j $49 - 14y + y^2$; k $25x^2 - 80xy + 64y^2$; l $9x^4 - 12x^3 + 4x^2$

Exercise 17A

1 7 2 10 3 $5\frac{1}{2}$ 4 −2 5 6 6 $3\frac{1}{3}$ 7 −$\frac{2}{3}$ 8 $2\frac{1}{2}$ 9 $1\frac{1}{2}$ 10 $11\frac{2}{3}$ 11 −$5\frac{1}{2}$ 12 2 13 12 14 15 15 −10 16 $11\frac{1}{2}$ 17 $2\frac{1}{3}$ 18 $1\frac{1}{4}$ 19 −$\frac{1}{2}$ 20 $\frac{3}{5}$ 21 3 22 17 23 −4 24 −$1\frac{1}{4}$ 25 $x < 4$ 26 $x > -\frac{1}{2}$ 27 $x \leqslant 3$ 28 $x > 1\frac{2}{3}$ 29 $x < 12$ 30 $x \geqslant -1\frac{1}{5}$ 31 $x < \frac{3}{4}$ 32 3, 4, 5 33 8, 9, 10 34 2, 3 35 2, 3, 4, 5 36 $1 < x < 5$ 37 $-4 \leqslant x < 3$ 38 $2 < x < 13$ 39 $1\frac{1}{2} \leqslant x \leqslant 6\frac{1}{2}$

Exercise 17B

1 2 **2** $-4\frac{1}{2}$ **3** -1 **4** 5 **5** 6 **6** 0 **7** $-2\frac{1}{3}$ **8** -2 **9** $-\frac{2}{3}$ **10** 5 **11** 2 **12** $4\frac{1}{2}$
13 $\frac{1}{2}$ **14** -14 **15** 6 **16** $3\frac{1}{3}$ **17** $6\frac{1}{2}$ **18** $-1\frac{1}{3}$ **19** $-5\frac{3}{4}$ **20** $-2\frac{2}{3}$ **21** $-2\frac{1}{5}$ **22** 12
23 $5\frac{1}{3}$ **24** $1\frac{3}{4}$ **25** -3 **26** $x < 2$ **27** $x > 1\frac{1}{2}$ **28** $x \geq -4$ **29** $x < -3$ **30** $x \leq 7$
31 $x > 4\frac{3}{4}$ **32** $x < 2\frac{4}{5}$ **33** $-3, -2, -1, 0, 1$ **34** $-7, -6, -5, -4$ **35** 2, 3
36 $-3, -2, -1, 0, 1, 2$ **37** $6 < x < 10$ **38** $x > 3$ **39** $5 < x \leq 14$ **40** $-8 < x < 2$

Exercise 18A

1 **a** $(3x + 4)$ km; **b** 28 **2** **a** £$(2x - 10)$; **b** $x = 8$, cost price = £18, selling price = £24
3 **a** $(x + 10)$ years, $(x + 7)$ years; **b** $x = 9$, ages are 9 years, 6 years **4** **a** $(18N + 20)p$; **b** 10
5 **a** $p = 50$, angles are 130°, 62°, 32°; **b** $p = 39$, angles are 108°, 51°, 21° **6** **a** $n, n + 2, n + 4, n + 6,$
$n + 8$; **b** 120, 122, 124, 126, 128 **7** **a** £$(x + 100)$, £$(2x + 200)$; **b** $x = 2100$, Mrs Maxwell gets £4400
8 **a** $(6x + 40)$ m; **b** 340 m; **c** $x = 70$, perimeter = 460 m; **d** $x = 85$, width = 115 m **9** **a** $7y + 80$;
b 8 **10** **a** $(2x + 18)$ cm, $(7x + 6)$ cm²; **b** 2·4 **11** **a** $x = vt$; **b** $(6v + 10)$ km; **c** 65 **12** **a** $(35 - 3t)$ h;
b 9 **13** **a** $2x - 1, 4x - 3$; **b** $7x - 4$; **c** 65, 129, 257

Exercise 18B

1 **a** £$2x$, £$(x - 20)$; **b** £120, £100; **c** $x = 90$; amounts earned are £90, £180, £70 **2** **a** $60 - 7x$; **b** 7
3 **a** 9; **b** 13; **c** 8 **4** 35, 36, 40 **5** **a** $(18n - 18)p$; **b** 22 **6** **a** $x - 3, x + 3, x + 6$; **b** $4x + 6$;
c 32 **7** **a** $p - 30, 3p - 90$; **b** $p = 270$, dictionary has 720 pages **8** **a** 11; **b** 17 **9** **a** 4; **b** 12
10 **a** $1\frac{1}{2}$; **b** 1·8 **11** $1\frac{1}{2}$ **12** **a** $2 + x, 2 + 2x, 4 + 3x$; **b** $x = 9$; terms are 2, 9, 11, 20, 31

Exercise 19A

1 $(x + 2)(x - 2)$ **2** $(3 + y)(3 - y)$ **3** $(2p + 7)(2p - 7)$ **4** $(1 + 4a)(1 - 4a)$ **5** $(mn + r)(mn - r)$
6 $(10 + t^2)(10 - t^2)$ **7** $(w^3 + 5z^3)(w^3 - 5z^3)$ **8** $(9a^8 + 8b^5)(9a^8 - 8b^5)$ **9** $(6xy^2 + 11)(6xy^2 - 11)$
10 $(1 + 3p^3q^4r^5)(1 - 3p^3q^4r^5)$ **11** $2(x + 3)(x - 3)$ **12** $5(1 + y)(1 - y)$ **13** $m(m + 1)(m - 1)$
14 $2p(p + 4)(p - 4)$ **15** $3xy(1 + 2xy)(1 - 2xy)$ **16** $5y^2(3 + y^3)(3 - y^3)$ **17** $2ty^3(5t^2 + 2y)(5t^2 - 2y)$
18 $(x + 2)(x + 4)$ **19** $(y + 3)(y + 12)$ **20** $(p + 1)(p + 20)$ **21** $(w + 4)(w + 15)$
22 $(t + 1)(t - 3)$ **23** $(x - 2)(x + 5)$ **24** $(y - 2)(y - 16)$ **25** $(v + 1)(v - 6)$ **26** $(r - 4)(r - 6)$
27 $(s - 6)^2$ **28** $(4 + x)(5 - x)$ **29** $(1 - y)(15 + y)$ **30** $(4 - a)(9 - a)$ **31** $(p - 1)(12p + 1)$
32 $(1 - 5f)(1 + 8f)$ **33** $(3w - 1)^2$ **34** $(x + 3)(2x + 1)$ **35** $(m + 1)(2m - 5)$ **36** $(p - 1)(3p - 7)$
37 $(y + 2)(2y - 3)$ **38** $(r + 4)(3r - 1)$ **39** $(2x - 1)(3x - 4)$ **40** $(2w - 3)(4w + 3)$
41 $(2 - 5t)(4 + t)$ **42** $(2 - 3y)(5 - 4y)$ **43** $(x + 2y)(2 + a)$ **44** $(x - 3)(t + 5)$
45 $(4m - 5n)(1 + 2m)$ **46** $(3r - p)(p + 1)$ **47** $(2a + 3b)(2a - 3)$ **48** $(5x + 2)(1 - 3y)$
49 $(t - 4v)(t - 3)$ **50** $(7xy - w)(2w - 3x)$

Exercise 19B

1 $(p + 5)(p - 5)$ **2** $(8 + a)(8 - a)$ **3** $(10y + 3)(10y - 3)$ **4** $(1 + 2rs)(1 - 2rs)$
5 $(12 + m^2)(12 - m^2)$ **6** $(t^4 + 14v^3)(t^4 - 14v^3)$ **7** $(7p^6q^5 + 1)(7p^6q^5 - 1)$
8 $(16x^{10} + 13y^8w^9)(16x^{10} - 13y^8w^9)$ **9** $3(x + 1)(x - 1)$ **10** $7(1 + 2y)(1 - 2y)$ **11** $2w(2 + w)(2 - w)$
12 $5x(x + 5)(x - 5)$ **13** $2y^3(3 + y^2)(3 - y^2)$ **14** $b^2(a + cd)(a - cd)$ **15** $3xy(7 + 4y^4)(7 - 4y^4)$
16 $10ps(3p^2 + 10rs)(3p^2 - 10rs)$ **17** $(x + 2)(x + 10)$ **18** $(w + 3)(w + 11)$ **19** $(y + 3)(y + 16)$
20 $(p + 4)(p + 20)$ **21** $(t + 2)(t - 14)$ **22** $(r - 5)(r + 7)$ **23** $(a - 6)(a - 9)$ **24** $(f - 3)(f - 17)$
25 $(8 - p)^2$ **26** $(10 + m)(10 - m)$ **27** $(6 + v)(15 - v)$ **28** $(y - 7)^2$ **29** $(5 + w)(6 - w)$
30 $(x - 3)(x - 21)$ **31** $(p - 1)(8p + 1)$ **32** $(1 + 4r)(1 - 6r)$ **33** $(4w - 1)^2$ **34** $(x + 1)(2x + 7)$
35 $(y + 5)(3y + 1)$ **36** $(a + 1)(5a - 2)$ **37** $(t - 3)(3t - 2)$ **38** $(p - 3)(5p + 4)$
39 $(2g - 1)(3g + 4)$ **40** $(1 - 2m)(8 + 5m)$ **41** $(2 - 3s)(3 - 4s)$ **42** $(x + 6)(4x - 3)$
43 $(x + 2)(4 + y)$ **44** $(5 - p)(p + 2r)$ **45** $(3w - 2x)(1 + x)$ **46** $(ar - 3w)(ar + 1)$
47 $(x + 4)(y - 3)$ **48** $(2mn + 3)(2m - 5n)$ **49** $(3t - 4)(t - v)$ **50** $(6xy - 5p)(2xr - 3p)$

Exercise 20A

1 $-1, -5$, 2 $-4, -5$ 3 $2, -9$ 4 $-3, 8$ 5 $6, 7$ 6 $2, 15$ 7 $0, 5$ 8 $0, \frac{3}{4}$ 9 4
10 $4, -12$ 11 $1, -\frac{1}{6}$ 12 $\frac{1}{2}, \frac{1}{4}$ 13 $1, -1\frac{1}{2}$ 14 $\frac{1}{2}, 1$ 15 $1\frac{1}{2}, -2\frac{1}{2}$ 16 $-2, 7$ 17 $-2\frac{1}{2}, 6$
18 $0, -3$ 19 $1\frac{1}{3}, -5$ 20 $\frac{5}{6}, 2$ 21 $-0.59, -3.41$ 22 $1.14, -6.14$ 23 $7.12, -1.12$
24 $13.16, 0.84$ 25 $-0.11, -4.39$ 26 $3.32, -0.72$ 27 $0.58, -1.16$ 28 $1.61, 0.53$ 29 $4\,s$
30 $26, 34$ 31 12 32 $14, 12\,\text{cm}, 16\,\text{cm}, 20\,\text{cm}$

Exercise 20B

1 $-2, -8$ 2 $4, 10$ 3 $5, -6$ 4 $-5, 13$ 5 $3, 18$ 6 $0, -9$ 7 $0, \frac{2}{3}$ 8 $-4, 25$ 9 $6, -8$
10 2 11 $\frac{1}{3}, -\frac{1}{4}$ 12 $6, 10$ 13 $-\frac{1}{3}, -7$ 14 $\frac{1}{2}, 4$ 15 $-\frac{1}{2}, 4\frac{2}{3}$ 16 $-1, 2$ 17 $-\frac{1}{2}, 5$
18 $0, 2\frac{1}{2}$ 19 $4, -4$ 20 $\frac{1}{4}, -1\frac{1}{3}$ 21 $-0.76, -5.24$ 22 $1.19, -4.19$ 23 $6.45, 1.55$
24 $2.30, -1.30$ 25 $-0.53, -3.81$ 26 $0.89, -2.06$ 27 $0.19, -1.39$ 28 15 29 $3\,s, 9\,s$
30 $10\,\text{cm}, 12\frac{1}{2}\,\text{cm}$ 31 $2.5, 5$

Exercise 21A

1 $2y - a$ 2 $4x$ 3 $\dfrac{5}{p}$ 4 $\dfrac{3w}{2}$ 5 $3y^2$ 6 $\dfrac{rs^2}{2}$ 7 $\dfrac{t+w}{y}$ 8 $-\dfrac{5a}{3r}$ 9 $\dfrac{5w+2xw}{6x}$ 10 $\dfrac{8yq-3}{3p}$

11 $\dfrac{y}{2}$ 12 $\dfrac{2}{5s}$ 13 $\dfrac{r(r+s)}{2}$ 14 $\dfrac{2s-ut}{t}$ 15 $\dfrac{2m^2-3y}{ay}$ 16 $-\dfrac{2x}{3}$ 17 $\dfrac{4a+5y}{a}$

18 $\dfrac{3aw+5wx}{2a}$ 19 $\dfrac{3y}{y-ax}$ 20 $\dfrac{6mx+x}{2v}$ 21 $\dfrac{w^3-y}{2w}$ 22 $\dfrac{y-9}{2}$ 23 $\dfrac{4p}{r^2}$ 24 $\dfrac{4-3a^2x}{a^2x}$

25 $\pm\sqrt{\dfrac{4y+p}{p}}$ 26 $\dfrac{\pm\sqrt{w^2-x^2}}{y}$ 27 **a** $p = 2l + 2b$; **b** $l = \dfrac{p-2b}{2}$; **c** $24\,\text{cm}$ 28 **a** $y = \dfrac{p-400x}{25}$;

b 218 29 **a** $r = \sqrt{\dfrac{A}{\pi}}$; **b** $4\,\text{cm}$; **c** $2.52\,\text{cm}$ 30 **a** $p = 20 + 16y + 2x$; **b** $y = \dfrac{p-20-2x}{16}$; **c** 3;

d $A = 2xy + 80y$; **e** $x = \dfrac{A-80y}{2y}$; **f** 3.25

Exercise 21B

1 $3 + x$ 2 $at - 7$ 3 $\dfrac{y}{4x}$ 4 $\dfrac{p}{2}$ 5 $8fh$ 6 $2ax$ 7 $\dfrac{5+z}{y}$ 8 $\dfrac{2c-6ab}{5a}$ 9 $\dfrac{x+6w}{2w^2}$

10 $\dfrac{5xz-6z}{6x}$ 11 $\dfrac{bc}{a}$ 12 $\dfrac{2x^2}{y}$ 13 $\dfrac{7mr-r^2}{m}$ 14 $\dfrac{y-z}{2}$ 15 $-\dfrac{2xy}{5}$ 16 $\dfrac{a+4b}{2}$ 17 $-\dfrac{7f}{g}$

18 $\dfrac{5xz+2yz}{3x}$ 19 $m+3$ 20 $\dfrac{5x-av}{xv}$ 21 $\dfrac{2sx-w}{4s^2w}$ 22 $-x^2$ 23 $\dfrac{r}{3x^2}$ 24 $\dfrac{4x-y}{x}$

25 $\pm\sqrt{\dfrac{m-3a}{m}}$ 26 $\dfrac{\pm\sqrt{9w^2+x^2}}{2x}$ 27 **a** $p = y - nx$; **b** $x = \dfrac{y-p}{n}$; **c** £15 28 **a** $h = \dfrac{3v}{\pi r^2}$;

$r = \sqrt{\dfrac{3v}{\pi h}}$; **c** 8·29 cm; **d** 4·56 cm **29 a** $A = \dfrac{1400 + nx}{x + y}$; **b** $y = \dfrac{1400 + nx - Ax}{A}$; **c** 24

30 a $d = 20t + vT$; **b** $T = \dfrac{d - 20t}{v}$; **c** 13

Exercise 22A

1 $\dfrac{y}{2 - w}$ **2** $\dfrac{ab + d}{3 + d}$ **3** $\dfrac{4}{2r - a + 5}$ **4** $\dfrac{xp}{p - x}$ **5** $\dfrac{m}{2m - t}$ **6** $-\dfrac{7y}{3}$ **7** $\dfrac{y^2}{2 + y}$ **8** $\dfrac{9af + 6f}{2a - 6f}$

9 $\dfrac{7rp^2 + 3r}{4p}$ **10** $-\dfrac{2x}{x + 1}$ **11** $\dfrac{xw}{w - x}$ **12** $\dfrac{r}{6r + 4}$ **13** $\dfrac{3a^2}{2a - 4}$ **14** $\dfrac{2av}{6a + 1}$ **15** $\dfrac{y}{5}$ **16** $\dfrac{7r^2}{2r^2 + 4}$

17 $\pm\sqrt{\dfrac{q}{a - 2}}$ **18** $\pm\dfrac{2x}{\sqrt{1 + x^2}}$ **19** $\pm\dfrac{y}{\sqrt{4 - w^2}}$ **20** $\sqrt[3]{\dfrac{r^2}{r + 1}}$

Exercise 22B

1 $\dfrac{z}{3 - x}$ **2** $\dfrac{5s}{2r + 3}$ **3** $\dfrac{c}{1 - d - ac}$ **4** $-\dfrac{3xy}{2x + y}$ **5** $\dfrac{r}{4r + 3}$ **6** $\dfrac{8b}{3}$ **7** $\dfrac{wx}{wp - x}$ **8** $\dfrac{2tv + 3t}{v + 2}$

9 $\dfrac{a^2}{2a - d}$ **10** $\dfrac{8}{p - 6}$ **11** $\dfrac{2x^2}{2x - 3}$ **12** $\dfrac{3v}{5}$ **13** $2a$ **14** $\pm\dfrac{q}{4}$ **15** $\dfrac{w^2}{x^2 p}$ **16** $\dfrac{8b + 3fk^2}{k^2 - 4}$

17 $\pm\sqrt{\dfrac{3x}{a + 3}}$ **18** $\pm\dfrac{yr}{\sqrt{y^2 - r^2}}$ **19** $\pm\dfrac{rw}{\sqrt{3r^2 - 8}}$ **20** $\pm\dfrac{m}{u}\sqrt{m^2 + 2}$

Exercise 23A

1 $x = 2, y = 1$ **2** $p = 5, q = 2$ **3** $a = 3, b = -1$ **4** $v = 7, w = -4$ **5** $f = 6, g = -2$
6 $x = -1, y = -2$ **7** $a = 3, b = 1$ **8** $r = 20, s = 10$ **9** $t = 2, v = 3\frac{1}{4}$ **10** $x = 4, y = 6$
11 $r = 2\frac{1}{2}, s = -1\frac{1}{2}$ **12** $x = 25, y = -30$ **13** $p = \frac{5}{8}, q = \frac{3}{4}$ **14** $x = -3, y = -2\frac{1}{2}$
15 $a = \frac{2}{5}, b = 1\frac{1}{5}$ **16** seven 2p coins, eight 5p coins **17** 20p, 35p **18** 40 **19** $x = 12, y = 16$
20 $10 \text{ km h}^{-1}, 6 \text{ km h}^{-1}$

Exercise 23B

1 $a = 2, b = 4$ **2** $x = 7, y = 1$ **3** $p = 3, q = 10$ **4** $t = 2, v = -3$ **5** $r = -10, s = 4$
6 $x = 1, y = 8$ **7** $a = \frac{1}{2}, b = -3$ **8** $v = 1\frac{1}{2}, w = 2\frac{1}{2}$ **9** $f = -5, g = -6$ **10** $x = -12, y = -8$
11 $x = \frac{3}{4}, y = \frac{1}{4}$ **12** $a = 2, b = 1\frac{1}{3}$ **13** $p = 3\frac{1}{3}, q = 6\frac{2}{3}$ **14** $x = 4, y = -1$ **15** $v = 2\frac{1}{4}, w = 1\frac{1}{2}$
16 £3·50, 75p **17** $A = 3, B = -2$ **18** $x = 6\frac{1}{2}, y = 3\frac{1}{2}$ **19** 18, 6 **20** $90 \text{ km h}^{-1}, 120 \text{ km h}^{-1}$

Exercise 24A

1 a $y = kx$; **b** 4; **c** 30; **d** 1·4 **2 a** $y = kx^2$; **b** $\frac{1}{2}$; **c** 18; **d** 76·88; **e** ± 10; **f** $\pm 2·72$ **3 a** $p = \dfrac{k}{q}$;
b 6; **c** 2; **d** 24; **e** 1·25 **4 a** 192; **b** 0·081 **5 a** 0·875; **b** 350; **c** $\pm 1·16$ **6 a** 0·5; **b** 220·5;
c ± 3; **d** $\pm 0·5$ **7 a** 28 min; **b** 270 m²; **c** 16 min **8 a** 4; **b** $\frac{1}{4}$; **c** 25; **d** $\frac{1}{100}$ **9 a** 4 hours;
b 100 km h^{-1}; **c** 1 h 40 min **10 a** 7·11 ohms; **b** 0·21 mm; **c** 0·87 ohms; **d** 0·16 mm

Exercise 24B

1 **a** $y = kx^2$; **b** $y = \dfrac{k}{x^2}$; **c** $y = \dfrac{k}{x}$; **d** $y = kx^3$ **2** **a** 15; **b** 140 **3** **a** 0·5; **b** 8 **4** **a** 10; **b** 0·5
5 **a** 36; **b** ±0·75; **c** 64; **d** ±2·5 **6** **a** 2; **b** $\tfrac{1}{32}$; **c** 2·29 **7** **a** 0·25; **b** 16; **c** 0·04; **d** 100
8 **a** 941 g; **b** 6·04 cm **9** **a** 1·5 amps; **b** 20 ohms; **c** 7·5 amps **10** **a** $y \propto \dfrac{1}{x^2}$; **b** $y = \dfrac{2}{x^2}$; **c** 50; **d** 0·4

Exercise 25A

1 $\dfrac{2a^2}{15}$ **2** $4x^2y$ **3** $\dfrac{3}{q}$ **4** $6t^2$ **5** $\dfrac{6a}{5}$ **6** $\dfrac{5s^2t^2v}{8}$ **7** 3 **8** $\dfrac{1}{6x^2}$ **9** $\dfrac{q}{3}$ **10** $\dfrac{xy}{2}$ **11** $\dfrac{8t}{r}$ **12** $\dfrac{3y}{4w}$
13 $\dfrac{a+2}{2(a-3)}$ **14** $\dfrac{3}{2(p+3)}$ **15** $4(x+4)$ **16** $\dfrac{9a-8}{20}$ **17** $\dfrac{k-6}{6}$ **18** $\dfrac{3m+13}{35}$ **19** $\dfrac{17x-1}{12}$
20 $-\dfrac{x+4}{6}$ **21** $\dfrac{t+18}{24}$ **22** $\dfrac{2y^2-3x^2}{6xy}$ **23** $\dfrac{b}{a+b}$ **24** $\dfrac{4r}{r-2}$ **25** $\dfrac{x+6}{2x}$ **26** $-\dfrac{5s}{2(2r+s)}$ **27**
28 $\tfrac{1}{2}$

Exercise 25B

1 $\tfrac{1}{2}$ **2** $\dfrac{1}{a^2}$ **3** $16x^2$ **4** $\dfrac{3}{2t^2}$ **5** xw **6** $\dfrac{3a}{10b}$ **7** $\tfrac{2}{3}$ **8** $\dfrac{3}{p}$ **9** $\dfrac{9y^2}{2x^2}$ **10** $\dfrac{4m^2v^2}{3}$ **11** $\dfrac{3ab^2}{4cd}$ **12**
13 $\dfrac{m}{(n+v)^2}$ **14** $\dfrac{r}{r+s}$ **15** $\dfrac{6(a+b)^2}{7(a-b)}$ **16** $\dfrac{7x+17}{12}$ **17** $-\tfrac{5}{6}$ **18** $\dfrac{y+4}{6}$ **19** $\dfrac{w+24}{35}$ **20**
21 $\dfrac{2x}{45}$ **22** $\dfrac{3y+4x}{4xy}$ **23** $-\dfrac{2b}{a+2b}$ **24** $\dfrac{f-3g}{f-g}$ **25** $\dfrac{19y-6}{5(3y-2)}$ **26** $\dfrac{7ab}{2(3a-2b)}$ **27** $\dfrac{7}{18x}$ **28** $\tfrac{1}{3}$

Exercise 26A

1 **a** (−1·5, 0); **b** 2; **c** 2·8; **d** −3; **e** (1·4, 5·8); **f** $x = 1·4, y = 5·8$ **2** **a** 160 km, 290 km, 340 km;
b 50 km; **c** 85, speed in km h⁻¹; **d** $d = 85t + 50$ **3** **a** (3, 0), (0, 6); **b** (−6, 0), (0, 4); **c** (6, 0), (0, 1·5);
d (−2·5, 0), (0, 5); **e** (0·3, 0), (0, 0·6) **4** **a** 3·9; **b** 1·7, −1·7; **c** 0·9 < x < 1·3; **d** 1·7 **5** $x = 3·5$,
$y = 2·5$ **6** **a** 5·9 m; **b** 1·5 < x < 2·4; **c** 3·2; **d** $y = x$ **7** **a** −3·5; **b** 4·7, −0·7; **c** −4; **d** $x = 2$
8 **a** $\tfrac{1}{2}$, rate of growth in cm day⁻¹; **b** $h = 3 + 2·3t$; **c** 2·8 days, 9·4 cm; **d** 2 days **9** **a** 5, 1·6, −0·8;
b (−1·4, 7), (1·4, 7); **c** 1·4; **d** (2·54, 2·54)

Exercise 26B

1 **a** −1; **b** $x + y = 2$; **c** 1·5; **d** $x = -1·8, y = -0·2$ **2** **a** (12, 0) (0, 4); **b** (2, 0), (0, −4);
c (−1·5, 0), (0, 9); **d** (0·25, 0), (0, 0·5); **e** (0·4, 0), (0, −0·2) **3** **a** 12·1 m³; **b** 1·67; **c** 2 ⩽ x ⩽ 2·8
4 $x = 1·6, y = 3·8$ **5** **a** 104 million; **b** 3·6 years; **c** 116 million; **d** 6 million per year **6** **a** 2·29;
b 0·27, 3·73; **c** 2; **d** −3 **7** **a** 3·6 s; **b** 1·5, rate of gain of speed, or acceleration; **c** $v = 14 - \dfrac{3t}{4}$;
d 3·1 s **8** **a** 56·25 cm²; **b** 34·2 cm²; **b** 4·6, 10·4; **d** 3·5 ⩽ x ⩽ 11·5

Exercise 27A

1 **a** $m = 2, c = 3$; **b** $m = -1, c = 5$; **c** $m = \tfrac{1}{2}, c = -4$; **d** $m = -1\tfrac{1}{2}, c = 2$; **e** $m = \tfrac{3}{4}$,
$c = -1\tfrac{1}{3}$; **f** $m = \tfrac{2}{5}, c = \tfrac{4}{5}$ **2** **a** $m = 2, c = 4$; **b** $m = -1, c = 6$; **c** $m = \tfrac{1}{2}, c = -5$; **d** $m = \tfrac{1}{4}$,
$c = 1\tfrac{1}{2}$; **e** $m = -3, c = 6$ **3** **b** 0·32 m s⁻², −0·25 m s⁻²; **c** 100 m, 120 m, 128 m **4** **a** (1, 4), ($\tfrac{1}{2}$, 3),

$\frac{5}{2}$, 1); **c** 1·3; **d** 1·7 ≤ y ≤ 2·4 **5** **a** The missing values of y are 6·75, 7·66, 8, 7·59, 6·25, 3·78; **c** The gradient increases to a maximum value of about 6, then decreases to zero; **d** 1·35, 2·53; **e** x = 0·81, y = 2·8; x = 2·67, y = 4·7 **6** **a** 4r − 5t = 200; **b** 15 000 **7** **b** (1, 2), (1, 3), (2, 2), (2, 3), (2, 4), (3, 1), (3, 2); 22, 6 **8** **a** The missing values of y are 3·2, 1·78, 1·25, 1·47, 2·45, 4; **c** 1·23; **d** The graph to draw is y = x + 4; the solutions are 0·17, 1·12; **e** 0·21 < x < 0·88; **f** 0·27, 0·73

Exercise 27B

1 **a** m = 5, c = 2; **b** m = 1, c = −7; **c** m = −$\frac{2}{5}$, c = 3; **d** m = $\frac{2}{3}$, c = 4; **e** m = −2$\frac{1}{2}$, c = 3$\frac{1}{3}$; **f** m = −1$\frac{1}{4}$; c = −$\frac{1}{2}$ **2** **a** y = 3x; **b** y = 8 − 2x; **c** 3y = 2x − 18; **d** 2y = x + 12; **e** y = 3 − 2x **3** **a** 4 m s^{-2}, 0 m s^{-2}, 12 m s^{-2}; **b** 74 m; **c** v = 20 − 4t **4** **b** 7·4; **c** 3·8 ≤ x ≤ 10·2 **5** **b** r = 40 − 2t; **c** 320 Square units; the area represents the total volume of water delivered, which is therefore 320 litres **6** **a** (−1, 4), (−1, 5), (0, 3), (0, 4), (0, 5), (0, 6), (0, 7), (1, 2), (1, 3); **b** 49, 44 **7** **a** (ii); **b** (i); **c** (iv); **d** (iii) **8** **a** The missing values of y are 1, 2·31, 3, 3·06, 2·5, 1·8, 1; **c** (i) 0·42, 3·58 (ii) 0·45, 2·22; **d** 0·63 < x < 2·37; **e** (0·77, 2·58)

Geometry

Exercise 28A

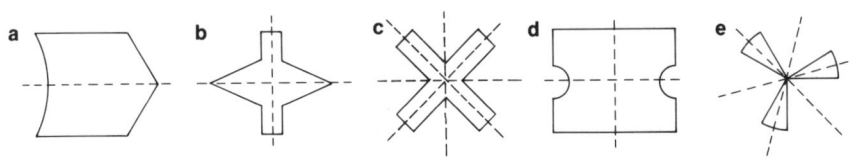

1 x = 65°, y = 50° **2** x = 30° **3** x = 130° **4** x = 66°, y = 14°, z = 43° **5** x = 36°, y = 54° **6** x = 38° **7** x = 20°, y = 12° **8** x = 50°, y = 25° **9** x = 40°, y = 140° **10** x = 18°, y = 12°
11

12 **a** 3; **b** 2; **c** 4; **d** 2; **e** 5 **13** **a** One axis, no rotational symmetry; **b** No symmetry; **c** Rotational symmetry only; **d** Two axes and rotational symmetry **14** **a** 1; **b** 2, 2; **c** 1; **d** 5, 5; **e** 6, 6 **15** **a** 360°; **b** 60°; **c** 40°; **d** 120°; **e** 140°; **16** **a** 150°; **b** 24; **c** 8; **d** 168°; **e** 20 **17** 30°, 60° **18** 30°, 45°, 15° **19** 105°, 55° **20** 76°

Exercise 28B

1 x = 40°, y = 15° **2** x = 37°, y = 32° **3** x = 58°, y = 122° **4** x = 50° **5** x = 36°, y = 56° **6** x = 39°, y = 51°, z = 90° **7** x = 30°, y = 25° **8** x = 68°, y = 28° **9** x = 20° **10** x = 40°, y = 20°
11
12 **a** Yes, order 2; **b** No; **c** Yes, order 8 **13** **a** B, W, E; **b** X, O; **c** X, N, O **14** **a** x = 0, y = 2, y = x + 2, y = 2 − x; **b** 4 **15** **a** 72°; **b** 108°; **c** 144°; **d** 156° **16** 72° **17** 80°, 120°, 70° **18** 108°, 86° **19** 130°, 64°

Exercise 29A

1 **a** D; **b** E, H **2** **a** Triangle AFM; **b** Quadrilateral FEDM; **c** Quadrilateral AFEB **3** **a** Triangle CDF; **b** Triangles CEF, FGC **4** (5, 5) **5** D is (1, 2), E is (3, 0), F is (3, 2) **6** **a** Yes; **b** No; **c** Yes **7** **a** No; **b** Yes; **c** Yes; **d** No

175

Exercise 29B

1 a Shapes A and F, shapes B, E and H, shapes D and G; **b** Shape C **2 a** Triangle AHE; **b** Triangle AFC; **c** Quadrilateral FEDC **3 a** Triangles DCE, CBD; **b** Triangle BCE **4** (2, 2) **5 a** (7, 3); **b** (1, −1), (7, −1) **6 a** No; **b** Yes; **c** No **7 a** Yes; **b** Yes; **c** No; **d** No

Exercise 30A

1 a 5:3; **b** 3:5; **c** 20 cm; **d** 15 cm **2 b** (i) (12, 3), (9, 6) (ii) (4, 4), (0, 8) **c** 1 cm², 9 cm², 16 cm²; **d** Ratio of areas = (scale factor)² **3 a** QR is parallel to BC, QR = 2BC; **b** 4 cm, 3 cm; **c** 3 cm²; **d** Triangles OAC, OPR; triangles OBC, OQR **4** 3, (0, 4) **5 a** 5:2; **b** 20 cm; **c** 27 cm; **d** W, 2·5 **6 a** (4, 6), (8, (2, 8); **b** (2, 8), (8, 8), (−1, 11); **c** 3, (2, 2) **7 a** (i) 1:9 (ii) 1:27; **b** 108 **8 a** 2:5; **b** 8:125; **c** 128 cm **9** 1⅓, 60 cm, 57 cm, 66 cm **10 a** (12, 9), (0, 5); **b** (−1, 2), (−2, 4); **c** −¼, (−0·8, 3·4)

Exercise 30B

1 a B; **b** WX; **c** XL = 10 cm; **d** AB = 10·5 cm **2 a** (3, 3), (6, 3), (3, 6), 9:1; **b** (4, −5), (8, −5), (4, −1); **c** (2, 2), (8, 2), (2, 8); **d** 1·5 **3 a** 4; **b** RS is parallel to BC, RS = 4BC; **c** 22·5 cm; **d** 176 cm 165 cm² **4** 2·5, (−3, 8) **5 a** 1⅔; **b** 100 m; **c** 64 m; **d** 90 m **6 a** (9, 6), (15, 18), (3, 12); **b** (4, 1), (5, 3), (3, 2); **c** ½, (−1, 0) **7 a** 125:27; **b** 1250 cm³ **8** 50 **9** −1·8, 108 cm, 90 cm **10 a** (8, 9), (2, 6); **b** (8, 11), (8, 7); **c** 1⅓, (−4, 3)

Exercise 31A

1 a Reflection in the y-axis; **b** Reflection in the x-axis; **c** Half-turn about 0; **d** Translation of 5 units downwards; **e** Translation of 8 units to the left **2 a** (−1, 1), (−4, 1), (−4, 2); **b** (−1, −1), (−4, −1), (−4, −2); **c** Reflection in the x-axis **3 a** (3, 3); **b** (−2, −2) **4 a** (0, 4), (−1, 4); **b** (5, 5), (5, 1), (6, **5 a** Translation of 1 cm to the right; **b** Reflection in the line MN; **c** Half-turn about the mid-point of AM **6 a** (2, 2), (3, 2), (2, 4); **b** (−2, −2), (−3, −2), (−2, −4); **c** Half-turn about 0 **7** Anticlockwise quarter-turn about 0 **8 a** (4, 5), (6, 5), (6, 4); **b** Translation of 6 units upwards **9 a** (−2, −2), (−5, −2), (−2, −3); **b** (2, −4), (5, −4), (2, −3); **c** Half-turn about the point (0, −3)

Exercise 31B

1 a Reflection in the x-axis; **b** Translation of 7 units to the right; **c** Half-turn about O; **d** Reflection in the y-axis; **e** Anticlockwise quarter-turn about O; **f** Clockwise quarter-turn about O **2 a** (0, 4), (1, 3), (2, 4); **b** (0, −4), (−1, −3), (−2, −4); **c** Half-turn about the origin **3 a** (5, 4); **b** (−2, −3) **4 a** (−2, 0), (−6, 0), (−6, −2); **b** (2, 4), (0, 4); **c** (−2, 4), (−4, 4); **d** Translation of 4 units to the left **5 a** Triangles QPO, SRO; **b** Triangle POQ; **c** Triangles PAS, RCQ; **d** Translation of 2 cm to the left and 1 cm upwards; **e** Reflection in the line OR; **f** Reflection in the line SO; **g** Half-turn about the mid-point of SP **6 a** (−3, 2), (1, 4); **b** (0, −3), (−2, −1); **c** Translation of 5 units to the right and 4 units upwards **7 a** (−4, 1), (−4, 2), (−2, 2); **b** (4, 1), (4, 2), (2, 2); **c** Reflection in the y-axis **8 a** Translation of 8 cm to the right; **b** Translation of 12 cm to the right; **c** Translation of 2x cm to the right **9 a** (−2, 1), (−4, 1), (−2, 0); **b** (−1, 2), (−1, 4), (−2, 2); **c** Anticlockwise quarter-turn about the origin

Exercise 32A

1 a 90°; **b** 24°; **c** 90°; **d** 66° **2 a** AC is a diameter, or AC bisects angle BAD, or AC bisects angle BCD; **b** 40°, 100° **3** $x = 55°, y = 53°$ **4** $x = 31°, y = 23°$ **5** $x = 26°, y = 36°$ **6** $x = 33°, y = 32°$ **7** $w = 61°, x = 29°, y = 50°$ **8** $x = 30°, y = 65°$ **9** $x = 40°, y = 25°$ **10** $x = 23°, y = 44°$ **11** $x = 42°, y = 24°$ **12** 36°, 18° **13** 65°, 126°

Exercise 32B

1 Angles ABD, BFD, BED, CBF; triangles ABE, OBC, OBF, OFD **2** $x = 32°, y = 29°$ **3** $x = 47°, y = 73°$ **4** $x = 65°, y = 40°$ **5** $x = 24°, y = 132°$ **6** $x = 30°$ **7** $x = 20°, y = 22°$ **8** $x = 45°, y = 27°$ **9** $x = 33°, y = 24°$ **10** $x = 36°, y = 142°$ **11** $34°, 124°, 22°$ **12** $30°$

Exercise 33A

1 a Angles ACE, ADE; **b** Angle ADC; **c** Angles ADC, AEC **2** $x = 80°, y = 160°$ **3** $x = 52°, y = 33°$ **4** $x = 62°, y = 34°$ **5** $x = 156°$ **6** $x = 37°, y = 74°$ **7** $x = 50°, y = 32°$ **8** $x = 24°, y = 30°$ **9** $x = 56°, y = 45°$ **10** $x = 22°, y = 46°$ **11** $x = 64°, y = 34°$ **12** $x = 42°, y = 28°$

Exercise 33B

1 a Angle ACB; **b** Angle OBA; **c** Angle ABC; **d** Angle BOC **2** $x = 26°, y = 54°$ **3** $x = 40°, x = 55°, y = 49°$ **5** $x = 50°$ **6** $x = 20°$ **7** $x = 61°, y = 61°$ **8** $x = 25°, y = 65°$ **9** $x = 60°, y = 100°$ **10** $x = 50°, y = 25°$ **11** $x = 36°, y = 48°, z = 18°$ **12** $x = 30°, y = 10°$

Trigonometry, Pythagoras' Theorem

Exercise 34

1 a 6·43 cm; **b** 18·5 m; **c** 15·9 cm; **d** 6 m; **e** 16·9 m; **f** 7·13 cm **2 a** 66·4°; **b** 44·4°; **c** 43·2°; **d** 63·4°; **e** 28·0°; **f** 34·8° **3 a** 3·61 m; **b** 10·3 cm; **c** 6 cm; **d** 13·0 m; **e** 191 m; **f** 43·3 cm **4 a** 8·97 cm; **b** 16·5 m; **c** 13·8 m; **d** 24·3 cm; **e** 1·46 m; **f** 0·694 cm **5 a** $x = 5·91$ m, $\theta = 61·7°$, area = 7·28 m²; **b** $x = 5·73$ m, $y = 6·28$ m, area = 18·0 m²; **c** $x = 20·9$ cm, $\theta = 48·6°$, area = 248 cm²; **d** $x = 86·6$ m, $y = 34·4$ m, area = 1370 m² **6 a** 4·36 m; **b** $x = 8·54$ cm, $\theta = 69·4°$; **c** 49·6°; **d** $x = 21·6$ cm, $y = 8·93$ cm; **e** 35·1 m **7 a** $\tfrac{4}{5}, \tfrac{3}{4}$; **b** $\tfrac{5}{13}, \tfrac{12}{13}$; **c** $\tfrac{24}{25}, 3\tfrac{3}{7}$; **d** $\tfrac{15}{17}, \tfrac{8}{17}$; **e** $\tfrac{1}{2}, \sqrt{3}$; **f** $\dfrac{3}{\sqrt{10}}, 3$

Exercise 35A

1 a 18·2 m; **b** 18·6° **2 a** 53·9 km; **b** 112° **3 a** 21·3°; **b** 96·6 m **4 a** 220°; **b** 99·2 km; **c** 80·9 km; **d** 91·4 km **5 a** 72·1 cm; **b** 112·6°; **c** 66·6 cm; **d** 2400 cm² **6 a** 18·0 km; **b** 24·5 km; **c** 054° **7 a** 17·5 m; **b** 67·3 cm; **c** 869 m² **8 a** 2·89 m; **b** 4·20 m; **c** 1·31 m **9 a** 9·06 m; **b** 8·94 m; **c** 63·1 m² **10 a** 8·83 m; **b** 3·73 m; **c** 1·35 m **11 a** 130°; **b** 121 km; **c** 278 km; **d** 194°

Exercise 35B

1 a 560 m; **b** 600 m **2 a** 29·7°; **b** 7·28 m **3 a** 80·3 km; **b** 74·2 km; **c** 227° **4** 14·6 m **5 a** 3·86 m; **b** 57·1°; **c** 21·2 m² **6** 60·8 km, 125° **7 a** 5 cm; **b** 12 cm; **d** 9·6 cm; **e** 7·2 cm **8 a** 20·7°; **b** 30·7° **9** Angle AEF = 60°; **a** 6 cm; **b** 10·4 cm; **c** 31·2 cm²; **d** 249 cm²; **e** 374 cm² **10 a** 33·2 m; **b** 25·2° **11 a** 30·3 km; **b** 060°; **c** 72·2 km; **d** 164 km

Exercise 36A

1 a 4·85 m; **b** 13·3 m; **c** 46·7° **2** 88 cm **3 a** 35·7 m; **b** 215° **4 a** 241 km; **b** 145 km; **c** 031°, 146° **6** 246 cm² **7** 43·1° **8 a** 96·9 km h⁻¹; **b** 55·9 km, 140° **9 a** $\tfrac{5}{13}, \tfrac{12}{13}$; **b** 25 cm; **c** 39 cm **10 a** 117 m; **b** 35·6°

Exercise 36B

1 a 9·46°; **b** 11·7 m; **c** 36·6° **2 a** 58·8 km; **b** 297°; **c** 253°; **d** 027° **3 a** 24·1°; **b** 22·4° **4 a** $\frac{7}{24}$; **b** 672 cm² **5 a** 41·2 cm; **b** 46·7°; **c** 56·3° **6 a** 52·2 km; **b** 94 min; **c** 84·2 km; **d** 31 min **7** 15·3 m, 339° **8 a** 22·2 cm, 28·4 cm; **b** 314 cm² **9** 528 cm² **10 a** 29·0°; **b** 054°

Exercise 37A

1 a 53, 127; **b** 204, 336; **c** $210 < x < 330$; **d** $0.7 < y < 1$ **2 a** A translation of 90 units in the direction of the positive x-axis **b** 45, 225 **3 a** 72; **b** 104; **c** 124; **d** 115 **4 a** The gradient increases from zero to a maximum value of approximately 0·02, then decreases to zero; **b** 76 **5 a** 1·4, 135; **b** $103 < x < 167$ **6 a** 122; **b** 66; **c** 27

Exercise 37B

1 a 63, 297; **b** 143, 217; **c** $78 < x < 282$; **d** $-0.7 < y < 0.7$ **2 a** No axes of symmetry, rotational symmetry about the point (180, 0); **b** Symmetry about the line $x = 180$, no rotational symmetry; **c** No axes of symmetry, rotational symmetry about the point (180, 0) **3 a** 28; **b** 38; **c** 37·5; **d** 20·6 **4 a** $-1, 45$; **b** -0.05 **5 a** 0·29, 24·7; **b** $12 < x < 35$

Exercise 38A

1 a $x = 1.58$ cm, $y = 3.24$ cm, area = 2·36 cm²; **b** $x = 5.52$ m, $\theta = 38.1°$, area = 13·6 m²; **c** $x = 6.02$ c $\theta = 43.8°$, area = 5·00 cm²; **d** $\theta = 32.6°$, $\alpha = 98.9°$, area = 222 m² **2 a** 20·3 km; **b** 38·2 km **3 a** 16° **b** 22·3 m; **c** 14·9 m **4 a** 1·78 m; **b** 3·75° **5 a** 307 m²; **b** 30·8 m; **c** 446 m² **6 a** 136 km; **b** 149 km **7 a** 1940 m²; **b** 73·3 m; **c** 336° **8 a** 25 cm; **b** 23·6°; **c** 199 cm² **9 a** 74·2 m; **b** 24! **10 a** 14·1 miles; **b** 11·5 miles; **c** 11·47 a.m.; **d** 11·37 a.m.

Exercise 38B

1 a $x = 21.2$ cm; $y = 37.3$ cm, area = 390 cm²; **b** $x = 12.9$ m, $\theta = 66.6°$, area = 41·5 m²; **c** $\theta = 34.0°$, $\alpha = 107.7°$, area = 11·6 mm²; **d** $x = 34.2$ m, $\theta = 45.0°$, area = 230 m² **2 a** 25·0 miles; **b** 21·5 miles **3 a** 24·6 m; **b** 18·5 m **4 a** 15 m; **b** 97·0°; **c** 181 m² **5** 1·56 miles **6 c** 23·8 cm² **7 a** 54·6 km; **b** 216°; **c** 44·0 km **8 a** 19·7 m; **b** 29·9° **9 a** 12 cm; **b** 62·0°; **c** 26·9 cm² **10 a** 57·1 km h^{-1}; **b** 85·6 km; **c** 18·07 h; **d** 18·31 h

Mensuration

Exercise 39

1 a 30 cm, 75 cm²; **b** 44 cm, 154 cm²; **c** 126 m, 1260 m²; **d** 5·4 m, 2·43 m²; **e** 88 mm, 616 mm²; **f** 8·58 cm, 5·85 cm² **2 a** 60 m²; **b** 16·5 cm²; **c** 414 m² **3** figures **b** and **e** **4 a** 96 cm³, 136 cm²; **b** 3 m³, 14 m² **5 a** 104 cm³; **b** 180 m³ **6 a** 36 m³, 84 m²; **b** 42 cm³, 86 cm²; **c** 277 cm³, 295 cm²; **d** 1·44 m³, 8·64 m² **7 a** triangular prism; **b** 240 cm³, 276 cm² **8 a** 2830 cm³, 1170 cm²; **b** 178 cm³, 184 cm² **9 a** 3·57 cm; **b** 5·89 cm; **c** 1·36 cm **10 a** 100; **b** 1000; **c** 10⁴; **d** 10⁶; **e** 10⁶; **f** 10⁹; **g** 10⁴; **h** 10⁸

Exercise 40A

1 a 339·3 cm³; **b** 115; **c** 180 cm³ **2 a** 20·8 cm³; **b** 45 **3 a** 7·54 cm; **b** 302 cm; **c** 26 **4 a** 101 m²; **b** 112 m² **5 a** 45 m²; **b** 540 m³; **c** 18·1 m; **d** 367 m² **6 a** 972π cm³; **b** 27 cm; **c** 18 cm **7 a** 396 cm³; **b** 293 g **8 a** 246 m; **b** 3660 m²; **c** 3070 m² **9 a** 0·102 mm²; **b** 0·00102 cm **c** 24·6 m **10 a** 0·385 m³; **b** 2·585 m²

Exercise 40B

1 a 216 cm^3; **b** 264 cm^2; **c** 140 **2 a** 750 cm^3; **b** 9·09 cm **3 a** 86·8 cm; **b** 82·9 cm^2 **4** 0·141 m^3 **5 a** 1200 cm^3; **b** 560 cm^2 **6 a** 125 cm; **b** 19·9 cm **7 a** 50 cm; **b** 10·7 cm **8 a** 0·156 m^3; **b** 3510 cm^3; **c** 7·81 g cm^{-3} **9 a** 101 m; **b** 606 m^2

Exercise 41

1 a 4·19 cm, 8·38 cm^2; **b** 5·50 cm, 19·2 cm^2; **c** 7·08 cm, 9·20 cm^2; **d** 89·5 cm, 851 cm^2; **e** 62·2 cm, 48 cm^2 **2 a** 47·7°; **b** 320·9°; **c** 107·4°; **d** 40° **3** 49·7 cm^2 **4** 40·4 cm^2 **5** 10·4 cm^2 **6** 1220 cm^2 **7 a** 382 cm^3; **b** 3·63 cm **8 a** 1810 cm^3; **b** 2·07 cm; **c** 104 cm^3 **9 a** 0·54 m^3; **b** 1490 cm^3; **c** 77·8 cm^3 **10 a** 302 cm^2; **b** 75·4 cm^2; **c** 767 cm^3

Exercise 42A

1 a 2·51 cm; **b** 1·51 cm^2 **2 a** 64π; **b** 16 cm **3 a** 754 cm^3; **b** 415 cm^2 **4** 153° **5 a** 452 cm^3; **b** 4 cm; **c** 134 cm^3; **d** 318 cm^3 **6** 40·3 cm **7** 1720 cm^2 **8 a** 4 cm; **b** 17·5 cm **9** 65·3 cm **10** 5·57 cm **11** 4·12 to 1

Exercise 42B

1 a 628 cm^3; **b** 408 cm^2 **2** 22·6 m **3 a** 16·3 cm^2; **b** 100 **4 a** 256 cm^3; **b** 117; **c** 0·16% **5 a** 19·6 cm; **b** 24·1 cm^2 **6** 8·77 cm, 483 cm^2 **7 a** 8 cm; **b** 19·5° **8 a** 2220 cm^3; **b** 592 cm^2; **c** 8·54 cm **9** 118 cm **10** 169° **11** 61·2 cm^2

Matrices

Exercise 43A

1 a 1×3; **b** 3×2; **c** 2×2 **2 a** (9 −5); **b** (0 14); **c** (−12 9); **d** (−42 14) **3 a** $\begin{pmatrix} 2x \\ y \end{pmatrix}$; **b** $\begin{pmatrix} 0 \\ 7x^2y \end{pmatrix}$; **c** $\begin{pmatrix} -2x^2 \\ 3x \end{pmatrix}$ **4 a** (−2 1½); **b** $\begin{pmatrix} 4½ \\ -2 \end{pmatrix}$; **c** $\begin{pmatrix} 2 & -2½ \\ 4 & 1½ \end{pmatrix}$; **d** $\begin{pmatrix} -4 \\ -2 \end{pmatrix}$ **5 a** $x=4, y=-1$; **b** $x=2, y=3$; **c** $x=-1, y=4$; **d** $x=5, y=2$ **6 a** (33); **b** (1); **c** (4xy); **d** (−y) **7 a** $\begin{pmatrix} 6 \\ -5 \end{pmatrix}$; **b** (−7 4); **c** $\begin{pmatrix} 0 & 50 & 10 \\ 25 & -75 & -15 \end{pmatrix}$; **d** $\begin{pmatrix} -5x & 2x & -4x \\ 15x & -6x & 12x \\ 10x & -4x & 8x \end{pmatrix}$ **8 a** No; **b** No; **c** Yes, $\begin{pmatrix} 12 \\ 9 \end{pmatrix}$; **d** Yes, $\begin{pmatrix} 1 & 24 \\ -8 & 33 \end{pmatrix}$; **e** No; **f** Yes, (3 −35); **g** Yes, $\begin{pmatrix} -15 & 0 & 6 \\ -10 & 0 & 4 \end{pmatrix}$ **9 a** $x=-2$, **b** $x=-7, y=-5$; **c** $x=2½, y=-3$; **d** $x=9$ or $-1, y=9$; **e** $r=1⅔, t=2⅓, v=-1, w=2$ **10 a** $\begin{pmatrix} 3 & -2 \\ -7 & 5 \end{pmatrix}$; **b** Singular; **c** $\begin{pmatrix} 1½ & 1 \\ 2½ & 2 \end{pmatrix}$; **d** $⅓\begin{pmatrix} -3 & 3 \\ -8 & 7 \end{pmatrix}$; **e** $\begin{pmatrix} -1 & 3 \\ -2 & 7 \end{pmatrix}$; **f** Singular; **g** $\begin{pmatrix} 1 & 2¼ \\ 1 & 2 \end{pmatrix}$; **h** $-\begin{pmatrix} 5 & 8 \\ 4 & 6 \end{pmatrix}$; **i** $-\begin{pmatrix} 3 & 8½ \\ 3 & 9 \end{pmatrix}$

Exercise 44B

1 **a** 6×3; **b** 5×1; **c** 3×3; **d** 1×7 **2** **a** $\begin{pmatrix} -6 \\ -2 \end{pmatrix}$; **b** $\begin{pmatrix} -9 \\ 8 \end{pmatrix}$; **c** $\begin{pmatrix} 17 \\ 2 \end{pmatrix}$; **d** $\begin{pmatrix} 5 \\ \end{pmatrix}$

3 **a** $(-5x \quad 11y)$; **b** $\begin{pmatrix} -tw \\ 6t - 2w \end{pmatrix}$; **c** $\begin{pmatrix} 2r^2 \\ 5r \end{pmatrix}$ **4** **a** $(2\tfrac{1}{2} \quad -4 \quad 1\tfrac{2}{5})$; **b** $\begin{pmatrix} 10 \\ -8\tfrac{2}{3} \end{pmatrix}$; **c** $\begin{pmatrix} \tfrac{1}{2} & 2 \\ -1 & 3 \end{pmatrix}$

5 **a** $x = -1, y = -4$; **b** $x = 4, y = -3$; **c** $x = \pm 4, y = \pm 2$; **d** $x = 3, y = 5$ **6** **a** (0); **b** $(-18$

c $(-t)$ **7** **a** $\begin{pmatrix} -3 \\ 1 \\ 5 \end{pmatrix}$; **b** $(-5 \quad 30 \quad -20)$; **c** $\begin{pmatrix} 3 & 25 \\ 1 & 9 \end{pmatrix}$; **d** $\begin{pmatrix} 8 & -6 & 12 \\ -4 & 3 & -6 \end{pmatrix}$ **8** **a** Yes, 3×1;

b No; **c** No; **d** Yes, 3×3; **e** No; **f** Yes, 2×1; **g** No   **9** **a** $\begin{pmatrix} 13 & -12 \\ 16 & -11 \end{pmatrix}$; **b** $\begin{pmatrix} -14 & 7 \\ 21 & 14 \end{pmatrix}$;

c $(-3 \quad 5)$ **10** **a** $p = 2$; **b** $x = 4, y = -1$; **c** $p = -3, q = 4$; **d** $t = \tfrac{1}{2}, w = 16, x = 2, y =$

11 **a** $\begin{pmatrix} 4 & -3 \\ -9 & 7 \end{pmatrix}$; **b** $\tfrac{1}{3}\begin{pmatrix} 11 & 6 \\ 5 & 3 \end{pmatrix}$; **c** Singular; **d** $\begin{pmatrix} -\tfrac{1}{2} & -1 \\ 1 & 3 \end{pmatrix}$; **e** $\begin{pmatrix} 0 \cdot 2 & 0 \cdot 06 \\ -0 \cdot 1 & 0 \cdot 02 \end{pmatrix}$

f $\tfrac{1}{4}\begin{pmatrix} -9 & 5 \\ -8 & 4 \end{pmatrix}$; **g** Singular; **h** $\begin{pmatrix} 1 & 2 \\ 1 & 1 \end{pmatrix}$; **i** $\begin{pmatrix} -5 & 3 \\ 9 & -5 \end{pmatrix}$

Exercise 45A

1 **a** A' is $(2, -2)$, B' is $(6, -2)$, C' is $(6, -4)$; **b** Reflection in the x-axis **c** $\begin{pmatrix} 1 & 0 \\ 0 & 1 \end{pmatrix}, \begin{pmatrix} 1 & 0 \\ 0 & -1 \end{pmatrix}$. Two successive applications of **M** are equivalent to the identity transformation. This means that **M** is its own inverse   **2** **a** Clockwise (or negative) quarter-turn about O; **b** Reflection in the line $y = x$; **c** Half-tur about O; **d** Reflection in the x-axis; **e** Anticlockwise quarter-turn about O   **3** $(3, -1), (-2, 5)$
4 **a** Anticlockwise quarter-turn about O; **b** $\begin{pmatrix} -1 & 0 \\ 0 & -1 \end{pmatrix}$, half-turn about O; $\begin{pmatrix} 0 & 1 \\ -1 & 0 \end{pmatrix}$, clockwise quarter-turn about O; $\begin{pmatrix} 0 & 1 \\ -1 & 0 \end{pmatrix}$, clockwise quarter-turn about O   **5** **a** $\begin{pmatrix} -1 & 0 \\ 0 & 1 \end{pmatrix}$; **b** $\begin{pmatrix} 3 & 0 \\ 0 & 3 \end{pmatrix}$

c $\begin{pmatrix} 0 & 1 \\ -1 & 0 \end{pmatrix}$ **6** **a** $(-4, 0), (-4, 2), (-8, 2)$; **b** $(0, -4), (-2, -4), (-2, -8)$; **c** Reflection in the x-a:

$\begin{pmatrix} 1 & 0 \\ 0 & -1 \end{pmatrix}$ **7** **a** Reflection in the y-axis, $\begin{pmatrix} -1 & 0 \\ 0 & 1 \end{pmatrix}$; **b** Clockwise quarter-turn about O, $\begin{pmatrix} 0 & 1 \\ -1 & 0 \end{pmatrix}$

8 **a** $(4, 4), (3, 5)$; **b** Anticlockwise rotation of $45°$ about O, scale factor $= \sqrt{2}$ **9** **a** Reflection in the x-axis, scale factor $= 3$; **b** Reflection in the line $y = x$, scale factor $= 5$; **c** Clockwise rotation of $45°$ abo O, scale factor $= 2\sqrt{2}$ **10** **a** Reflection in a line or point; **b** Reflection in the line $3y =$

11 **a** $\begin{pmatrix} 1 & 0 \\ 0 & 1 \end{pmatrix}, \begin{pmatrix} 0 & 1 \\ -1 & 0 \end{pmatrix}$; **b** $\begin{pmatrix} 16 & 0 \\ 0 & 16 \end{pmatrix}, \begin{pmatrix} -128 & 0 \\ 0 & 128 \end{pmatrix}$ **12** Clockwise rotation of $127°$ about O. Th product of two reflections in lines inclined at an angle of θ is a rotation of 2θ about the point of intersecti of the lines.

Exercise 45B

1 **a** P' is $(-2, 0)$, Q' is $(-2, 2)$, R' is $(-6, 2)$; **b** Reflection in the line $y = -x$; **c** $\begin{pmatrix} 0 & -1 \\ -1 & 0 \end{pmatrix}$

2 **a** Half-turn about O; **b** Reflection in the x-axis; **c** Reflection in the line $y = -x$; **d** Clockwise quarter-turn about O 3 **a** $(2, -1)$; **b** $(3, -1)$; **c** $(2, 3)$ 4 **a** Enlargement of centre O and scale factor 2; **b** Enlargement of centre O and scale factor $-\frac{1}{2}$; **c** Translation of $\begin{pmatrix} -6 \\ -1 \end{pmatrix}$ (i.e. 6 units to the left and 1 unit downwards) 5 **a** $\begin{pmatrix} 1 & 0 \\ 0 & -1 \end{pmatrix}$; **b** $\begin{pmatrix} 0 & -1 \\ 1 & 0 \end{pmatrix}$; **c** $\begin{pmatrix} -3 & 0 \\ 0 & 3 \end{pmatrix}$ 6 Reflection in the y-axis, $\begin{pmatrix} -1 & 0 \\ 0 & 1 \end{pmatrix}$, $\begin{pmatrix} 0 & 1 \\ 1 & 0 \end{pmatrix}$, $\begin{pmatrix} 0 & 1 \\ -1 & 0 \end{pmatrix}$ 7 **a** Reflection in the line $y = -x$, $\begin{pmatrix} 0 & -1 \\ -1 & 0 \end{pmatrix}$; **b** Half-turn about O, $\begin{pmatrix} -1 & 0 \\ 0 & -1 \end{pmatrix}$

8 **a** $(8, 6)$, $(5, 10)$; **b** 37°, scale factor $= 5$ 9 **a** $\begin{pmatrix} 1 & 0 \\ 0 & 1 \end{pmatrix}$, $P^{-1} = P$; **b** Reflection in the line $3y = 2x$

10 **a** $\begin{pmatrix} 1 & 0 \\ 0 & 1 \end{pmatrix}$; **b** $\begin{pmatrix} 0 & 1 \\ -1 & 0 \end{pmatrix}$; **c** $\begin{pmatrix} 64 & 0 \\ 0 & 64 \end{pmatrix}$; **d** $\begin{pmatrix} 0 & 128 \\ 128 & 0 \end{pmatrix}$ 11 **a** $y = 2x$, $3y = x$; **b** 45°;

c $RS = \begin{pmatrix} 0 & -1 \\ 1 & 0 \end{pmatrix}$, anticlockwise quarter-turn about O; $SR = \begin{pmatrix} 0 & 1 \\ -1 & 0 \end{pmatrix}$, clockwise quarter-turn about O 12 $\begin{pmatrix} -0.6 & -0.8 \\ 0.8 & -0.6 \end{pmatrix}$

Vectors

Exercise 46A

1 (a) $-\mathbf{b}$; (b) $\mathbf{a} + \mathbf{b}$; (c) $\frac{1}{2}\mathbf{a}$; (d) $\frac{1}{2}\mathbf{a} + \mathbf{b}$; (e) $\mathbf{b} - \frac{1}{2}\mathbf{a}$ 2 (a) $\vec{PR}$; (b) $\vec{QP}$; (c) $\vec{PQ}$; (d) $\vec{RS}$; (e) $\vec{RQ}$; (f) $\vec{SR}$
3 (a) $-\mathbf{f}$; (b) $\mathbf{e}$; (c) $\mathbf{0}$; (d) $\mathbf{c}$; (e) $-\mathbf{e}$
4 (a) 24 cm; (b) 10 cm 5 (a) 2 cm; (b) 22 cm; (c) 10 cm; (d) 11.3 cm

6 (a) $\begin{pmatrix} 7 \\ 1 \end{pmatrix}$; (b) $\begin{pmatrix} -2 \\ -5 \end{pmatrix}$; (c) $\begin{pmatrix} 5 \\ -4 \end{pmatrix}$; (d) $\begin{pmatrix} -5 \\ 4 \end{pmatrix}$ 7 (a) $\begin{pmatrix} 2 \\ -1 \end{pmatrix}$;

(b) $\begin{pmatrix} 5 \\ 1 \end{pmatrix}$; (c) $\begin{pmatrix} -4 \\ 2 \end{pmatrix}$; (d) $\begin{pmatrix} 1 \\ -4 \end{pmatrix}$ 8 (a) $\begin{pmatrix} -18 \\ 15 \end{pmatrix}$; (b) $\begin{pmatrix} 4 \\ 2 \end{pmatrix}$; (c) $\begin{pmatrix} -22 \\ 29 \end{pmatrix}$ 9 (a) 5; (b) (13;

(c) 11.3; (d) 28 10 (a) $(6, -2)$; (b) $(-15, 5)$; (c) $(6, 7)$; (d) $(1, -4)$ 11 (a) 2; (b) $\begin{pmatrix} -12 \\ -16 \end{pmatrix}$

12 (a) $(9, 6)$; (b) LK is parallel to OJ, LK = 2OJ; (c) Trapezium; (d) $\begin{pmatrix} 4 \\ 5 \end{pmatrix}$, OJKM is a parallelogram

Exercise 46B

1 (a) $-\mathbf{p}$; (b) $\frac{1}{2}\mathbf{q}$; (c) $\mathbf{p}+\mathbf{q}$; (d) $\mathbf{p}-\mathbf{q}$; (e) $-3\mathbf{q}/2-\mathbf{p}$ **2** (a) $\overrightarrow{BP}$; (b) $\overrightarrow{PA}$; (c) $\overrightarrow{CB}$; (d) $\overrightarrow{AB}$;
3 (a) $\mathbf{b}$; (b) $\mathbf{0}$; (c) $-\mathbf{d}$; (d) $\mathbf{h}$; (e) $-\mathbf{f}$ **4** (a) $2\mathbf{x}$; (b) $2\mathbf{x}+2\mathbf{y}$; (c) $\mathbf{x}-\mathbf{y}$; (d) $-\mathbf{x}-2\mathbf{y}$
5 (a) 25; (b) 5; (c) 15; (d) 20   **6** (a) $\begin{pmatrix}-4\\3\end{pmatrix}$; (b) $\begin{pmatrix}2\\1\end{pmatrix}$; (c) $\begin{pmatrix}-2\\-4\end{pmatrix}$; (d) $\begin{pmatrix}6\\1\end{pmatrix}$ **7** (a) (
(b) $\begin{pmatrix}-2\\-2\end{pmatrix}$; (c) $\begin{pmatrix}-9\\16\end{pmatrix}$ **8** (a) (4, 1), (−2, 5), (6, 5); (b) Isosceles trapezium   **9** (a) 25; (b) 17·9
(c) 17; (d) 38   **10** (a) (6, 4); (b) (−8, −6); (c) (3, 5); (d) (4, −2)   **11** (a) 5, −1; (b) $\begin{pmatrix}60\\-25\end{pmatrix}$
12 (a) (−1, 4), (2, 7), (6, 4); (b) BA = BC, BA is perpendicular to BC; (c) Kite; (d) (5, 4), square

Exercise 47B

1 (a) $-\mathbf{a}$, $-\mathbf{p}$; (b) Parallelogram   **2** $\frac{2}{3}$ **3** (b) 5, 5; (c) Isosceles trapezium   **4** 3   **5** (a) $3\mathbf{a}+$
$3\mathbf{b}-6\mathbf{a}$, $2\mathbf{b}-4\mathbf{a}$, $2\mathbf{a}+2\mathbf{b}$; (b) 2   **7** (a) $\mathbf{b}-\mathbf{a}$, $\frac{2}{3}\mathbf{b}-\frac{2}{3}\mathbf{a}$, $\frac{1}{2}\mathbf{a}-\mathbf{b}$, $\frac{1}{3}\mathbf{a}-\frac{2}{3}\mathbf{b}$ **8** Parallelogram   **9** (a)
(b) $\frac{2}{3}$; (c) $\frac{7}{10}\mathbf{a}-\frac{3}{5}\mathbf{b}$ **10** (a) 3; (b) $\frac{1}{3}$

Answers to GCSE Specimen Papers

Paper 3

1 a 15 400; **b** 23 950, 24 049 **2 a** 48 m^2; **b** 252 m^2 **3** 9.3×10^7 **4** 155° **5 a** (12, 0); **b** (0, 5); 13 **6 a** 99 km; **b** 15°, 075°; **c** Angles are 90°, 35°, 55°; **d** (i) 16.4 km (ii) 79.6 km **7 a** 20; **b** 7; $a = \dfrac{v-u}{t}$ **8** 64 **9** £112.50 **10** Draw 1, $\frac{3}{4}$, $\frac{1}{4}$; draw 2: $\frac{4}{7}$, $\frac{3}{7}$, $\frac{3}{7}$, $\frac{4}{7}$ **11 a** 3^{-2}; **b** $\frac{1}{9}$ **12** (−1, −1), (−5, −1), (−5, −3); **b** (5, −1), (1, −1), (1, −3); **c** (−1, 1), (−5, 1), (−5, 3); Translation of 6 units to the right; **e** Reflection in the x-axis **13 a** 51°; **b** 20.8 **14 c** 2; **d**, −0.73, −.73 **15 a** £3x; **b** £500; **c** £1400 **16 a** 1.18 cm; **b** 4.8 cm^2; **c** 14.4 cm^3, 14 400 000 cm^3 **17 a** 14 cm; **b** 70°; **c** Triangle ACD or triangle CED; **d** Triangles CAB, CDB **18 a** 8; **b** $\frac{1}{8}$ **19 a** (i) 90° (ii) 28°; **b** (i) 9.4 cm (ii) 10.7 cm

Paper 4

1 $3(x+4)(x-4)$ **2 a** 36°, 10 sides; **b** 48 cm **3 a** 23°; **b** 23° **4 a** (i) 4 (ii) $\frac{1}{2}$; **b** 7 **5 a** $\begin{pmatrix} 6 & 13 \\ -8 & 8 \end{pmatrix}$; **b** $\begin{pmatrix} 10 & 5 \\ 5 & 5 \end{pmatrix}$ **6** 28.4 cm^3 **7** 8 **8** 25.12 cm^2 **9 a** (i) −30 (ii) −30; **b** (i) 3, −8 (ii) 0, −5 **10 a** 32.5 m; **c** (i) 25.4 m (ii) 24° **11 a** 3; **b** 7; **c** (i) 15 (ii) 6; **d** Shade the region which is outside A and S but inside W. This represents the set of girls who can only use the word-processor **12 a** (i) $\frac{1}{2}$ (ii) $\frac{1}{6}$ (iii) $\frac{1}{3}$; **b** $\frac{1}{6}$; **c** $\frac{1}{8}$ **13 a** 3; **b** $g = \dfrac{4\pi^2 l}{T^2}$ **14 a** (i) 306 cm (ii) 7140 cm^2; **b** 28.6% **15 a** y values are 2.25, 1, 1.16, 1.58, 3; **d** 1.4, 3.2 **16 a** (i) $\begin{pmatrix} 3 \\ 0 \end{pmatrix}$ (ii) $\begin{pmatrix} 0 \\ -2 \end{pmatrix}$; **b** (i) Triangle with vertices (−2, 2), (−2, 4), (−5, 4) (ii) Triangle with vertices (−2, −2), (−4, −2), (−4, −5); **c** (i) Reflection in the y-axis (ii) Reflection in the line $y = -x$ (iii) Anticlockwise quarter-turn about the origin; **d** Translation of $\begin{pmatrix} 2 \\ -3 \end{pmatrix}$ **17 a** (i) $\frac{1}{3}\mathbf{a} - \mathbf{b}$ (ii) $\frac{1}{5}\mathbf{a} - \frac{3}{5}\mathbf{b}$; **b** $\frac{3}{5}$; **c** (i) 20 cm^2 (ii) 12 cm^2 (iii) 12 cm^2